BULIMIA

The Binge-Purge Compulsion

BULIMIA

The Binge-Purge Compulsion

JANICE M. CAUWELS

DOUBLEDAY & COMPANY, INC., GARDEN CITY, NEW YORK

Library of Congress Cataloging in Publication Data

Cauwels, Janice M.
Bulimia: the binge-purge compulsion.

Bibliography: p. 233.
Includes index.
1. Bulimarexia. 2. Women—Mental health.
I. Title.
RC552.B84C38 1983   616.85′2
ISBN 0-385-18377-1
Library of Congress Catalog Card Number 82–45538

CONTENTS

ACKNOWLEDGMENTS

I have changed the names, ages and identifying details of all bulimics quoted or mentioned in this book and thank them for generously sharing their experiences with me.

I am grateful to the following professionals who discussed their findings with me:

John A. Atchley, M.D.	American Anorexia Nervosa Association, Inc.
Christopher Athas	Anorexia Nervosa and Associated Disorders, Inc.
Barton J. Blinder, M.D.	University of California, Irvine
Marlene Boskind-White, Ph.D.	George Junior Republic, Freeville, NY
Judith Brisman, Ph.D.	Center for Bulimia, New York City
William Davis, Ph.D.	Center for the Study of Anorexia and Bulimia, New York City
Elke D. Eckert, M.D.	University of Minnesota, Minneapolis
Gretchen Goff, M.P.H.	University of Minnesota, Minneapolis
Meir Gross, M.D.	Cleveland Clinic Foundation
David B. Herzog, M.D.	Massachusetts General Hospital, Boston

Hans F. Huebner, M.D.	New York Hospital–Cornell Medical Center, New York City
Craig Johnson, Ph.D.	Michael Reese Medical Center, Chicago
Jack L. Katz, M.D.	Montefiore Hospital, Bronx, NY
Karen Lee-Benner, R.N., M.S.N.	University of California, Los Angeles
Vivian Meehan, R.N.	Anorexia Nervosa and Associated Disorders, Inc.
Estelle B. Miller, M.S.W.	American Anorexia Nervosa Association, Inc.
Lloyd L. Miller, D.D.S.	Tufts University, Medford, MA
John H. Rau, Ph.D.	Long Island Jewish–Hillside Medical Center
David Rudnick, M.D.	University of California, Los Angeles
Ellen Schor, Ph.D.	Center for Bulimia, New York City
Anita B. Siegman, Ph.D.	University of Southern California, Los Angeles
Michael Strober, Ph.D.	University of California, Los Angeles
William C. White, Jr., Ph.D.	Cornell University, Ithaca, NY
Joel Yager, M.D.	University of California, Los Angeles

The manuscript of this book profited from the corrections and suggestions of James E. Mitchell, M.D., and Richard L. Pyle, M.D., of the University of Minnesota, F. Douglas Whiting, M.D., and Brian Richard Boylan, whom I thank for their time and prompt attention. Kathy Baumhofer taught me how much writers owe to excellent typists.

Finally I wish to thank my agent, Carole Abel, and my editor, Marie-Denise Comas, for their confidence in this book and its author.

There has been a growing need for a detailed, straightforward book on eating disorders in recent years. This in part reflects increased awareness of eating problems in our culture but also reflects what appears to be a serious increase in the incidence of such problems in the general population. Conversations with our professional colleagues who are involved with studying or treating eating disorders confirm our own impression that information about these syndromes is being avidly sought by victims of eating disorders. Published articles to date in popular periodicals have often suffered as a consequence of deadlines, space restraints, preconceived ideas and a reliance on sensationalism. They are often limited by all-too-brief quotations, or at times misquotations, from knowledgeable professionals. Janice Cauwels has written a book which attempts to solve some of these problems.

Even though anorexia nervosa (an illness related to the subject here) has been studied for many years, there is still much to be learned about the causes and treatments of this disorder. Treatment has been directed at restoring lost weight without dealing with the psychological consequences of the disorder. Very little is known about the long-term consequences of this illness. Information concerning the syndrome of bulimia is even more lacking. While a great deal of attention has been given to this syndrome in the popular press, individuals who experience this disorder are often frustrated in their attempts to obtain useful information or treatment. Researchers are, at this point, just beginning to obtain basic information which will permit them to adequately characterize the syndrome and its clinical course. Despite the obvious need for effective treatment resources, there have been almost no research studies on treatment outcome. In our own region of the country, newspaper ads offering programs for the treatment of bulimia attest to the fact that many therapists, some of whom have had little, if any, experience in the treatment of eating disorders, are rapidly moving to fill this gap. People with eating disorders are asking the question, "What do I do for my problem now that I know I have it?" Lack of useful answers or useful treatments from professionals has led to considerable frustration and pain for those with eating disorders and has undoubtedly contributed to the formation of many self-help groups across the country. It would appear that many of these have been very beneficial for their members.

While this book is timely, it is perhaps also premature since it raises many more questions than we are able to currently answer. This is especially true of the bulimic syndrome which until recently was a "closet illness." How many people in our population are actually involved? Has this illness been increasing in frequency and if so why? What special groups does it affect more than others? Why does it seem to have a predilection for young females? Why, like alcohol usage, does it go out of control in some individuals and not in others? What is the role of genetic or familial factors in the development of severe forms of the syndrome? What are the neuroendocrine changes associated with the syndrome and are they causally related or only secondary features of disturbed eating habits? What is the role of depression in the development of eating disorders? Is it primary or secondary to the disorders? What is the course of the illness? Most important, what are the most effective treatments for bulimia? Some individuals who come to us for treatment say that they have previously received treatment for depression or for chemical dependency since they could not find a therapist who knew how to treat their eating disorder. For many people, existing treatment provides relief from the low self-esteem and depression that accompany the eating disorder, but not for the eating disorder and its associated problems. These include medical and dental complications, social isolation, financial and legal difficulties, and deterioration of relationships with family and friends.

This book provides a comprehensive overview of current thinking on these issues. It has value for professionals and non-professionals alike. The author's interest in bulimia goes back to 1980, when she prepared and later published one of the earlier articles on the eating disorder bulimia. Since that time, she has extensively reviewed the professional literature on eating disorders and traveled throughout the country to interview directly those persons who were involved in the study of eating disorders. The author's pursuit of accuracy and up-to-date information included extensive revision and updating by all those professionals who contributed their expertise to the book. The author also taped interviews with dozens of individuals experiencing the bulimic syndrome and anorexia nervosa throughout the country at many different treatment centers. This extensive use of vignettes from actual patient interviews, followed by updated information from multiple professional sources, adds greatly to the clarity and effectiveness of this work.

Although answers to many of the questions we have raised will await results of continuing research over the coming years, this book contains an up-to-date summary of currently available information and will help fill the void until more information is available.

James E. Mitchell, M.D.
Richard L. Pyle, M.D.
University of Minnesota

BULIMIA

The Binge-Purge Compulsion

Chapter 1

WHAT IS BULIMIA?

Consider these facts:

Anne, a forty-four-year-old recovered alcoholic, has started graduate school to earn a business degree. Between her classes, her part-time job as a clerk in the university bookstore, her five-mile daily run, her family, and her work in Alcoholics Anonymous, Anne literally hasn't a spare moment. As a matter of fact, she's afraid to take a vacation and relax because unscheduled time terrifies her. Not that she's worried about her drinking —she's been sober for eighteen years. Anne is scared of free time because she used to spend hours each day gorging herself on her favorite foods, then forcing herself to vomit until her stomach was empty. Although she overate and vomited daily for twenty-seven years, her husband and four children never found out—nor did Anne herself know of anyone else who behaved this way with food until she sought treatment for her closet illness.

Jessica, a thirty-six-year-old financial analyst for a company in California, overeats just as Anne did, but uses a different method to get rid of the food. Jessica takes three hundred laxatives a day. She has done this for sixteen years.

Thirty-seven-year-old Len, a law student in Boston, used to vomit by sticking a wooden spoon down his throat. This method no longer works for him. To keep from gorging himself, he now shops daily, buying only as much food as he needs for the one meal he will eat at exactly 6:30 P.M.

A teen-ager with anorexia nervosa—an eating disorder that strikes young women—alternately starved herself, gorged herself and made herself throw up. She finally sought help from an eating-disorders specialist, but it was too late—she died while retching and vomiting over a toilet bowl.

Natalie and Adrienne met at a group-therapy session in New York. Both had deliberately vomited most of what they had eaten over the past few years. Both had swollen salivary glands as a result of their gorging and vomiting, and both had been sent to oncologists (cancer specialists) by physicians who mistakenly thought they had Hodgkin's disease.

The names and other identifying details about these people (and others in this book) have been changed, but their experiences are true. Stories like these are becoming more and more common. What do they indicate? Who are these people? What kind of problem do they have? And what can they do about it?

These people have bulimia, also known in the media as "bulimarexia," "binge-vomiting" and "gorge-purging." Bulimia is an eating disorder similar to chemical dependency. The term comes from the Greek *bous limos*, meaning "ox hunger"—a misnomer, since true hunger has little to to with the illness. Bulimia victims regularly gorge themselves with food, especially high-calorie food, for periods lasting up to several hours. To avoid gaining weight, they purge themselves after each binge through self-induced vomiting and/or laxative and diuretic abuse. Some bulimics alternate their gorging with amphetamine-boosted fasts or excessive exercise. At some point their concern with weight becomes irrelevant, for they have become hooked on the tranquilizing effects of gorge-purging. Most of them eventually learn to vomit by simple reflex action, as though it were normal. They have condemned themselves to a routine cycle of guilt, self-loathing and devastating isolation.

Somewhere between 80 and 95 percent of bulimics are women; with apologies to bulimic men, who are in the minority, they are referred to here by the generic "she." Bulimic behavior ranges from occasional overeating at parties to consuming fifty thousand calories and vomiting twenty times a day. Many people experiment with binge-vomiting only to find that they dislike it intensely. Others are predisposed to become bulimic: their gorge-purging grows steadily worse and can reach a point where it takes control of their lives.

Thirty-one-year-old Natalie recovered from bulimia after four years. Thirty-seven-year-old Chris is still trying to end twenty-one years of binge-vomiting and swallowing up to sixty laxatives at a time. It is not difficult to find women who have suffered from bulimia for a decade or more. Bulimia is a closet illness—a shameful secret from family and friends—and most of its victims become expert at hiding it. Bulimics carefully map out their foraging routes so as not to stop in the same grocery, deli or bakery too often. They muse aloud at checkout counters about nonexistent husbands, children or parties for which they are buying cartfuls of food. While this secrecy saves the victim from embarrassment, it also isolates her. The majority of women interviewed for this book believed themselves unique in gorge-purging and beyond medical help. "Most of us didn't seek help until we were absolutely desperate," says Anne. "We thought that there was no help because there was no illness." Bulimia is one of the best-kept secrets in our society.

As such it contrasts with anorexia nervosa, the self-starvation that glamour-hungry young women inflict upon themselves because of their obsession with thinness. About half of anorexia victims have bulimia as one of their symptoms and are often referred to as bulimic anorectics. Chris, for example, vomited herself down to less than ninety pounds on a five-foot ten-inch frame before being packed off to a hospital. "I was terrified of gaining weight," she says. "They forced me to put on forty pounds before they let me out." The deep-seated and complicated relationship between bulimia and anorexia nervosa has caused controversy about whether they are variations of a single eating disorder.

There is little doubt, however, that bulimia is also an illness distinct from, and perhaps more prevalent than, anorexia nervosa. One study showed bulimia to be six times as common as anorexia nervosa among a sample of students diagnosed at the University of Washington Psychiatric Clinic; the investigators called these findings a conservative estimate of bulimia's incidence in the student population. The Eating Disorders Clinic at the University of California at Los Angeles (UCLA) originally opened to serve anorectics but quickly changed its emphasis when five times as many bulimics as anorectics showed up for help. So few women have been treated for bulimia, however, that its incidence in the general population is anybody's guess. Experts estimate that hundreds of thousands of women may have bulimia; magazine articles and talk shows on bulimia elicit thousands of letters and phone calls from victims desperately seeking help.

Because bulimia has only recently surfaced as a full-blown illness, the few women courageous enough to admit to it have often been greeted with disbelief, misunderstanding and contempt. Many former bulimics recovered because they sought help from chemical-dependency clinics, refusing to leave until they were treated. Others demanded treatment from psychiatrists experienced in treating anorexia nervosa, ignoring the hesitation of professionals to tackle a problem they had heard of but not encountered.

Still others took the initial step to recovery but were not so fortunate. Renee, a twenty-five-year-old secretary, checked herself into a psychiatric ward when psychiatrists advised her that it was the only way to conquer her bulimia:

> I was stuck in there for a month, and it made my problem much worse. I got hung up on a married man, and whenever we got passes we'd go out together and get as drunk as possible. And the staff made me do the craziest things. They told me that I was bulimic because I was afraid of getting pregnant, so I had to wear a pillow under my shirt for a week to get me used to

the idea of pregnancy. I always referred to my eating problem as "the thing," and they made me go around for a few days pretending that I was "the thing" and treated me like a disease instead of a person.

The only difference that hospitalization made in my life was that my insurance didn't cover it, so when I got out I had to file for bankruptcy.

At least Renee was fortunate to find psychiatrists familiar with bulimia; other women report that medical specialists they have approached have never heard of the illness.

Bulimia is subject to misunderstanding and prejudice partly because it has rarely been mentioned in medical literature. The few articles either refer to bulimia incidentally while explaining anorexia nervosa or insist that the subject needs further study. Bulimia has remained confusing and mysterious because of a vicious cycle: victims haven't come for help because physicians haven't understood and publicized their problem; physicians haven't understood the problem because they have had too few victims to study.

This situation is changing rapidly and dramatically as the medical profession becomes increasingly concerned about bulimia. Psychologists and psychiatrists are expanding eating-disorders programs at the University of Minnesota, UCLA, and elsewhere; research is also under way at New York Hospital–Cornell Medical Center, Michael Reese Medical Center in Chicago, and the Clarke Institute of Psychiatry in Toronto, to name only a few institutions.

Preliminary studies of bulimia victims reveal a smorgasbord of different backgrounds and personalities divided into subgroups sharing key emotional traits. The clinical diagnosis of bulimia includes depressed mood and self-deprecation; equally noticeable in some bulimics is perfectionism in appearance and performance that has doomed them to constant dissatisfaction. Consciously insecure and pathetically anxious to please, bulimics can be extremely sensitive to rejection, especially by men. "It's very definitely a dependence on others for self-esteem rather than getting it from within yourself. I set myself up for disappointment," says Chris. To make matters worse, many bulimic women learned from their families to hide their feelings and are simmering with rage and frustration that they stuff down during a binge. The binge releases them from, and the vomiting "restores," their self-control.

Ironically, some bulimics are the envy of their acquaintances. Known in the media as "bulimarexics," slender, meticulously groomed, beautifully dressed, poised and pleasant, they function well in life because of the very perfectionism that imprisons them. But many other bulimics seem to be chaotic, unhappy individuals whose personality disturbances and addictions to liquor or drugs have precluded their achieving personal, social or professional success.

How do these women start binging and vomiting? While the causes of the illness remain speculative, bulimics can usually identify particular circumstances that resulted in their first binges or experiments with vomiting. They mention family backgrounds that make them susceptible to social influences familiar to us all. One of these is the cultural pressure to be thin. Many bulimics have struggled with weight their entire lives or have been overly concerned about their bodies. They greatly enjoy food, but they fear its consequences because weight gain means imperfection, rejection, failure to live up to the expectations of family and friends. Dieting for a lifetime is not much fun, but it's exactly what many women do, perhaps maintaining a weight that is metabolically unsuitable for them. If they begin severe dieting or fasting to lose weight, they will feel compelled to binge. Twenty-eight-year-old Adrienne, a public-relations agent for a New York museum, had this problem:

> I used diet pills to fast for long periods and became elated at the weight loss. I'm five feet two inches and went from 155 to 108 pounds. The vomiting started when I'd get so hungry after fasting that I'd eat until I was ready to burst and, wanting both to relieve my discomfort and control weight, I stuck my finger down my throat. I later learned to vomit just as a reflex action. Being thin was so good for me—I loved it, but with my appetite I wouldn't stay there unless I vomited. I al-

ways felt guilty about failing at my diet, and suddenly I was free.

Bulimia can also start as a diet itself or as a weight-maintenance technique following a diet. The woman has been told that she would look terrific if she would just lose a few more pounds; she diets or fasts successfully and is lavishly praised for her new figure. She loves the compliments but is terrified that she can't maintain the weight, so she starts vomiting. Rita, a thirty-year-old high school music teacher, became bulimic in this way:

> I've never been more than ten pounds overweight, which is just enough for friends to tease me unmercifully about being plump. I pretended that it didn't bother me, but I was terribly sensitive and felt very self-conscious. The summer of my senior year in high school I had an appendectomy, lost the ten pounds and was blasted off on a giant ego trip because everybody, I mean *everybody*, showered me with praises. The problem was that I couldn't maintain the weight because I hadn't dieted and didn't know how to change my habits to avoid overeating. I felt anxious about that and about other pressures—going away from home for the first time to an Ivy League college and wanting to act very self-confident and strong while I was really insecure about my life and especially my appearance. I felt that I had to look and be perfect to fit in at college, so to stay thin I began vomiting up what I ate. I don't remember where I got the idea; maybe it was from how you're supposed to stick a finger down a child's throat to make it vomit if it swallows poison. That started a habit that would plague me on and off for the next twelve years. And doing it—even *thinking* about it —was so ugly to me!

Rita can't remember where she got the idea of vomiting. Other bulimics report that it would never have occurred to them had it not been for thin friends or a female role model. Twenty-

nine-year-old Yvonne could be said to have "inherited" the disorder:

> I first started vomiting when I was thirteen years old. I
> did it to imitate my mother, who used to vomit after
> dinner but always said that she wasn't sick. It was just
> something that she did. I would often overeat, then I'd
> vomit to relieve the discomfort. This would happen
> now and then until I got to be about seventeen, when I
> really started to get into true bulimia—I'd eat more be-
> fore vomiting, and I'd do it more often. There was a lot
> of turmoil going on in our family at the time, and that
> didn't help the situation any.

But bulimia need not necessarily start because of food or
weight issues. Some people seem always to have been "bulimic"
in a sense; their problems simply begin to center around food.
They may be accustomed to using food as a self-medication or
as a substitute for unmet needs. Before they know it, bulimia becomes their main obsession and source of tension as well as their
solace.

Researchers have found that a trauma (such as the loss of or
separation from a significant person) can cause an existing
conflict to rear its head and team up with food to cause bulimia.
Colleen, a thirty-two-year-old lawyer, attributes her illness to an
unpleasant experience:

> I had thought that my relationship with my boyfriend
> was going well, but he had been dissatisfied with a lot
> of things he had never mentioned to me. Finally, one
> day he asked me to meet him at a restaurant for lunch.
> Halfway through the meal he started laying all my
> faults out on the table between the clutter of little
> dishes. It was one of those elegant restaurants that is
> very quiet, and I'm sure that some of the other people
> could hear him. He made it quite clear that he wanted
> nothing to do with me anymore, asked for the check
> and left. He had arranged to meet me because he knew
> that I wouldn't make a scene in public and that he
> could leave me there when it was over.

I was stunned. I somehow left the restaurant, went home and cried myself sick. I had always had a weight problem and usually handled crises by overeating, but this time I was so upset that I felt as if I were gagging on what I had just eaten. I went to the bathroom, stuck my finger down my throat and brought up the whole lunch. I had not digested the food, so it didn't smell terrible, and I wasn't really nauseous. So I got the idea of vomiting to lose weight. I wanted to run away and thought of this in terms of getting out of my body by losing weight and leaving my present body behind. The next day I went and got my hair cut in a completely different style, bought all kinds of makeup and started vomiting up everything I ate. I was determined that I would never again look in the mirror and see the woman my boyfriend had rejected.

For Colleen, food is just one part of her attempt to escape from the person who was hurt by her boyfriend's behavior. Her body imprisons her in the pain; she believes that her only means of freeing herself is to make that body look as different as possible.

Similarly, bulimia can be a means of handling loneliness, unhappiness, tension and anger that its victims have never learned to express constructively. Denise, a thirty-eight-year-old gynecologist, had several pressures pile up on her at once:

I had always had a weight problem. I was one of your perfectionistic children, never angry, hostile or upset, always doing everything right. I was too good a girl to try liquor or drugs and always used food instead. The bulimia goes way back to when I had broken off with my fiancé and started out in private practice. A lot of new things were happening all at once, and I lost a lot of weight, but not with vomiting. I thought this was the magical answer—practice in San Francisco, new apartment, new figure—now I thought I would find the man of my dreams, and all kinds of magical things would happen. As I slowed down from all the energy of being really too thin for the first time, I thought I was the perfect woman. I was emaciated and thought I looked like a model. Things slowed down; the office fell through; the man of my dreams turned out to have lots of money and little emotional depth. I was angry about all this and started to overeat again. Somebody at a party suggested that I could vomit, and it sounded like a good idea. It became a terrible habit that I usually indulged in at around 2 A.M.

These circumstances are much too common to explain bulimia completely; instead, they can be thrown into the recipe along with the emotional and physiological causes of chemical dependencies like alcoholism. Bulimics and bulimic anorectics often are alcoholics with family histories of alcoholism and weight problems. Researchers are trying to verify a correlation between alcoholism and bulimia; alcoholic bulimics, on the other hand, don't need statistics to prove to them that the addictions are similar. As a recovered alcoholic bulimic, Anne is in a good position to explain why:

At first I was anorectic. I began vomiting one day after worrying that I had eaten too much. It took only a few months for me to become locked into the whole binge-vomiting cycle. Initially my weight was my primary concern, but once I got into the habit, that concern was lost. I was really dependent on binging. It was like alcoholism in that I used food as a coping mechanism for everything. I just binge-vomited regularly, four or five times a day, regardless of how my life went. One of the hardest things I ever did was to go through treatment for alcoholism when I was twenty-six. I really knew that my main problem was not alcoholism but binge-vomiting, for which there was no treatment, and it was a terrible position to be in.

Adrienne feels that bulimia is just like alcoholism:

When you're alcoholic, the first drink makes you feel euphoric. The second drink brings you down. Not taking a second drink also brings you down. The same holds true for binge-eating. The first few bites made me experience pleasure—not joy or satisfaction, just pleasure. Continuing to eat or not continuing both destroyed the pleasure. The consequence of the activity was pain—because I felt uncomfortably full, and because I knew that if I didn't get rid of the food I'd grow heavy.

Some bulimic women drink to try to curb their binge-vomiting, only to find that the two addictions blend together. Others find that eating sugar or white flour causes them to binge as readily as if these foods had set off a chemical reaction. "I could sit here with you and have coffee and a piece of cake," says twenty-one-year-old June. "And I could con it really well—you'd never know that anything was wrong. And when I left here I'd go straight to a store and buy a big cake, and take it home and eat the whole thing. One taste of sugar is enough to do it." This reaction is one of the several puzzles that investigators are trying to solve to determine whether there is a biochemical basis to bulimia. New research on carbohydrates, neurotransmitters and related subjects suggests that the illness may start not in the stomach but in the brain.

Bulimic women also have problems with drugs, often after trying diet pills to lose weight. Jennifer, a forty-year-old nurse with bulimia, recalls how her aspirations toward the perfect final grades and the perfect figure turned her into a speed freak:

I wanted the top score in my major exams, and diet pills—amphetamines—made me feel energetic and able to organize my work, concentrate and persevere. More importantly, they both made me feel like the kind of person other people wanted me to be and took away my appetite. I lived on almost nothing except fluids and was able for the first time to stabilize my weight. After graduating with honors in biology, I got a job as a medical receptionist and could get all the speed I wanted. I used it for the next ten years.

The loss of self-control common to alcoholism, drug addiction and bulimia shows up in a bad habit many bulimic women pick up—stealing. Hoarding is a symptom of anorexia nervosa; stealing, ranging from pilfering trifles to outright shoplifting, is a symptom of bulimic anorectics and bulimics. They first develop problems with eating and then start stealing food. In depriving their bodies of food, vomiting enhances its attraction: the compulsion to steal food is the next step beyond that of gorging on it. Betty, a twenty-one-year-old college student, found her bulimia and her stealing escalating during her senior year at a private boarding school:

> It got to be a real bitch because I didn't have the privacy to vomit as much as I wanted, and I had a hard time sneaking food into my room sometimes. I'd stuff my pockets with cafeteria food and thought nothing of stealing food from other girls who got care packages. I lived one dorm away from a friend of mine whose father owned a cookie factory. He'd send her crates containing boxes of assorted cookies that she'd keep in her room. I'd stop in whenever I went by her building and steal a box at a time. One of the girls living down the hall from her was chubby, so my friend suspected her of taking the cookies but never confronted her.
>
> I've done things like that since then with food—walking through grocery stores eating fruit or candy and conveniently forgetting to pay for it. Occasionally it has crossed my mind to steal something major—for me that would be a blouse, maybe—but I haven't, because I've been too scared of getting caught.

Natalie was less able to resist temptation:

> I stole food while working at one of those drive-in chains. I'd gobble down fifteen hamburgers, six orders of french fries and two giant malts in a single evening. Later, when I was married, I'd charge things I needed and use cash to buy groceries so my husband couldn't track down where the money went. I also lied to him

about my salary and deposited less in our checking account than I actually earned. He finally figured out
what was going on when I started going into department stores and charging bulk orders of candy because
I could no longer help myself.

Severely ill bulimics steal money to finance their habit, just like
drug addicts. Others get caught in department stores stealing
clothes, jewelry and similar items that they don't need. They
describe their shoplifting as compensation for whatever might
have been missing from their lives.

Psychiatrists are investigating bulimia's relationship to other
addictions, hoping to find a common factor that might enable
them to understand bulimia. Bulimia victims may lack the ability to control their strong impulses, making it easy for them to
start abusing liquor, drugs or food. What appears to be perfectionism in some bulimics may actually be constructive compul-
siveness—an "uncontrollable" need to perform and appear well.
This quality may help explain why victims of eating disorders
and chemical dependency show intriguing similarities in background, personality, behavior and everyday problems.

What is bulimia? It is not simply a perverse idiosyncrasy of attractive, successful career women; rather, it is what Overeaters
Anonymous calls a "cunning, baffling, powerful" illness that no
woman, no matter how adventuresome, would want to flirt with.
"Bulimics become centered on binging and purging, slaves to a
symptom that completely envelops their lives and affects them
socially, emotionally and sexually," according to Michael Strober
of the UCLA Neuropsychiatric Institute. Many bulimics do little
except binge and vomit and seek food for the next binge. They
binge-vomit throughout pregnancy. If a bathroom is not available, they vomit outdoors or into plastic bags for later disposal.
They lose their jobs because they stay home from work to binge
or can no longer concentrate. They get arrested for shoplifting.
They can end up ruined—financially, socially and professionally.

And as if these problems weren't bad enough, many bulimic
women suffer serious physical effects from their body abuse
—metabolic imbalances, decayed teeth, general ill health, spastic
colons—and some have even died.

Is there a way out of bulimia? Yes—in fact, the majority of bulimia victims quoted in this book have not binge-vomited for at least several months. Treatment for bulimia is not an easy process; it requires a commitment to therapy and a strong sense of personal responsibility—but it works.

Although still experimental, bulimia therapy follows certain basic principles. One is that the best approach is multidisciplinary and highly individualized. Bulimia victims are contracting for combinations of group, individual and behavioral therapy, pharmacotherapy, hypnotherapy, family therapy and nutritional counseling. Their choices between reputable (as well as disreputable) self-help groups, workshops and eating disorders clinics are steadily increasing. Each of these disciplines and methods has many problems and limitations, however, and none provides the magic cure that many bulimics want.

Bulimics often become discouraged in therapy when a fight with the family, a work deadline or a dreary day makes them want to binge. And many of them set up special obstacles to their therapy, most notably the unhealthy spirit of competition they develop in group therapy. A bulimic who is neither the longest abstinent nor the worst binge-vomiter in her group will feel less than "perfectly" good or bad. "I was placed in a group after being treated in a hospital for anorexia nervosa," says Patricia, a nineteen-year-old college student. "I recall being terribly jealous of another woman in the group who looked as thin as I was when hospitalized. I thought, 'Why wasn't *she* made to gain weight?' And it turned out that she had taken over a hundred laxatives at a time, which was more than I had done. I no longer felt unique, and I hated that."

Fortunately, a hallmark of recovery from bulimia is a powerful sense of altruism toward other victims. Much bulimia therapy borrows from the format used by Alcoholics Anonymous and Overeaters Anonymous in the sense that abstinent volunteers work with those who are still struggling. Every bulimic interviewed for this book was delighted to discuss his or her experience; most of them insisted that bulimia can be cured. They enjoy the satisfaction of being liberated from addiction and of turning that experience to constructive use.

A theme common among bulimia victims is: "I wish someone

had confronted me about bulimia, or had even questioned my behavior. I wish I had known that it was a real illness." Until recently they saw no way out of their dilemma and thought of themselves as freaks. Fortunately, bulimics need no longer struggle with loneliness, ignorance and despair.

Chapter 2

SEMANTICS AND SNAKE PITS:
THE STATE OF THE ART

Only a few years ago nobody knew about bulimia; now most people have heard of binge-vomiting even if they don't know its medical term. Women's magazines and talk shows are now busily informing the public about the horrors of binge-vomiting and the joys of recovery. Anorexia nervosa associations have hastened to assure us that their services cover "related eating disorders." Mothers, daughters, sisters, wives and girlfriends are coming out of closets to discuss their food problems. There is little doubt in anyone's mind today that hundreds of thousands of women are having serious trouble with bulimia.

This barrage of publicity has drawbacks as well as advantages. "Articles on bulimia accomplish absolutely nothing," says one recovered bulimic, "not just because eating disorders are so overdone already, but because our being written about makes people with bulimia feel special. That means absolutely nothing unless you're getting better—wanting to be special is part of what got us into trouble in the first place." Limited by their authors' restrictions of time and space, articles in popular magazines are simplistic—not a primary source of information about a disorder as complicated as bulimia. Many bulimics are offended by what they see in print. And since purging is learned from imitation, publicity on bulimia might well tempt other women to try vomiting or laxatives. On the other hand, it's important to inform women struggling with bulimia where to go for help and what to expect when they get there.

Psychiatrists and psychologists are not at all sure exactly what bulimia is; in fact, the amount of dogmatism one hears on the subject is usually inversely proportional to the speaker's qualifications to pontificate. This is not surprising—although anorexia nervosa is the subject of many medical books and articles, no one is quite sure what *that* is either. Eating disorders are not merely symptoms of dieting gone haywire; they are extremely complicated illnesses with biological, psychological and cultural components. "With both anorexia and bulimia there are so many variables that just a listing of the symptoms seems contradictory," says Vivian Meehan, founder and president of Anorexia Nervosa and Associated Disorders, Inc. (ANAD) in Highland Park, Illinois. The prevalence and seriousness of bulimia are just starting to be recognized, and without long-term, direct, complete follow-up studies, therapists find it very hard to evaluate their treatment methods. Researchers attacking this puzzling illness are scattered across the country; each clinic treating bulimia is likely to attract a particular rather than a representative group of patients. With few medical articles and conferences on bulimia, there is not much opportunity to compare study results and arrive at a consensus about its causes and cures.

Not many experts care to draw conclusions about bulimia; most refuse even to speculate without the data to back them up. Others have data that they are anxious to publish and therefore reticent to discuss, even generally, with a writer. Those who do speak request (and have had) the chance to review their carefully guarded statements before these go into print. At the opposite extreme are therapists of dubious qualification who have jumped into the eating-disorders field with as much caution as one would approach a gold mine, broadcasting confidently that they can help victims of anorexia nervosa and bulimia. Let the bulimic beware: there are plenty of charlatans out there who are very interested in your problem—and your purse.

Bulimia is so complicated a subject that even naming it has caused controversy. The fact that it is often misnamed in the media merits some explanation.

Semantics

THE MANY NAMES OF BULIMIA

The term "bulimia" has been around for a long time. Recently a New York newspaper columnist ran a letter from a doctor in Manhattan explaining that the Talmud refers to bulimia and implies that the early Hebrew sages thought of it as a disease. Over the past several decades psychiatrists and psychologists have used "bulimia" to mean a pathological craving for food (as did Robert Lindner in describing the case of Laura in *The Fifty-Minute Hour* *). As they encountered more and more cases of bulimia, however, clinicians began to recognize that it was not just a food craving but also an extremely complicated disorder (a "disorder" or "syndrome" has an intricate pattern of symptoms). Because the term "bulimia" seemed a simplistic label, they attempted to specify their findings by replacing it with more cumbersome terms: "bulimia nervosa," "desperate overeating," "dietary chaos syndrome," and "abnormal normal weight control syndrome." Dr. A. H. Crisp, of St. George's Hospital in London, an internationally known specialist in eating disorders (and the inventor of this last phrase), wrote recently: "No one descriptive term is ever likely to do justice to this multifaceted condition."

Bulimia seemed perplexing not just in itself but also in relation to anorexia nervosa. For some time psychiatrists had noticed episodes of overeating in anorectic patients and viewed bulimia as a symptom, a chronic phase or an aftermath of anorexia nervosa induced, in part, by prolonged starvation itself. "Bulimic patients may be said to exemplify the worst fears of the anorexic patients come true," wrote Dr. Gerald Russell of the Royal Free Hospital in London. But bulimia was not anorexia nervosa, and it involved purging as well as overeating. Marlene Boskind-White and her husband William C. White, Jr. noticed these

---

* Lindner, Robert, "Solitaire: The Case of Laura," *The Fifty-Minute Hour* (New York: Holt, Rinehart & Winston, Inc., 1954).

differences when they began studying binge-vomiting at Cornell University in 1975. "Descriptions of bulimia at that time never referred to purging," says Boskind-White. "We'd give our patients descriptions of both anorexia nervosa and bulimia, and they couldn't relate to either one." She solved this problem by coining the term "bulimarexia" to describe more precisely the binges, followed by guilt-induced compulsive purges, that the Whites discovered in their patients. Gorge-purging, they felt, was distinct from and somewhere in between both compulsive overeating and self-starvation.

Obviously, there was no point in having several names for one disorder. As clinicians and researchers were becoming more aware of bulimia, the American Psychiatric Association was in the process of revising their *Diagnostic and Statistical Manual of Mental Disorders* for its third edition (*DSM III*). The upshot was that the binge-purge disorder was considered for inclusion. The association redefined the traditional term "bulimia" according to the newer findings and established criteria by which a psychiatrist or psychologist could diagnose the syndrome as a bona fide psychiatric illness.

In 1980 *DSM III* appeared with a definition of bulimia that distinguished it from anorexia nervosa or any physical disorder. The diagnostic criteria for bulimia listed in the manual are:

A. Recurrent episodes of binge-eating (rapid consumption of a large amount of food in a discrete period of time, usually less than two hours)
B. At least three of the following:
    (1) consumption of high-calorie, easily ingested food during a binge
    (2) inconspicuous eating during a binge
    (3) termination of such eating episodes by abdominal pain, sleep, social interruption or self-induced vomiting
    (4) repeated attempts to lose weight by severely restrictive diets, self-induced vomiting, or use of cathartics or diuretics
    (5) frequent weight fluctuations greater than ten pounds due to alternating binges and fasts
C. Awareness that the eating pattern is abnormal and fear of not being able to stop eating voluntarily

D. Depressed mood and self-deprecating thoughts following eating binges

E. The bulimic episodes are not due to anorexia nervosa or any known physical disorder†

"It's amazing that bulimia is in the diagnostic manual at all with so little data published during the development of *DSM III*," says Dr. Richard L. Pyle of the University of Minnesota. Although it established "bulimia" once and for all as the correct term for binge-purging, the *DSM III* definition (which covers a few pages) has several esoteric weaknesses and contradictions. For one thing, it still allows the term "bulimia" to refer to a symptom of anorexia nervosa and obesity, even though bulimia is also a unique illness. It makes no reference to bulimic behavior like vomiting up every few mouthfuls, chewing food and spitting it out, fasting, abusing amphetamines or exercising excessively. It doesn't point out how important vomiting is. It states that bulimia seldom incapacitates its victims.

But the definition is intended basically as a starting point. The diagnostic criteria form a basis for medical research, assuring that different investigators are looking at the same behavior and that their statistics for different patients are therefore truly comparable. (A recent study by Dr. Katherine A. Halmi and her colleagues at New York Hospital–Cornell Medical Center has initially confirmed the accuracy of the criteria.) As it stands, the *DSM III* definition includes the binge (or what the victim perceives as a binge) and the diverse methods of weight-gain restriction—"dieting" (by whatever means), vomiting, laxatives and diuretics. Until further studies show that it needs revision, it will have to do.

BULIMIA VS. BULIMAREXIA

But if "bulimia" is the formally approved term for binge-vomiting, why do the media refer so often to "bulimarexia"? The Whites noted that the new definition of bulimia included purg-

† American Psychiatric Association, *Diagnostic and Statistical Manual of Mental Disorders,* 3rd edition (Washington, D.C.: American Psychiatric Association, 1980), pp. 70–71. Reprinted by permission.

ing but were greatly relieved that their preferred term had not
been adopted for *DSM III*. Marlene Boskind-White was strongly
opposed to having binge-purging categorized as a psychiatric illness:

> I don't even want to call bulimarexia an illness. We be-
> lieve that bulimarexia is a habit. Like cigarette smoking
> and alcohol abuse, it may be a very serious habit, but
> still it's a habit. It has been learned, and it can be
> unlearned. Many of these women learn to gorge and
> purge by imitation after having heard of someone else
> doing it. "Illness" implies the whole medical model.
> These women don't have a psychopathological prob-
> lem; they're normal, healthy women who want to be
> skinny, and most of them would be terrified to think
> that they had a psychiatric illness. Even labeling the
> habit "bulimarexia" was the least palatable part of our
> work, because we felt women could use it as a safe
> edifice, a medical illness to hide behind until they
> found therapists on whom to shift their own respon-
> sibility for binging.

Boskind-White describes an isolated habit that a woman can
give up on her own (regardless of other problems) rather than a
disorder woven into the psychological and emotional fabric of
her personality. The Whites feel that a woman must already be
sustaining herself in life reasonably well to be treated successfully for binge-vomiting. Among other things, their treatment involves working in the present to stop the binge-vomiting rather
than reaching into the past to find and analyze its causes.

The Whites are courteous and accommodating to interviewers
and often quoted. Since they are open about their viewpoint and
their treatment methods for "bulimarexia," their intensive weekend workshops are likely to attract those binge-vomiters who
view their behavior in the same way. The Whites have seen hundreds of successful, attractive, intelligent, perfectionistic women
who keep their gorge-purging an unsuspected secret in their
seemingly desirable lives. While *some* bulimics may fit this pat-

tern, many—possibly the majority—do not; but the media have
picked up the subgroup of "perfectionistic bulimarexic women,"
and this stereotype has stuck.

"Bulimia" and "bulimarexia" shouldn't be used inter-
changeably. Although both terms refer to the same gorge-purging behavior, they are not synonyms. The Whites (and presum-
ably other therapists who use the term "bulimarexia") see
binge-vomiting as a habit that can be broken through a few
days' intensive therapy. Other therapists, however, think that
binge-vomiting is a very different kind of experience—a psychiatric disorder that requires long-term therapy. "Bulimia" and
"bulimarexia" can be understood as two labels for two different
approaches to binge-vomiting.

Obviously, this book presents binge-vomiting as a psychiatric
illness. Many bulimics, frustrated by attempts to have their disorder taken seriously, are infuriated by the suggestion that it's
just another fad diet. "It's not just a habit," says one victim, "it's
not like biting your nails; it's so tied in with everything; you
must understand and work out a lot of problems to stop binge-
vomiting for sure." But any therapeutic approach can be recom-
mended *if* it helps a person stop binge-vomiting and live a
healthier, happier, more fulfilling life.

IS IT EVER "NORMAL" TO BINGE-VOMIT?

The theoretical difference between bulimarexia the habit and
bulimia the psychiatric illness is one of *kind.* Another confusing
issue involves a difference of *degree.* Dr. Halmi's study found
that 13 percent of a sample of college students experienced all
the major symptoms of bulimia as outlined in *DSM III.* Meanwhile the media have had a field day citing statistics that 25 to
30 percent of college students, especially those on sports teams
or in sororities, occasionally binge and vomit. How many college
students, for example, are actually bulimic?

Nobody denies that many women use fasting, vomiting or
purging to control their weight. Some psychiatrists try to make
careful—and at this point dangerous—distinctions between bulimia (which meets *DSM III* criteria) and occasional overeating

and vomiting. Dr. David B. Herzog, Director of the Eating Disorders Unit at Massachusetts General Hospital, takes this view:

> Probably 95 if not 100 percent of people have some peculiar food behaviors or idiosyncrasies. I have no doubt that binge-vomiting, or just vomiting, is common in our society, especially among women in the college-age group—so common that it's verging toward some kind of norm. People who vomit to maintain weight may be engaging in something totally different from bulimia. If they are leading good lives, working, staying happy and sustaining good relationships, then their binge-vomiting is an idiosyncrasy, not an abnormality, although many of them may become frightened by articles and programs on bulimia telling them that they're sicker than they actually are.

Other psychiatrists describe occasional binge-vomiting (or "bulimoid behavior," as one would like to call it) as being more specific, conscious and self-directed than bulimia. Often experimental and confined to weekends or celebrations, it doesn't disrupt the practitioner's life. Some women may stop binge-vomiting once they hear of its medical and psychological dangers, and they may not need therapy at all.

The psychiatrists who make this distinction may or may not prove to be right. They have no way of knowing that these students won't end up very sick. And while comforting the "normal" binge-vomiters, such generalizations may just encourage them to become addicted to the whole gorge-purging process. The statements may likewise lead therapists to underestimate obvious cases of bulimia. Bulimia is a pernicious disorder that physicians and psychiatrists need to take more seriously than they have up to now. Far from being terrified at their diagnosis, as Marlene Boskind-White suggests, chronic bulimia victims feel enormously relieved to learn that their problem has a name enabling them to appeal for medical help. It makes little sense to downplay the real dangers of bulimia to protect either those flirting with it or those frightened by psychiatric medicine. Are people who feel down afraid to say, "I'm depressed," because depression is a psychiatric illness?

Another problem with the distinction is that reassuring experimental binge-vomiters of their normalcy also minimizes the risk involved. Some people sociably use cigarettes, alcohol or drugs, but they are not predisposed to addiction—the substance doesn't pull the proper switch, so they use it infrequently or not at all. They simply aren't attracted to gorging and purging. Others aren't as fortunate, says Dr. Joel Yager, Medical Director of the UCLA Eating Disorders Clinic:

> I would speculate that perhaps as many as 30 percent of women who go through college will try vomiting at least once to avoid putting on weight; 5 to 10 percent of them may develop bulimia. I use these figures for speculation because 5 to 10 percent is a reasonable guess as to the population figure for impulsive personalities, people for whom alcohol or drugs or bulimia might be symptomatic forms of expression. The figure is also consistent with Dr. Katherine Halmi's recent research. These people won't be able to shake it.

Dr. Yager acknowledges that his 5 to 10 percent figure for bulimia is speculation based on comparison with other compulsive disorders. The point is that *even if only* that many people develop bulimia, nobody can predict who they will be. Why encourage the entire 30 percent to believe that their behavior is normal?

In his book *Competing with the Sylph,* ‡ Dr. L. M. Vincent discusses the "normality" and "abnormality" of vomiting common among dancers who are trying to maintain weight. "To suggest that vomiting is necessarily addictive . . . would be as ludicrous as claiming that all social drinkers inevitably become alcoholics," he writes. The comparison to alcoholism is common and reasonable even though very little is known about bulimia.

‡ Vincent, L. M., M.D., *Competing with the Sylph: Dancers and the Pursuit of the Ideal Body Form* (Kansas City: Andrews & McMeel, Inc., 1979).

But recovered alcoholics and drug abusers unanimously claim that it was far more difficult for them to overcome their simultaneous addiction to binge-vomiting. Besides giving us our earliest ideas of nurturance, food is the only potentially addictive substance that is necessary for survival. The bulimic can't abstain or escape from food as she could from alcohol, cigarettes or drugs. The social pressures to use these substances are not as great as the social pressures to be thin: even the models in cigarette and liquor ads are as glamorously slim as those displaying the latest fashions. Food addiction has no moral, legal or apparent medical consequences; on the contrary, food is ubiquitous, loaded with warm connotations and just plain delicious. Enjoyment of both food and slimness creates a psychological and physiological cycle arguably more powerful than other forms of addiction. It may actually be safer to drink socially or to try drugs than it is to start binge-vomiting.

There is no dividing line between idiosyncrasy and abnormality that will keep a binge-vomiter with the right predisposition from going off the deep end. Occasional vomiting is not real addiction, just as occasional blues is not acute depression. But the gorge-purging cycle can corkscrew its way into a woman's personality until it is firmly attached to all aspects of her life. Like other addictions—for that matter, like all psychiatric illnesses—eating disorders are both entities in themselves and symptoms of the problems that cause them. And while bulimia can exist in a mild form, just like any other illness, it certainly has the potential to grow worse.

Of course, most of us probably misuse food in some way without even being aware of it. Most of us have been brainwashed into obsession with slimness; ironically, the health and fitness fad often includes thinness, which may not be healthy at all. But does a high incidence of this thinking and behavior make it normal? Or does it just signal a problem too huge for the psychiatric profession to accommodate? Is it really "normal" for a woman to be so terrified of gaining weight that she makes herself vomit?

People don't have to feel very down before they recognize that something is wrong and try to cheer themselves up. Therapists should be pointing out that repeated binging and vomiting likewise don't have to be incapacitating to indicate a real problem. The high incidence of binge-vomiting, occasional or otherwise, is a commentary on the "normalcy" of our weight-conscious, anxiety-provoking society.

Snake Pits

The brief history of bulimia represents more than just semantic squabbling and theoretical fuss. In some cases it has involved psychiatrists and patients in very unpleasant confrontations. Despite being newly recognized (and therefore viewed with suspicion by the medical profession), eating disorders have securely established their reputation for being extremely difficult to treat. As a result, many victims of anorexia nervosa and bulimia have until quite recently had their disorders ignored, avoided or mistreated by psychiatrists and physicians.

HOW TO IGNORE BULIMIA

Believing with the rest of us that thinner is better, physicians have been known to ignore anorexia nervosa in teen-agers of both sexes until the victims became so emaciated that they required hospitalization. The chronic bulimic tends to maintain a normal weight and looks reasonably healthy; unless the related problems are pulling her apart at the seams, she can have an even harder time getting medical attention. For years courageous bulimics have been describing their gorge-purging to physicians, only to have it disregarded. Marla, a twenty-two-year-old bookkeeper, found that some of the best oncologists in the country refused to acknowledge her bulimia:

> I had been bulimic for five years when I discovered a lump in one of my breasts. They did a biopsy that turned out to be negative, but I had had severely high fevers for months, and my lymph glands were swollen from vomiting, so my doctor was afraid of cancer. I live not far from a famous clinic and was sent there for tests. I told them that I was anorectic, that I had binge-vomited for five years and that I used ten to twelve lax-

atives a day. I thought those things could be causing my symptoms, but they refused to make the connection. I didn't push it; I wanted something to be physically wrong with me so that I wouldn't have to peg everything on the bulimia. I wanted them to cure me, but all they did was ignore what I said and wonder why my tests were negative.

Today eating-disorders specialists know that painless enlargement of the lymph or parotid (salivary) glands is a frequent consequence of bulimia, although this information has doubtless not filtered down to oncologists. Four years ago, however, a well-respected psychiatrist sent an article on parotid gland enlargement to one of the major medical journals, and it was turned down for publication because the editors simply didn't believe it.

Another bulimia victim had a similar problem in an emergency room:

For several months after I stopped vomiting and using laxatives, I had severe gastric problems, including abdominal spasms that once required emergency treatment. When I told the resident in the emergency room that I was recovering from bulimia, he asked, "What in hell is that?" So I explained what I had been doing instead of just using the medical term and got a better response from him. But he still had trouble connecting the symptoms that brought me there for treatment with the fact that I had been vomiting up most of what I ate for twelve years.

These examples are not unusual or extreme. Obviously, physicians have not been expecting a steady clientele of eating-disorders patients and have not educated themselves accordingly. But the point is that bulimics are horrified at the thought of revealing their illness, and some who mustered up the courage to tell their physicians have only prompted reactions ranging from facetiousness to disgust. Some physicians remark, "I wish I could do that"; others inquire, "Well, why don't you just stop?"

Sometimes a judgmental response from a physician can scare
away a bulimic patient for years.

The medical profession's track record of responses to eating-
disorders victims looks just as bad when we turn to therapists
themselves. Some therapists find bulimia repulsive and want
nothing to do with its victims. This is surprising, since therapists
treat murderers, rapists and sadomasochists without any qualms
whatsoever. The behavior itself ought not to be pertinent. And
until recently, this particular behavior has not been: before
bulimia became well known, many bulimics in therapy never
even mentioned their problem to their therapists. They either
sensed the possibility of a poor response or did not know that
binge-vomiting was a treatable illness. Many others, who
suffered from alcoholism as well as bulimia, found their eating
disorder disregarded in favor of the more familiar, treatable addiction or subjected to trial-and-error behavior-modification techniques. Twenty-three-year-old Andrea had both experiences:

> I was hospitalized on a chemical-dependency/food-
> disorder floor. The anorectics were all being forced to
> eat, while I was being driven crazy—pushed on the
> chemical-dependency route and told to get control over
> my alcoholism before trying to deal with food. My psy-
> chiatrist ordered family-style meals for me, then put
> me on a one-thousand-calorie diet. That didn't work,
> because whenever I got out on passes I'd binge. So they
> had me talk to another woman about my bulimia, eat
> what I wanted and then vomit into a pail in front of
> her while they videotaped the whole thing. I felt really
> uncomfortable about vomiting with someone there, but
> watching the videotape didn't bother me a bit. The
> food comes up so quickly and easily that it wasn't re-
> ally that gross. And my observer told me afterward that
> it was the quantity of food I ate, rather than my vomit-
> ing it, that bothered her about watching it.
> I kept insisting that booze was a problem but that it
> was food that was making me crazy. The psychiatrist

said that bulimia was not life-threatening, that I just needed control in my life and that food was part of that.

I got food easily while I was in the psych ward and was obviously vomiting. If they watched the bathroom, I'd throw up in the laundry basket, in the wastebasket, in the utility room, at the end of the hall—anywhere I could get away with it. I managed to steal food with a psychiatric aide along with me on one trip. I conned a retarded chemical-dependency patient into buying me food and made friends with a nurse who brought me food all the time. I was being treated for addiction, yet I was always desperate. In five weeks of treatment there were eight days on which I did not binge and vomit. I even passed out in the bathroom a few times, probably because my electrolytes were off, but they didn't even scold me for sneaking in there. It was terribly frustrating, because they really didn't understand that I couldn't help myself and that I needed their help.

Things didn't improve much when I got out of the hospital, because I was put into two halfway houses for recovering alcoholics. I missed most of the activities in the first one because I was busy vomiting, but no one confronted me with that. I had found a psychiatrist who was pretty sophisticated about eating disorders, and he and I both explained to the administrator of the second house that I was bulimic, but their rules were such that I could not get out of kitchen duty. I had to prepare meals for thirty women. We'd bake about twenty dozen cookies at a time and store them downstairs, and I was always getting caught down there eating them. They thought I was incredibly stupid for disobeying the rules and wouldn't understand that I craved food and had no choice but to find it. So I got kicked out of that place because of my bulimia, just as I had been kicked out of the first place because I took diet pills. I hate halfway houses.

Andrea and others like her remember struggling with a disorder greeted with indifference, annoyance, ignorance and anger. Certainly some bulimics have been treated badly, some to the point of barbarism, and there is no excuse for that. Certainly the medical profession needs to be educated about bulimia. But consider the viewpoint of a competent, serious psychiatrist or psychologist confronted with a patient stubbornly determined to hang on to an unfamiliar, grotesque disorder. It can be a pretty unsettling experience. Therapists are not omniscient; nor are they omnipotent, although bulimics in particular often expect them to be.

THE OTHER SIDE

Psychiatrists, psychologists and psychiatric social workers don't always encounter bulimia in people obviously ill with other problems or addictions. They find it in anorectics, superficially the opposite of bulimics and complicated in themselves, or they may find it in attractive women who manage their lives well despite their tremendous difficulty with food. Professionals feel astonished by bulimia, bewildered that patients can't stop gorge-purging, concerned, disturbed by the disorder's high incidence and the desperation of its victims, and plain curious. They also feel compassion and a strong sense of helplessness. Some become eating-disorders specialists because a sister, daughter or friend developed anorexia nervosa. Others recovered from eating disorders themselves and find their mission in the field. "Having suffered and recovered from bulimia, I felt almost as if I had found my faith once I started treating other victims," says Ellen Schor of the Center for Bulimia in New York City. Without this personal perspective, however, eating disorders can be a terribly difficult, discouraging and, at times, unpleasant field in which to work.

Psychiatrists are people, as one of them points out in describing the activities of an anorectic patient:

> One of our earliest patients gave the nurses the impression that she was hoarding food, but we never quite caught her at it. One day a most violent stench began

to emanate from her room, so the head of the service ordered the nurses to strip the room and search it completely. We found twelve containers of rotting butter, all sorts of rotting vegetables and other foods hidden around the room. It was nauseating for both the doctors and the nurses. We're only human—we felt disgusted by the whole thing.

Dr. Jack L. Katz of Montefiore Hospital in the Bronx has treated anorectics for over a decade and offers an interesting summary of how he and his colleagues reacted to bulimia as a symptom of anorexia nervosa:

When we first learned of bulimia, we found it hard to believe for a couple of reasons. So little had been written about bulimia that when we first began to hear of bulimic episodes, we couldn't really reconcile them with the rest of what we knew about anorexia nervosa. Here these girls were starving themselves to emaciation, yet they also described binging, and it just didn't seem consistent. When we began to believe that it happened because we heard about it from so many anorectic patients, we then found the nature of the gorging hard to believe. So much food is eaten—and in a virtual dissociated state in which the woman is almost oblivious to the environment and totally incapable of terminating the binge at a reasonable point.

Yet when we first started to work with bulimic patients, we were probably more confident than we should have been. It was easier for us, in a sense, to relate to this behavior than to anorexia nervosa. Most of us don't starve ourselves, but we do often snack excessively—in front of the TV set, at a party, in a restaurant—so we felt binging to be more comprehensible than starving. We thought that all we'd have to do would be to identify what triggers the binges and then explore why the victims have so much trouble ending them. That's a major problem—to approach bulimia too confidently without recognizing how pernicious the symptoms are and how out of control the patient is.

The opposite is true as well: it's a major problem if the therapist is unsure of how much he or she has to offer bulimia victims. A therapist who communicates hesitation or confusion instead of confidence will soon be in trouble with the patient.

Many therapists avoid both problems by refusing to work with bulimic patients at all. One reason is the high failure rate in the treatment of eating disorders. Anita B. Siegman of the University of Southern California explains:

> Therapists have the same problem with bulimics that they do in treating alcoholics. As with alcoholics, the therapist can't be a savior, and individual therapy alone just doesn't work. Like physicians, therapists don't like to feel helpless, and the prognosis for curing eating disorders is not encouraging. There is that built-in failure, plus a lack of knowledge, because, again like physicians, therapists are not well trained in nutrition.

Therapists are squeamish about treating eating disorders also because both the starvation of anorexia nervosa and the gorge-purging of bulimia have serious medical consequences. Psychiatrists report having received panic-stricken calls from psychologists and social workers whose anorectic patients were complaining about possibly serious problems. Meanwhile the psychiatrists themselves worry about losing their medical sophistication and rely on internists for help.

The implications are obvious: there are far more bulimia victims who need help than there are therapists competent and willing to treat them. The Eating Disorders Clinic at UCLA, for instance, has a waiting list of over one hundred bulimics from the West Los Angeles area alone. The same is true elsewhere. And meanwhile quacks in search of lucrative business are hanging out their shingles.

In a sense, bulimia research is still in the dark ages. But like research on anorexia nervosa, it has picked up considerable momentum—people have been helped and progress has been made. In fact, after intensive work with bulimics, many therapists find that however troublesome they may be, bulimic women can also be fascinating, stimulating and very enjoyable to work with. These therapists also feel enormous compassion for their patients. "I always associate bulimia with the pain and stress I've seen in my patients—how miserable they must have felt to have to resort to these drastic means of helping themselves feel a little better," says Dr. Herzog. "My reactions to bulimia almost run the gamut," says one New York psychologist. "At first I felt elated, adventuresome, excited that we were going to do something new, probably feeding into the magic that the bulimics themselves feel about getting well. Lately I've been struck with some of the more realistic, difficult aspects of treatment and have had very deep feelings of powerlessness, helplessness, anger at their not letting me in at times." The commitment to treat eating disorders must be strong indeed.

Chapter 3

BULIMIA'S FAMILY

As a satisfier of hunger, a provider of body energy and nutrients and a medicinal agent, food means health and growth. The weight changes that ready us for birth also propel us into the traumas of puberty. The body shapes resulting from our food habits carry sexual and even moral connotations. Through its nourishing effects on our physiology, food determines our psychology as well, and most of us would admit that our thoughts and feelings about food are often more overpowering than its biochemical role in life would imply.

The sensation of being fed is our earliest perception of nurturance. Food later helps define our understanding of family, home and all their warm connotations. It is a chameleon of pleasure and sociability—a festive holiday dinner with all its fixings and fragrances, a cozy breakfast in bed or quiet candlelight supper for two, a potluck picnic seasoned with fresh summer air. We organize its delicious tastes into favorite menus and special memories of meals enjoyed with family and friends. Our food habits in part define our nationality, our religious beliefs, our notions of prestige, our systems of reward and punishment, our values. Food never stands alone—we always see it amid an entourage of implied meanings.

These associations help explain why some people become addicted to abusing food. It serves as a concrete substitute for evanescent pleasures or basic needs that are missing from their lives. It offers them a means of coping with stress, for a single binge can obliterate, for the time being, all their problems of living. Used in this way, food remains a daily necessity, but paradoxically it also threatens health and drastically impairs everyday life.

The psychiatric eating disorders are extreme examples of this problem. They may start with an adult's conscious decision to abuse food, or they may appear in children too young to know that they are ill. In either case, eating behavior becomes dangerous and unnatural, and the food itself becomes an addictive substance stripped of its positive symbolism.

The Eating Disorders

The five psychiatric eating disorders defined in *DSM III* are *anorexia nervosa, bulimia, pica, rumination disorder of infancy,* and *atypical eating disorder*. The last is a catch-all category for apparent disorders that do not exactly meet the other criteria; its ranks keep increasing as interesting varieties of anorexia and bulimia turn up. Pica is the repeated eating of a nonnutritive substance; it usually occurs in children who are retarded, deficient in minerals, neglected, or just poorly supervised—but is not limited to them. Younger children may eat paint, plaster, string, hair or cloth, while older ones sometimes eat animal droppings, sand, bugs, leaves or pebbles. Victims also eat normal food. The disorder is usually self-limiting.

Like pica, rumination disorder of infancy affects children of both sexes and is apparently rare. A baby suffering from rumination brings up its food without nausea or retching, usually after arching its spine and straining back its head. It then either spits out the food or chews and reswallows it. Sucking movements of the baby's tongue give the impression that it enjoys the rumination, although it may become irritable and hungry between episodes. The disorder can kill as many as 25 percent of the babies it affects—although the baby eats a great deal, it slowly starves to death if it does not keep food down. More commonly the disorder just goes away. Rumination can also occur in adults and be mistaken for bulimia. But the eating disorder most directly associated with bulimia is anorexia nervosa.

Before discussing bulimia's sister ailment, we must give passing acknowledgment to another eating problem—obesity. Obesity is not an eating disorder, at least not in the modern classification. It is rather a physical state that may result from an eating disorder or merely from some pattern of eating disturbance. Technically speaking, anorexia nervosa is a physical state also, as are the weight fluctuations characteristic of bulimia, but these disorders have psychological criteria that are not necessary for a diagnosis of simple obesity and that may indicate greater general disturbance.

This is not to underestimate the complicated problems with food and feelings that lead to obesity. Bulimia can be viewed as an extreme solution to them—one reason it seems especially bizarre is that its victims seldom have enough extra weight to divert attention from their binges themselves. The overeater and the bulimic may eat for similar reasons, but the overeater may unconsciously use fat to avoid attracting the opposite sex, for instance, while the bulimic is determined to look normal or svelte. While bulimics pay their unpleasant price to stay thin, overeaters may see advantages in being fat: they avoid sexual exploitation, vulnerability and "unpleasant" activities like exercising or socializing, or they fit society's image of what they should be—a plump grandmother, a jolly baker. Many overeaters resemble bulimics not just in their eating, which they may use to cope, but also in their interest in why they overeat, their discouragement about stopping their binges, their desire for a magic cure that does not require them to change.

Anorexia Nervosa

Anorexia nervosa can be traced back to the eleventh century, when the Persian physician Avicenna wrote about a melancholic young prince who was successfully treated for the disorder. Cases of anorexia nervosa appeared now and then through the Middle Ages, when it was attributed to possession and witchcraft. The disorder was finally named by British physician Sir William Gull in 1874. Despite its current fashionability, then, anorexia nervosa is by no means a new illness, but both its incidence and its recognition have increased dramatically over the past several decades. Some professionals speculate that it has be-

come more common now that there is less tuberculosis to cause
the emaciation that anorectics desire.

WHAT IS ANOREXIA NERVOSA?

The term "anorexia nervosa" implies loss of appetite due to a
nervous condition. On the contrary, the anorectic is obsessed
with food, craves it but stubbornly refuses to eat or retain it,
preferring to starve to the point of illness, invalidism and, quite
possibly, death. Dr. Hilde Bruch, professor emeritus of the
Baylor College of Medicine in Houston and an eminent author-
ity on anorexia nervosa, defines it simply as "the relentless pursuit of thinness." Anorexia is popularly known as "the starvation
syndrome," a term that evokes little of its complexity. Like many
psychiatric syndromes, anorexia nervosa may be the final common pathway taken by a variety of predisposing weaknesses. It
has inspired voluminous medical and popular articles and books;
here it deserves brief discussion because some therapists believe
that anorexia nervosa and bulimia are parts of a single illness
and because many anorectics have bulimia.

The diagnostic criteria for anorexia nervosa are:

A. Intense fear of becoming obese, which does not diminish as
   weight loss progresses
B. Disturbance of body image—e.g. claiming to "feel fat" even
   when emaciated
C. Weight loss of at least 25 percent of original body weight or,
   if under 18 years of age, weight loss from original body
   weight plus projected weight gain expected from growth
   charts may be combined to make the 25 percent
D. Refusal to maintain body weight over a minimal normal
   weight for age and height
E. No known physical illness that would account for the weight
   loss°

Other symptoms are closely associated with these criteria in the
diagnosis. Anorexia nervosa is difficult to classify as a psychiatric illness because starvation itself causes psychological
changes, so that causes and effects become blurred. This is why

° American Psychiatric Association, *Diagnostic and Statistical Manual
of Mental Disorders,* 3rd edition (Washington, D.C.: American Psychiatric
Association, 1980), p. 69. Reprinted by permission.

the anorectic must be persuaded to restore her weight to a certain level before she can begin psychotherapy. As she meanwhile grows thinner, she behaves increasingly like a starving person—but one who refuses food.

The anorectic acts like a hostile, stubborn tyrant over her body and eventually over her entire family. She will not eat, no matter how cajoled, threatened or painfully hungry she is. Like the chemically-dependent person, the anorectic persistently denies that she has a problem. She refuses to acknowledge that her body lacks nutrition, either defensively or because she has starved herself to the point of poor judgment. Her enjoyment of refusing food and losing weight is exhilarating; she becomes so terrified of a relapse that she views her body as an enemy, separate from herself, that must be harshly disciplined. Interestingly enough, she often takes over the cooking and forces others to eat, or she may hoard food, crumble it or push it around on her plate—anything but eat it. As she loses more weight, she becomes more and more withdrawn, unrealistic and persistent.

The anorectic's starvation is her revenge upon her hated body. She becomes hyperactive, exercises feverishly, and finds it difficult to sleep. All of her senses seem sharpened; she feels alive and energetic at first. But her body is panicking. She loses her menstrual period. Her scalp hair begins falling out, while elsewhere on her body soft, downy hair grows to help conserve heat, for she is always cold. Her blood pressure lowers, and her pulse slows. Her skin grows dry, and she becomes constipated. She develops sodium and potassium deficiencies that cause heart and muscle spasms. Eventually her desperate body begins feeding off its own muscle tissue, including that of the heart and other vital organs, until she becomes too weak to hold up her head.

Experts estimate that one in two hundred girls between the ages twelve and eighteen will develop anorexia nervosa, and that age category is broadening in both directions as more cases are being reported. As many as 20 percent of these young women may die; others may develop lifelong health problems. Approximately half of them develop bulimia as a symptom—their starvation makes them binge, and they purge out of deep guilt. Most anorectics—90 to 95 percent—are women, although the number of male cases seems to be increasing. The disorder is

harder to diagnose in men because their clothing more effectively
masks emaciation, and they have no menstrual periods to lose.
Interestingly, there seems to be a greater proportion of bulimics
among male anorectics than there is among females; like the
women, male bulimic anorectics have a significant incidence of
alcoholism, impulsive behavior and drug abuse. Men are less
likely than women to recover from anorexia, perhaps because
maleness itself tends to protect against a predominantly female
disorder, so that only the most vulnerable become ill.

WHAT CAUSES ANOREXIA NERVOSA?

The anorectic girl begins her diet just like any other teen-ager
but ends up in a suicidal regimen. What makes her resort to self-
starvation? Traditionally psychiatrists have attributed it to a
combination of long-standing and immediate problems—a complex intertwining of social and cultural pressures to be thin,
identity crises and family issues.

"The enigma of anorexia nervosa," Dr. Bruch writes in *The
Golden Cage*,† "is how successful and well-functioning families
fail to transmit an adequate sense of confidence and self-value to
these children. They grow up confused in their concepts about
the body and its functions and deficient in their sense of identity, autonomy and control." Dr. Bruch's statement summarizes a
classic psychiatric view of anorexia nervosa. The anorectic was
an ideal child—obedient, hardworking and perfectionistic. Her
apparent independence hides her essential immaturity, dependence, low self-esteem and chronic self-doubt. Unaware of and
unable to express what she wants, lacking an identity, the
anorectic changes to suit others' high expectations of her while
remaining isolated, self-absorbed, anxious and unhappy.

Like their child, the anorectic's parents hide severe family
problems under a façade of harmony and perfection. Demanding and overprotective, they exploit their daughter as a tool to
complete their own lives. They have a vested interest in seeing
her remain what psychotherapist Steven Levenkron calls "the
best little girl in the world."

This is one reason that anorexia nervosa has been thought to

† Bruch, Hilde, M.D., *The Golden Cage: The Enigma of Anorexia
Nervosa* (Cambridge: Harvard University Press, 1978).

be triggered by puberty. Adolescence brings with it all kinds of pressures to develop an individual, self-respecting identity, a natural transition that is nevertheless objectionable to some parents. In her desperation the girl seizes upon her body to exercise some control over herself and others' reactions to her. By starving, the anorectic at once makes herself worthier by becoming attractive (defined in our society as thin), rebels against her parents by refusing to cooperate with their attempts to feed her, and obliterates the body's signs of upcoming adulthood—what Dr. Crisp calls "the insult of puberty"—by transforming it back into the body of a child. It is her body shape and weight rather than food and its cluster of associations that preoccupy the anorectic—she feels that the advent of breasts, hips and menstruation is happening *to* rather than *within* her, that she is at the mercy not only of her parents and the world but even of her own flesh.

For some anorectics, growing thin precludes their confronting a terribly fearful aspect of adulthood—sexuality. Their fear of sexuality may be part of a more generalized reaction against society's definition of the adult role. Our society encourages self-indulgence and does not enforce restraints on impulse control; the women's liberation movement is increasing the means of self-expression available to women. Dr. Crisp has suggested that the teen-ager's self-imposed dieting may reflect her desire to be internally restrained, to supply a desperately needed sense of discipline that society fails to provide her. In other words, the anorectic could be reacting as much against society's sanction of sexual freedom as she is against her own emerging sexuality. Ironically, her self-imposed structure both compensates for the lack of imposed restraints *and* allows her to withdraw into total "self-indulgence." Alone in her little world, the anorectic makes all the rules.

But even within a strictly psychological context there is no specific formula for anorexia nervosa, as Michael Strober explains:

> Anorectics may *not* want to look less female or more neuter; *some* don't like their changes in shape at puberty. Anorexia nervosa is determined by many factors: in

some cases there is major anxiety about sexual development; in others it's much more complex. There are general changes that terrify these rigid girls; adolescent maturation triggers their terror of change and development. Their fear of being plain and average—a personality trait common in anorexia nervosa—becomes more crystallized. Dieting to emaciation sets them apart from others; the fundamental concern is that they see nothing else unique about themselves.

In other words, anorectics are afraid not of being fat but of being ordinary.

WHAT REALLY CAUSES ANOREXIA NERVOSA AND BULIMIA?

These theories about the causes of anorexia nervosa make a great deal of sense. After all, it's primarily an illness of teen-age girls. Newer theories, however, suggest that problems aggravated by the onset of puberty only partly contribute to anorexia. Dr. Bruch, for example, has proposed that feeding patterns during infancy (which may have more complicated implications for baby girls than for baby boys) can lead to anorexia nervosa later on. Other researchers have found eating differences between fatter and thinner newborn babies that predate any possible influence by their mothers. They instead suggest a strong biological component both in the babies' body compositions and in their eating that might contribute to bulimia as well as anorexia. In fact, researchers into the biochemistry of eating disorders are increasingly questioning the accepted psychological explanations for these illnesses. Anorexia nervosa is a favorite target for biochemical research, and certain findings about it have implications for bulimia as well.

Although traditionally viewed as an illness triggered by puberty, for example, anorexia is starting to show up in victims from all age brackets. Dr. David Rudnick, of the UCLA Neurological Research Center, reports having seen women who developed anorexia nervosa at ages fifty-nine and thirty-eight. Cases like these are difficult to reconcile with the conflicts about adulthood, sexuality and family usually thought to underlie the

disorder. Older anorectics may have had food or weight preoc-
cupations or family problems while growing up, but it's hard to
imagine these coalescing years later and causing the same kind
of syndrome that they do in adolescent girls. It's much easier to
speculate about a neuroendocrine or neuroanatomical disorder
that can have a number of trigger mechanisms.

Another blow to the puberty theory is the incidence of
Turner's syndrome among anorectic girls. Turner's syndrome is
a chromosomal abnormality by virtue of which a girl does not
develop breasts or menstrual periods. Despite their absence of
body changes to react to, girls with Turner's syndrome appear
just as vulnerable to anorexia nervosa as do their panic-stricken
sisters.

Age of onset and signs of puberty are not the only characteristics of anorexia nervosa that researchers have had to rethink.
Dr. Crisp has recently described a massively obese patient who
lost eighty pounds and developed anorexia at a weight of two
hundred and fifty.

Researchers have long studied metabolic irregularities in anorexia nervosa that they thought resulted from weight loss. Now
they're not so sure. They don't know whether certain hormonal
abnormalities, for example, precede, accompany or result from
excessive dieting. The abnormalities are important especially because the secretion of these hormones is believed to be controlled by the hypothalamus. The hypothalamus is an organ centrally located below the two major hemispheres of the brain that
activates, integrates and controls endocrine activities (internal
secretions), certain nervous system mechanisms, and various
body functions like water-balance regulation, temperature, sleep,
development of secondary sex characteristics, and food intake.
Mediating between different parts of the brain as well as other
parts of the body, the hypothalamus connects our sensations, our
emotions and our hormonal responses to them, freeing our conscious minds for other pursuits.

The hypothalamus seems to be a master switching device that
processes the body's messages about hunger. Its satiation center
sends out information on fullness; researchers speculate that le-
sions in this area cause eating to continue beyond the normal

stopping point. Either food scarcity or dieting alerts the hypothalamus and the central nervous system to tell the body that it needs food fast and that it had better binge or otherwise compensate for what's missing. Dieting may also relate somehow to the secretion patterns of some hormones produced or regulated by the hypothalamus.

Anorectics consistently show abnormalities in gonadotropins and possibly in thyrotropins. Thyrotropins are hormones that stimulate the thyroid gland, which regulates metabolic rate. Gonadotropins stimulate the reproductive organs; in women, two of them—follicle-stimulating hormones (FSH) and luteinizing hormones (LH)—cause ovulation and estrogen/progesterone secretion. The patterns of FSH and LH in anorectics are like those of much younger girls, and even after an anorectic restores her weight to normal, the patterns persist until the rest of the syndrome disappears.

These patterns help explain an interesting observation that several researchers have made. "Many anorectics develop amenorrhea before they lose any weight," says Craig Johnson, Director of the Anorexia Nervosa Project at Michael Reese Medical Center in Chicago. "Amenorrhea occurs in other starvation conditions, but the menses disappear later and return earlier with refeeding than they do with anorexia nervosa." This tendency may result from hormonal aberrations caused, in turn, by other symptoms of anorexia nervosa like depression, insomnia or excessive exercise, the last of which also usually precedes the acute illness and persists after recovery.

The implication of all this is that anorexia nervosa may be caused by some as yet undefined brain disorder. Some anorectics show abnormalities in body temperature and water regulation as well as in their endocrine functions; all these problems persist after the anorectic gains weight. Even more interesting, some of these irregularities don't show up in other starvation victims or in other psychiatric patients who are not terrified of becoming fat. This evidence, together with the anorectic's hyperactivity, suggests a disorder in the central nervous system—a neuroendocrinological mystery that is as difficult to unravel as the medical adjective is to pronounce.

FROM ANOREXIA NERVOSA TO BULIMIA

But these biochemical findings do not yet form a workable hypothesis. Dr. Katz and his colleagues, for instance, have inadvertently thrown a monkey wrench into the theoretical machinery. "We have observed many of the same hormonal aberrations in normal-weight bulimics as we have in underweight anorectics," he says. "We don't know what that means—it's a whole issue in itself. Our earlier findings and those of other investigators suggested that hormonal aberrations were strictly secondary to the weight loss. That conclusion is no longer valid." Neither is the conclusion that anorexia nervosa and bulimia are as distinct as *DSM III* would like us to believe they are. While these findings imply some relationship between the two disorders, they don't further explain either one. These bulimics could have all the characteristics of anorectics except the willpower to diet, or they could be former anorectics who regained their weight. If the latter is true, why or how did they switch from one eating disorder to another? No one knows.

Anorexia Nervosa and Bulimia

Bulimia could well owe its status as a rapidly up-and-coming disorder to the fascination with anorexia nervosa evident over the past several years. Many earlier writers on anorexia overlooked bulimia, probably because they were too inexperienced and naïve to see it. Because bulimia represents loss of control, anorectics in particular are very ashamed of it. But the more therapists looked for bulimia, the more they found it, especially among the more chronic anorectics. About half of all anorectics have episodes of bulimia, which give them a poor prognosis for recovery. But if bulimia is also a distinct illness, how is it related to anorexia nervosa?

The fact that people can have both anorexia and bulimia makes it difficult to discuss either illness. Studies headed by Dr. Regina C. Casper, of the Illinois State Psychiatric Institute, Dr. Paul E. Garfinkel, of the Clarke Institute of Psychiatry in Toronto, and Michael Strober, of the Neuropsychiatric Institute at UCLA, separately offer (and basically agree upon) provocative comparisons between "restrictor anorectics" (those who starve themselves) and "bulimic anorectics" (those who alternate starving with occasional bouts of binge-purging). But even though many anorectics develop bulimia, there may be many more normal-weight bulimics than there are anorectics of either type. Dr. Halmi's study, for example, concluded that bulimia was more likely to occur *without* the symptoms of anorexia nervosa and that it tended to strike people who had been overweight in the past or were heavy within their normal weight range. We need studies comparing restrictor and/or bulimic anorectics with "pure bulimics" (normal-weight bulimics who have no history of anorexia nervosa). Pure bulimics have so wide a range of personalities and in many ways seem so different from anorectics that the results of such a study—if performed scientifically on a large enough sample of people—are hard to imagine. Meanwhile it is impossible to discuss "pure" bulimia or anorexia in any reasonable, helpful terms without irritating qualifications. It's tempting to use anorexia nervosa as a common denominator and say, at least, that restrictor and bulimic anorectics share personality and family characteristics that are "anorectic." But this would be a gross oversimplification—especially since in some respects (such as self-control) certain pure bulimics resemble restrictor anorectics more closely than bulimic anorectics do.

What follow, then, are the safest comparisons that the medical profession has made between "bulimia" and "anorexia nervosa."

THE SISTER AILMENTS

Bulimics and anorectics are similar in both their attitudes toward food and some of their personality traits. Obviously, both disorders feature abnormal eating habits (bulimic anorectics eat smaller meals and binge-vomit less frequently and predictably than do pure bulimics) and resistance to eating. Obsessed with food, both the anorectic and the bulimic are fearful and anxious about losing control over their eating and therefore getting fat. Both anorectics and bulimics have distorted body images that differ, of course, in degree. While both groups are preoccupied with body *shape*, the anorectic is more fanatical about body *weight* as well. In their desperate attempts to diet, neither group recognizes that their methods are robbing their bodies of vital nutrients and possibly endangering their lives.

Personality similarities and differences between victims of the sister ailments cut through and isolate certain populations within each group. Many bulimics share with anorectics abnormally low self-esteem, feelings of ineffectiveness and poor assertion skills. Like anorectics, some bulimics have been raised to be good girls, destined to fulfill high expectations imposed by other people, and become overactive hard workers as a result. Many bulimics are perfectionistic, and both groups share important family problems. Both anorectics and bulimics feel confused about their emotions and their identities; they are troubled by their lack of inner control or direction in life. Many bulimics, and probably many anorectics, drift through difficult times of moodiness, depression and anxiety.

Unlike anorectics, bulimics turn *toward* food rather than *away* from it to handle stress, and the difference is obvious in their appearances. Anorectics must lose at least 25 percent of their total body weight to be diagnosed as such, while bulimics tend to range around normal weight. Because of their low weight, anorectics stop menstruating, while bulimics often skip a period or two. This may have significant implications psychologically as well as physically: anorexia is associated with a rejection of femininity and its monthly reminder; although professionally bulimics can be successful, active, ambitious and "liberated," they also tend to be strongly oriented toward traditional femininity.

Rather than starving themselves consistently, bulimics gorge and purge themselves; some of them may eat normal amounts of food between binges. Their personalities and their stronger appetites make bulimics less successful at simple dieting, so they resort to extreme measures to maintain weight (while anorectics may have had their natural hunger signs short-circuited by starvation). Anorectics seem confident, even exultant, over their mastery of food (handling and cooking but not eating it), but bulimics are anxious about and afraid of food because they are more likely to give in to hunger. This may be because bulimia is much more often associated with childhood and parental obesity than is anorexia, suggesting that bulimics may be biologically programed to gain weight. The emaciated anorectic is easily identified but resists treatment for her illness. The bulimic keeps her illness a secret, but although she shares the anorectic's pride in the uniqueness of her grotesque eating habits, she is often extremely relieved to find that others engage in them too.

Bulimia may start at a later age or last longer than anorexia nervosa, although so many young teen-age bulimics are showing up that this may not be true. Superficially, at least, bulimics seem more mature than anorectics. In contrast to the dependence and social withdrawal characteristic of anorectics, bulimics often display a sense of independence and even professional success. Bulimics seem more outgoing, socially adept, sexually involved and sensitive in relationships than anorectics. But in these terms the comparison actually starts to break down. Psychiatrists, psychologists and psychiatric social workers can't seem to agree on which group has their act together the most—pure bulimics, bulimic anorectics, or restrictor anorectics—because observations and studies keep leading different people to different conclusions. Researchers and clinicians agree that pure bulimics and restrictor anorectics are at opposite ends of a spectrum, but they can't decide what the spectrum is or which end of it indicates the greatest disturbance. (The same confusion is evident in comparisons of "pure" alcoholics and drug addicts with bulimics who have these problems.)

The question is whether the pathological self-control of the anorectic represents greater disturbance than the lack of self-control that afflicts bulimics. While the lives of restrictor anorectics have enabled them somehow to construct consolidated, tightly knit defense systems that permit them to remain rigid, bulimics have no such luck. Because of various defects in their development, bulimics are more prone to serious personality problems. They suffer from anxiety, tension and depression—feelings that overthrow their control systems and in response to which they may start to binge. Anorectics, on the other hand, can be prone to feelings of aggression. Bulimics complain more often than anorectics do about aches, pains and life in general, and they feel more worried, discouraged, guilty, irritable and restless. They are unstable victims struggling in webs of their own disturbances—alcoholism, drug addiction, shoplifting, promiscuity or other manifestations of poor impulse control. Their food habits help express this general chaos, in which they cycle haphazardly between indulgence and penance.

The control difference that seems most basically to differentiate anorectics and bulimics goes back to their respective childhoods. The anorectic was the angelic child; the bulimic was the hellion. Moody, prone to tears, likely to misbehave or fight with other children, self-conscious about her persistent chubbiness, the bulimic seems to have been even less equipped to face puberty with good grace than was her anorectic sister.

WHO WILL RECOVER?

For both anorectics and bulimics, recovery means learning to live all over again. Chronic anorectics must restore their weight at once to correct the effects of starvation. They are confined to hospital beds and earn privileges as they gain weight. Those anorectics who are less severely ill are permitted to gain weight gradually as their family and/or individual therapy progresses. Bulimia treatment resembles anorexia treatment in methods like using behavioral therapy and changing the eating pattern before psychotherapy begins. The prognoses for anorexia and bulimia depend on who is defining recovery, since therapists who have spent years treating these disorders disagree completely on this matter. Despite the constancies of each illness, there is little telling how a particular person may respond to therapy.

Some therapists feel that bulimics are easier to treat than anorectics. Pure bulimics seem to have the best chance for recovery as far as the eating itself is concerned. Rather than denying their problem, as do anorectics, bulimics are repulsed and frightened by their behavior. Once they have admitted to it, they don't resist treatment like anorectics—on the contrary, they feel an urgent need to get control of themselves. Having maintained normal weight and a more reasonable image of what their bodies look like, bulimics are more likely to develop normal eating patterns.

Bulimics tend to relate better in therapy. They are warmer, more open, better developed emotionally, less withdrawn than anorectics. They get involved in treatment and establish rapport with therapists more readily. They are aware of their need for social and sexual relationships, have richer fantasy lives and can benefit from therapy in their personal relationships, self-esteem and general functioning.

Despite these advantages, many therapists find that the bulimia itself frequently refuses to cooperate. On the contrary, anorectics who give in to treatment may improve their eating dramatically but stay restricted in other areas of their lives (and if their therapists don't recognize this, their patients may experience a relapse). But bulimics too may have difficulty with therapy because of their overlaying personality disturbances, impulse-control problems and family backgrounds. Anorectics can capitalize on the security they feel in their self-control; some try to become more flexible about life. Meanwhile bulimics are overwhelmed by all the problems that cause them to binge.

Anorexia and bulimia form patterns with each other in their long-term outcomes. Dr. Elke D. Eckert, of the University of Minnesota, has proposed a theoretical model: a normal-weight woman who develops anorexia may recover without becoming either overweight or bulimic. A restrictor anorectic can be treated and return to normal weight without developing bulimia; a bulimic anorectic, on the other hand, can return to normal weight and still have problems with bulimia. If the woman was overweight before becoming anorectic, she has a greater chance of becoming bulimic afterward; perhaps the bulimia was part of the obesity, since bulimics and obese people behave similarly. If she doesn't develop the complete bulimic syndrome, she may become overweight.

BULIMIA AND ANOREXIA NERVOSA—SIAMESE TWINS?

What can we conclude about the relationship between anorexia nervosa and bulimia? Therapists insist that they have seen many pure bulimics, and the Whites report that 90 percent of the binge-vomiters they have treated never had classic anorexia nervosa. Many bulimics claim that they have no desire to be emaciated; they just want to cope without vomiting and laxatives. For that matter, many dieters haven't got it in them to binge-vomit. But psychiatrists and psychologists known for their research on anorexia see many bulimic anorectics and feel that the kinship between the illnesses is unknown but powerful. Dr. Katz explains:

> Initially it seemed as if there was a very direct relationship between anorexia and bulimia. We have, however, also observed cases of women who, while they were diet conscious, never really passed through a true anorectic phase. Instead they went from dieting without emaciation directly into a bulimic phase. *DSM III* makes precisely this differentiation between anorexia and bulimia. Yet, on the whole, I don't think the distinction is as great as the terminology implies. For one thing, the overwhelming majority of bulimics do have a history of chronic anorexia. For another, even those bulimics who were never emaciated give a history of having been diet conscious and wanting to lose weight.

These comments imply that bulimics are more or less failed anorectics.

The anorexia associations likewise assume a close association between anorexia and bulimia. Since they are primarily in the anorexia business, they are perhaps likely to be approached by bulimic anorectics rather than pure bulimics, giving them a biased sample from which to judge. But the fact is that many bulimics went through an anorectic phase too brief even to be noticeable—they regained weight for some reason or other, but their underlying problems were not dealt with. Estelle Miller, founder of the American Anorexia Nervosa Association in Teaneck, New Jersey, reports that several of her patients seesaw back and forth between anorexia and bulimia and that they tend to get hung up on labels—"bulimia is better because it sounds more adult." And Vivian Meehan makes an interesting point:

> One ANAD study shows that 60 percent of bulimics experienced an appreciable weight loss before they began binge-purging. Anorectics can become bulimic, and bulimics can become anorectic. It's true that many starvers and vomiters never change to the other behavior, but our guess is that the incidence of bulimia in

anorexia nervosa is very high. It should be emphasized that symptoms can occur in any conceivable combination.

As they seem to do with their weight loss, anorectics may predispose themselves to bulimia through suggestibility. Most anorectics think that if they ever allow themselves to eat as much as they want, they will lose control; they reinforce to themselves the idea that appeasing their hunger will make them binge. Whether the anticipation of bulimia leads into bulimia or whether there are other physiological or psychological reasons for it is not known.

Perhaps the bottom line is that an activity as extreme, unpleasant and unhealthy as chronic purging is one that would occur only to an anorectic fanatically determined to be thin. Or perhaps the opposite is true—that bulimia itself is so powerful that it transcends the whole issue of weight, just as anorexia itself offers an escape from problems other than weight-related ones. Gretchen Goff, a recovered bulimic who is now the Coordinator for the University of Minnesota Bulimia Treatment Program, suggests this in describing her experience with both disorders:

When I was anorectic, I always wanted a big safety factor in my weight for fear that I might lose control, eat too much, and gain weight. When I started to binge and vomit, the vomiting took over as my safety factor, and I didn't have to keep pushing my weight down further. Most bulimic women are not intent on being super thin; they're average weight. Some women who stop binge-vomiting find it harder to keep their weight up—they worry about a safety factor.

Our experience does not support the idea suggested by some researchers that weight gain will help stop the binging. Even overweight women or those who gain weight while bulimic continue the behavior. They are more prone to binge-vomit at a lower weight, but that's just one factor. I think that the proclivity to binge is there no matter what you weigh.

Hanging labels on these illnesses is less constructive than understanding them as symptoms—abnormal behaviors that disguise deeper problems. And bulimia, which is rapidly edging anorexia nervosa out of the psychiatric limelight, is more overwhelming than mere comparison with its sister illness could explain.

Chapter 4

THE CLOSET ILLNESS

If we try to study bulimia as an illness distinct from anorexia nervosa, what do we find? Not much. "One thing I have become is an expert on the experts from having listened to everybody," says Dr. John A. Atchley, President of the American Anorexia Nervosa Association. "Nobody knows what causes bulimia. Nobody knows what causes anorexia nervosa. Nobody even knows that bulimia is a separate entity, although it is in the *DSM III*." This is one of the reasons that binge-vomiting is so often referred to as a syndrome—a set of mingled signs and symptoms that may be viewed apart from their causes. Like anorexia, bulimia is a grab bag full of contradictory characteristics.

DEFINING BULIMIA

The signs and symptoms of bulimia are easily observed. Assembling these observations into a workable definition of bulimia is another thing altogether. On the one hand, bulimia has not been common enough for psychiatrists to pursue clinical studies; on the other, researchers who try to investigate bulimia become more and more puzzled by its complexities. "The question of what bulimia is would have been much easier to answer a number of years ago, I think, because the more we look into it, the more variations we see among the women," says Craig Johnson. "There are many different social, characterological and biological components that contribute to the cause of the disorder."

Although fascinating new research is in progress on the bio-chemistry of bulimia, for the time being mental-health professionals are treating it as an emotionally based illness. As such, bulimia is a reliance on and simultaneous fear of food—the victim uses food to escape stress and fears while trying to maintain a façade of control and self-sufficiency. In her ambivalence toward food the bulimic resembles the anorectic. In fact, much is made of the idea that bulimia and anorexia represent degrees of disturbance on a continuum, but no one knows what the continuum is. Is it eating or weight-related disorders, with anorexia nervosa at one end and morbid obesity at the other? Is it anorexia nervosa itself? Is it eating style? Or is it even more general—a continuum of addictive disorders, the choice of which is based on the victim's background and personality? Or a continuum of character structure?

The lack of a precise definition makes it difficult for psychiatrists and psychologists to empathize with the experience of bulimia. Binge-vomiting seems to serve as a tranquilizer, an antidepressant, a reward, a self-medication that produces specific desirable effects. While binging, bulimic women are in a solitary narcosis of repetitive motion—they are "reowning" themselves, defining their otherwise fuzzy boundaries within an activity all their own. Craig Johnson recommends swimming to his patients because it's one of the few activities that can compete with binging in being repetitive, isolating and soothing. Many recovered bulimics recall having eaten themselves into numbness, to the extent that they often can't remember when or how the bulimia started. Aside from knowing that it escalated, some of them also can't recall how often or how violently they binged because starting to eat was like entering a fog. It's as if the mind as well as the body surrenders to the food, emerging from its anesthesia to feel shame, self-disgust and fear of the next binge.

Among other reasons, binging is a problem because it is so different and cut off from ordinary experience. Many bulimics control most areas of their lives; their food problems are so discrepant with how they see themselves that it's very difficult for them to acknowledge how bad those problems are. The bulimia becomes split off from other realms, such as good judgment and reasonableness, and they become demented around it.

BULIMIA'S INCIDENCE

One of the favorite areas of speculation about bulimia is its incidence, the interest in which seems to be a chicken-and-egg phenomenon. Certainly self-induced purging is not a new practice; for thousands of years it has been used both medicinally and socially. The ancient Egyptians purged themselves monthly as a prophylactic against sickness. The Romans invented the vomitorium, where guests could empty their stomachs after overindulging at a heavy banquet and return for more feasting. Purging was a purification rite for sportsmen in the nineteenth century, by which time people were resorting to such dubious weight-reducing techniques as having their stomachs pumped and swallowing sanitized tapeworms. In this century mothers still gave their children castor oil or enemas once a week to clean out their systems. All kinds of health beliefs can be associated with eating disorders. Some anorectics and bulimics develop a distaste for meat and become vegetarians before they become ill, or they start following different food fads.

We know that anorexia nervosa has been around for hundreds of years; probably some of its victims were bulimic anorectics. We know also that some women have suffered from full-fledged bulimia for over twenty-five years. Its incidence seems to be increasing in part because psychiatrists, psychologists, magazine editors and talk show hosts are now recognizing and publicizing it. It's possible also that our exquisitely weight-conscious society has driven more women to a "bulimoid" breaking point.

There are several problems involved with determining bulimia's incidence, the greatest of which is its secrecy. It's not unusual to find women who, like Anne, have gorge-purged for decades without their families finding out. For twenty-three-year-old Mary, her seven-year illness was literally a closet disorder:

> Once I was at home binging when I heard someone
> unlocking the front door. I threw all the food I could

grab into the cabinets and ran and hid in a closet just as my boyfriend walked in. I had no idea what he was doing home and was terrified that he would see my distended stomach. I spent three hours in that damn closet before he left, terribly anxious that the food would be absorbed and that I wouldn't be able to get rid of it afterwards.

If unexpected visitors came while I was binging, I just wouldn't answer the door. The binge was all the company I wanted.

The favorite time for binging, especially for those who share living quarters, is at night. And many bulimics are not counted by therapists because it just doesn't occur to them to seek help. Thirty-two-year-old Rea, an office worker from Virginia, ended a fifteen-year bout with bulimia because of a lucky accident:

I always used to flip on the TV for company while I dressed for work in the morning. One day one of the morning programs ran a piece on bulimia. I heard someone mention binge-vomiting and stopped dead in my tracks. They were talking about an illness with a name, and I just couldn't believe it! I was both dazed and incredibly relieved to find out that I could be helped. I wrote immediately to the clinic they mentioned on the program and also went to the employee assistance counselor at my company and told her about my behavior. She asked me whether I had any idea how many women came in and told her the same thing.

Despite these difficulties, experts who rely on their instincts for such things are convinced that bulimia is common and widespread. "A lot more women have bulimia than we think," says Craig Johnson. "Not a lot more than we *know*, a lot more than we *think*." "I'm not sure about the general population, but I think there's no doubt that among college-age women the incidence of bulimia is quite substantial," says Dr. Katz. "It's certainly not the rarity we once thought it was. I suspect that it was too hidden to be diagnosed and also that the actual incidence has since increased dramatically." "I've treated patients in their late thirties or early forties who have concealed their bulimia since adolescence. They came to treatment because someone finally suspected them," says Dr. Barton J. Blinder, Director of the Eating Disorders Program at the University of California at Irvine. "They've spent most of their lives in a *modus vivendi* with the bulimia, but I can see ways in which it restricted their full potential for personal or professional achievement." "In response to a recent article in *Seventeen,* we've had thousands of letters from young girls, fourteen to sixteen years old, saying that they've binge-vomited for six years and that the article was the first they'd heard of bulimia," says Karen Lee-Benner, a psychiatric nurse specialist who is Coordinator of the UCLA Eating Disorders Clinic. "These letters come from all over the country, and the girls pour themselves out desperately and passively—'Tell me what to do,' they plead." "I'm sure that there are hundreds of thousands of bulimics walking around today, and only those who are severely ill or find that bulimia is interfering with their lives will go for help," says Estelle Miller.

Surveys of college campuses conducted by psychiatrists at the University of Minnesota indicate that 50 percent of college students go on occasional eating binges, 6 percent of them have tried vomiting, and 8 percent have used laxatives at least once. These percentages are slightly higher for college women: 60 percent binge; 7 percent have vomited, and 10 percent have taken laxatives. The researchers found that 1.2 percent of female college freshmen they surveyed had both the characteristics of bulimia and a history of gorge-purging at least weekly. Eight percent of these women (4 percent of all the students) responded much like bulimics and could have a predisposition to or mild symptoms of the disorder.

The study in which Dr. Halmi and her colleagues found a 13 percent incidence of bulimia surveyed a more diverse student population. Dr. Halmi's group found that 87 percent of the bulimics were women, and 13 percent were men. (Although the incidence for men may be surprising, it is close to that found in another study. Dr. Ronnie S. Stangler and Adolph M. Printz conservatively estimated nearly a 4 percent incidence of bulimia among patients at the University of Washington Psychiatric

Clinic for students—89.5 percent of them women, 10.5 percent of them men.) An average of 10 percent of all the students surveyed in Dr. Halmi's study used self-induced vomiting or laxatives for purging—the two methods were strongly correlated. "The results of this survey indicate that the prevalence of binge-eating is higher than that previously reported . . . [and] . . . that binge-eating may be a much more serious public health problem than was previously thought," concluded the research team. They also pointed out that many of the students who did not return their questionnaires might nevertheless have bulimia.

Rumors about the incidence of bulimia are naturally even more impressive than study results. Anorexia Nervosa and Associated Disorders in Illinois reports that they receive about five hundred letters a week, mostly from bulimics. The American Anorexia Nervosa Association in New Jersey says that over 50 percent of the people in their self-help groups are bulimic. "Over the past eighteen months, between five and seven thousand women have contacted our project by mail or over the phone. We've had about two thousand questionnaires returned to us," says Craig Johnson. A news program on bulimia telecast in Minneapolis, Minnesota, resulted in two thousand calls within two days. An article on bulimia in *Glamour* brought an equal number of letters to the UCLA Eating Disorders Clinic within a few weeks. The Whites report that they have been inundated with requests for help over the past several years.

Both the anorexia associations and clinical psychiatrists and psychologists insist that bulimia can strike women of any class, from any location, at any age from early teens to retirement, and with varying degrees of intensity. And that's just in the United States. ANAD has received letters from people suffering from eating disorders in various parts of the world, as Vivian Meehan explains:

We were told of a small mountain town in Italy that had six cases of anorexia and/or bulimia. We have received letters about eating disorders from Japan, Holland, France, Indonesia, Malaysia, Guam, Colombia,

Mexico, San Salvador, and many from Puerto Rico. One support group in Holland is currently functioning because of initial information from us. We've also referred them, as well as others, to Anorexic Aid in England.

"The longer I'm involved with bulimia, the less bizarre I think it is," says Gretchen Goff. "I really think it's logical. Why wouldn't somebody try it? Everyone I know binges occasionally, and I think that many people experiment with vomiting and for some reason find it so aversive that they don't get into it. Others find it very reinforcing."

THE BULIMIC EXPERIENCE

How reinforcing can be seen by studies of gorge-purging behavior conducted at Michael Reese Medical Center and the University of Minnesota. Both studies found that bulimia usually starts around age eighteen (significantly enough, the age at which many of us break away from home) and that women wait from four to six years before seeking help. Seventy percent of the bulimics studied at Michael Reese binge-vomited more than once a day; 21 percent did so more than two hours a day. They spent an average of eight dollars and fifty cents per binge.

Dr. James E. Mitchell and his colleagues at the University of Minnesota studied a sample of bulimic women and found that the average length of their binges was slightly over an hour, although some binged for as long as eight hours straight. Each of the bulimics binged an average of twelve times a week. Most of them binged at least once a day and spent almost fourteen hours a week binging. Half the bulimics consumed over thirty-four hundred calories during a typical binge, and a few of them consumed fifty thousand calories a day. The usual time for binging was late afternoon or evening, and most of the women preferred to binge alone. Almost all of them ended their binges with vomiting, an average of twelve times a week. (The psychiatrists noted in the study their strong suspicion that the subjects underreported the frequency of their vomiting and the severity of their illness.) The foods they ate most often during their binges were ice cream, bread, candy, donuts, soft drinks, salads, sandwiches, cookies, popcorn, milk, cheese and cereal. In another study the researchers reported that two thirds of a different sample of bulimics exercised daily, although comparatively few of them used laxatives or diuretics. On the other hand, Craig Johnson has seen a woman who used six hundred laxatives a day for twenty years.

Dr. Halmi's study found that about 85 percent of the students who vomited did so less than once a month, while about 9 percent vomited one or more times a day. Besides vomiting, about 5 percent of all the students exercised, about 8 percent dieted, a few were in therapy or used weight-gain aids, and slightly over 1 percent belonged to diet organizations. Most of these students had distorted body images: they stated on their questionnaires that they considered themselves overweight even when the weights they reported indicated otherwise.

A real expert on this kind of experience is Miriam, a petite, attractive woman who looks younger than her thirty-six years. She grew up in South Dakota and now lives in the South with her husband and three children. She works part-time training and grooming horses. Miriam was bulimic for twenty-one years and addicted to diet pills for sixteen years. She arrived for her interview carrying a shopping bag containing seventeen volumes of diaries recording her ordeal. Most of the diary pages were blank, she explained, because during the most terrible times she could not bear to write about her sickness. What she did record were moments in her long history of fasting (up to two weeks at a time), pills, binges, despair and torment, resolves and prayers to get well, happiness and energy when she controlled her eating. Some entries follow:

April 20, 1963
    Today I wallowed. I officially proclaimed this day a free-for-all until tomorrow 2:00. Boy, did I let go. Mom bought lots of groceries—visited all the stores. At home I made a cheese cake—it was delicious. I did only one continuous thing from the moment I got up till bed. God forgive me and Miriam it's up to you and you alone.

October 31, 1969

Started early in the morning, felt horrible after three days of abstinence. Oatmeal, Post Toasties, toast, terrible boring day at office, time just stopped. Bubble gum, eight six-ounce packages of caramel corns, roll, cookies. Home 4:30, two ham sandwiches with glass of milk. Returned slacks. 1½ dozen donuts. Three Musketeers. Picked up kids. Went to Wards and charged three pounds of candy. Sick. Treats. Home. Five hamburgers. Salad. Four popovers.

Sick
No
No
No

October 12, 1972

I think I've reached the state to accept Step 1 [of the Overeaters Anonymous Twelve Steps]. I cannot control my compulsive eating. I've spent over $100 on groceries, $15 Pay Day Loan this week, paid $15 PDL last week. At noon I spent $5 on a bag of Snickers, taffy and junk and ate it all day long. At home I ate pizza and salad till it was gone and four batches of molasses cookies. I'm so sick of myself. This mess is every night. That's all I do with this precious life God has given me. I weigh 125, and my face is bloated. My thinking is confused. My self image is terrible. This neurotic behavior has got to stop. Please, Miriam, fight, don't give in. As soon as you eat that extra bite, you're lost. Lord please forgive me and help me fight. Please.

November 30, 1975

NO MORE! NO MORE! For Christmas. Please, Miriam, what can I write to plead with you to stop this. You are neurotic. Your whole life is food, and it's going down the drain with your self-respect. Your money, your time—precious time with your husband and children—you spend thinking, baking, shopping, eating, purging. You spent $130 last week, $70 rest of weekend and we still had to go to the store every nite to get

something for supper. Eight dollars of $20 left for to-
morrow.

Whatever you have to do to stay on your abstinence
—*Nothing hurts like this wasteful life—no more.*

July 3, 1979
    ENOUGH. I ate all day long. Tons of food: $2.25
gum, $1.80 junk, $4.00 candy at work, $1.00 at drug,
$2.00 at Burger King—ate all night long. It's terrible.
Miriam, you're a sick woman. Tomorrow is Independence Day. No pain is as awful as overeating, so stop
trying to eat yourself to death. You're 34, and you've
got to get hold of yourself. The guilt from your family
and from the money you borrowed is enormous. Please
Lord help me help myself.

An interesting feature of these entries is the way in which
Miriam views food as she writes. Her savored memory of a
cheesecake is only two sentences away from a plea for for-
giveness and a statement of resolve. She lists her gorging along
with other mundane activities like returning clothes and picking
up children, as though it were a fact of life as obvious as anything else.

Such entries contrast with others in which Miriam lyrically
congratulates herself for having fasted or dieted enough to lose
weight. Many bulimics are able to control their eating when absolutely necessary and according to how their lives are going.
Fluctuations in the frequency of their binge-vomiting are related
to separation, rejection or change—losing a boyfriend, fighting
with parents, leaving home or moving to a new apartment, going
to school or getting a new job. They cut down the binge-vomiting
when life is good, reacting to events that determine the level of
their self-esteem. Even so, many bulimics just binge routinely.
Thirty-one-year-old Merle, an underwriter for a large insurance
company in Boston, is an example:

It seems really funny to me now to look back and see
how obvious a problem I had with bulimia. When my
circumstances enabled me to enjoy life, I became less

preoccupied with binge-vomiting. If I was not only enjoying myself but also doing something at which I felt capable, I didn't think about food at all. And yet I was able to rationalize the bulimia during my happy times by telling myself that it was just something else I enjoyed, so it fit right in. It never occurred to me to use my good times as a way of weaning myself away from binge-vomiting.

FORMS OF BULIMIA

Bulimia manifests itself in different ways among different women, some of whom resist allowing themselves to be categorized. "I don't vomit that much," they'll say, or, "I don't use laxatives," or, "I'm from the South, and we don't act that way." Regardless of how or whether the woman purges after binging, she is still bulimic, staying thin by using pills, fasting or exercising. Thirty-three-year-old Alison, a nurse practitioner from Florida, disagrees:

> I don't consider myself truly bulimic. Other women in my bulimia group binge and vomit. I binge and then fast, exercise and use diuretics for long periods. My group coordinator says that I'm bulimic because my fasting serves the same purpose as vomiting and for the same reasons.
>
> I have been overweight since childhood, and my parents always made me feel very conscious of it. I sneaked and hid food to eat and got into fasting because of the terrible guilt I felt over my weight gain.
>
> My food problems were really reinforced when I was seven years old. Our next-door neighbor, my father's good friend, abused me sexually for two years. I dealt with the stress of trying to avoid him by overeating. My parents either didn't believe me when I told them about it or didn't know how to handle it until he moved away. Meanwhile I felt guilty, dirty, frightened, ashamed and furious with my parents, so I ate in part to deal with those feelings.

In high school I got into fasting for periods of up to fifteen days. I got the idea from friends who fasted occasionally to diet. They were thin, so I figured I could lose weight too. I'd get into prolonged binging for days between fasts, and the length of the fasts depended on how much weight I had to lose. I'd buy a half gallon of ice cream and a dozen apple fritters, eat half until my stomach hurt, rest, go out and run, then eat more. I could lose as much as seventy-five pounds in three months. I think altogether I must have lost the weight of three or four people. The slimmest I've been is twenty-five pounds overweight, and when I get compliments at that weight I get really angry because I'm a perfectionist and feel that I'm still fat. The compliments would make me binge more. The most I've weighed is three hundred and ten pounds. I'm five feet five inches.

During my fasts I'd drink lots of fluids and take diuretics. I'd go running for as long as I dared with my high blood pressure, and I'd do yoga and calisthenics for a few hours. I'd run myself to exhaustion, and even if my muscles got sore I'd go out and run the next day. It was my way of dealing with my feelings, especially anger.

I'd eat until my stomach hurt. With my weight fluctuations, I've got skin like a zebra's with stretch marks all over it. Fasting made me feel dizzy and faint, and I had small seizures. It also altered my blood sugar level. I've tried avoiding sugar for five years because one bite can start me binging.

I financed this habit with money from my parents and later my husband. Or I'd write bad checks and steal money and food. Between my eating, my medical bills and my drinking, I managed to go bankrupt.

Needless to say, the sexual abuse had affected my relationships with men because I had little sense of self-worth. I got married at seventeen to a man who, like myself, was an alcoholic, terribly dependent on his parents, and a binge-eater, although he's one of those skinny types that never gains an ounce. He used to sabotage my fasting by taking me out to eat or by getting a pizza or something and waving it under my nose. We had two little girls who were suffering a lot through all this, and when I finally decided to do something about my food problems and my alcoholism, I put them in foster homes.

I first saw a doctor about my eating around nine years ago. He referred me to a psychiatrist, but I wasn't ready for that and instead went to a local mental-health center, where I didn't get much help. I did go for chemical-dependency treatment, however, and have been sober for two years now.

I have gone through about seven Overeaters Anonymous groups unsuccessfully, because of my own insecurities and problems with the groups, because of the groups' instability, and because binging is much harder to cure than alcoholism. That's been really hard on my ego—to be able to quit one addiction and not the other. But finally I heard a recovered bulimic speak at an OA meeting and through her managed to get into a bulimia group. I felt different because, as I said, I don't really think that I'm a bulimic, but I was lucky enough to get into a stable bulimia group that provides me with good support. Before, I had never gone for more than two months without binging, and in the past five months I've had only four binges. But I tend to condemn myself for that.

I've tried to take my recovery day by day, and I'll start seeing a psychiatrist soon. I'm getting divorced, because I discovered that without our mutual addictions my husband and I have absolutely nothing in common. My only way of pleasing him was to cook him large meals. My main problem now is that I think I'm getting well for my kids' sake, and I need to want to get well for myself. It's funny—I always wanted to be superwife and supermom, and now I no longer want to take care of a man, and I'm trying to get over my guilt about giving up my kids.

Alison's honesty betrays her as a bona fide bulimic, since she reveals so many characteristics of the illness: extreme measures to undo the effects of her binging, childhood obesity and weight fluctuations, anger and other feelings that she tries to exercise away, and stealing to support her binging. (Some bulimics also report having been sexually abused as children, although their incidence of this experience may actually be no greater than that within the general population.) Bulimics like Alison who don't purge are no easier to treat than those who do, since they just figure out other ways to avoid getting fat.

THE IMPORTANCE OF VOMITING

About 90 percent of bulimics who purge do so by vomiting—another area of controversy. Some professionals believe that the binging itself is the main problem, since people who don't overeat don't feel guilty, uncomfortable and compelled to get rid of the food. "I know that some investigators have attached all sorts of unconscious symbolic significance to the vomiting; it may secondarily become infused with such meaning, but I strongly doubt the validity of such a formulation at the time the vomiting is initiated," says Dr. Katz. "The women we've interviewed state that the binging is the meaningful symptom; they learn to vomit by hearing about it from friends or discovering it fortuitously by themselves, and at the beginning, at least, it is purely an appendage that makes the binging more bearable."

And yet recent studies show otherwise. "For a long time we formulated that these women vomit in order to binge, but our research shows a whole group of women who binge so that they can vomit," says Craig Johnson. "Through some transformation, the binging becomes only a means to the vomiting, which is more important to them." Johnson documented this transformation by equipping a group of bulimic women with electronic beepers that they carried around with them for a week. Every few hours, from 8 A.M. to 10 P.M., Johnson's staff would beep each woman randomly. When beeped, she was instructed to stop what she was doing and record on a series of rating scales contained in a diary her thoughts, feelings and behavior at that moment. These data were fed into a computer and compared to those of a control group of women who ate normally in order to isolate emotional patterns specific to bulimics. The beepers enabled Johnson's staff to catch many of the women in binges and purges and to record the feelings that preceded them. By averaging out the bulimics' mood states over the week in comparison with those of the control group and those preceding, accompanying and following binges, Johnson found some surprising results.

For these women the typical binge occurred around mealtimes because they had to interact with food, so logically enough they felt hungry before a binge. Two hours before a binge their anger and guilt were high, while their feelings of control and adequacy were low, and they were starting to feel somewhat drowsy—almost as if a certain kind of altered state of consciousness were developing.

During the binges, significantly, all these feelings got worse. The women felt less in control, more inadequate; their alert/drowsy states remained steady, but they felt angrier, less hungry and more guilty. "The binge itself aggravated an already unhappy experience," says Johnson. "These findings contradict our classic formulations about overeating as a soothing, gratifying experience."

The purges, however, showed a reestablishment of control and adequacy; the bulimics felt less angry, more alert, with their feelings shifting back toward the base line. Two hours after the binges, their feelings still had not returned to the base line; the purges themselves were the points at which they seemed least angry. Johnson explains his conclusion:

> We must suspect, then, that the purge is the most important, most gratifying part of the sequence. Clearly it's some kind of cathartic, reinforcing experience that restores their sense of reality · orientation and allows them to feel in control and adequate again. The binge becomes a means to vomit: we've had women tell us that they binge beyond their satiation points to make it easier to vomit and that they select foods that are easiest to bring up.

Johnson's staff also did a survey of five hundred bulimic women who were asked to select adjectives that described their experience while binging and after purging. While they were binging, the women felt mainly disgust, helplessness, guilt and panic. After the purge, they still felt guilty and disgusted, but with a shift over to relief and calmness—the panic was gone. It's hard to tell whether this peace of mind arises from their having prevented themselves from gaining weight or whether the vomiting itself actually creates a different biochemical state.

Johnson's data have been corroborated by others who have treated or been in contact with many bulimics. "One of the most astounding things about bulimia is that many women will tell you that they enjoy vomiting," says Vivian Meehan. "That's part of the reason it's so very hard for these particular women to give it up." "I don't think vomiting is secondary, because I've treated people who didn't binge and still vomited—they'd throw up every little thing they ate," says Estelle Miller. "They admit that they love it—they claim that the frustration and release of tension are both similar to those experienced during an orgasm. They feel purged, clean, empty and spaced-out, and find it easier to sleep." Other therapists have similarly reported that their patients vomit most often when they are sexually frustrated. And other patients claim that their binging involves persecuting themselves with unpleasant feelings and devouring them, while vomiting results partly from the natural disgust—at the situation and the self—that these feelings evoke.

If researchers continue to find that vomiting is just as important, or more so, than binging, then the *DSM III* criteria for bulimia, which include but do not emphasize vomiting, will need to be revised. Moreover, the therapeutic approach to bulimia will have to involve unlinking the binging and vomiting and concentrating on the latter. The woman who stops binging may still vomit up what little she does eat, while the woman who can stop vomiting (without switching to fasting or exercise) will have to take responsibility for eating less and holding the food down. Without that sense of responsibility, it is very hard to stop purging.

Bulimics don't *intend* to become addicted to vomiting any more than anorectics *intend* to starve themselves to death—but they do. They may not be aware of how vomiting affects their feelings, but they do start out by viewing it as the solution to a lifelong struggle. "At last," they think, "I don't have to restrain myself or fight with food anymore; I don't have to pay the price of the foods and quantities I would love to eat." This is an enormous relief to them and the main element in bulimia's allure. One of the more tiresome clichés heard in the world of bulimia is that of "having your cake and eating it too"; clearly bulimic women think at first that they're getting away with something.

Unfortunately, the bulimia that starts situationally regresses into an ongoing activity. Any kind of restrained behavior that has no consequences increasingly becomes unrestrained. All of us would like to eat unlimited amounts of our favorite foods without paying for this indulgence. Bulimic women feel that way and probably eat in response to tension or unhappiness as well. Now they don't have to worry about getting fat. Once they start vomiting, their eating becomes more unrestrained. As that happens, they increase the vomiting, which in turns makes the eating even more unrestrained, and they start to spiral down.

Usually at some point along the way bulimics recognize that they're out of control, with a corresponding decrease in their self-esteem. Some biological patterning occurs that takes on a life of its own. Whenever they feel hungry or mealtime approaches, they know that they are about to binge and feel inadequate, uncontrolled and terribly guilty. A basic physiological response, or even a time of day, suddenly becomes a dreaded, panic-stricken experience for them. At this point they're in trouble—they can't avoid hunger, so instead they try avoiding food. Avoiding food of course fuels them toward food physiologically. So they're trapped.

The trap is so strong because it is set biologically—almost as if the body, weary of its mistreatment, has decided to take revenge.

Chapter 5

BIOCHEMICAL CAUSES, IMITATORS AND EFFECTS

Victims of bulimia find it hard to face up to their illness partly because binge-eating has very negative connotations. Gluttony is, after all, one of the seven deadly sins, and someone who can't stick to a diet is generally regarded as sloppy and self-indulgent. Most therapy programs for bulimia, like those for other addictive behaviors, emphasize the victim's responsibility for what she puts into her body. But psychiatrists and psychologists are hypothesizing that in some respects binge-eaters may be let off the hook. The prevalence of eating disorders is often attributed to cultural pressures, but researchers logically wonder why some people break under the strain and others don't. They persistently suggest that anorectics and bulimics may be victims of physiological idiosyncrasies that force them to behave strangely about food. Bulimia may be partly a matter of biological factors, ranging from simple food allergies (causing the victim to crave the food to which she is allergic) to gastrointestinal or even neurological problems. But these possibilities don't absolve the binge-eater from all responsibility, since gorge-purging has important medical consequences that no one should inflict upon herself.

Possible Causes of Bulimia

One relevant and well-substantiated area of research is that of biologically set weight. The proper weight for each of us is metabolically coded as a result of our genes and the total number of our fat cells, which may be greater in those of us who were fat as infants or children. This weight can vary within a certain range, but beyond that we must rely on pretty drastic measures to keep it at an abnormal level. This is important because any-one who drops below her set weight will want to binge as the body's natural protest. The body can't tell whether its owner is starving herself to be svelte or because she has nothing to eat; in either case it's going to let her know that it wants food. "People who drop below a biologically set weight should not be surprised by their stronger desire to eat," says Dr. Hans F. Huebner of the New York Hospital–Cornell Medical Center. "If you hold your breath, then begin breathing again, you'll hyperventilate in spite of yourself because the brain refuses to adjust to a lower oxygen level; the same thing occurs with food and proper body weight. Binge-eating occurs partly as a natural compensatory mecha- nism." As we have seen, the anorectic's diet itself predisposes her to binge, and attitude can help this process along. Most bulimics say that once they go off their diets by as much as a single bite, they give up. "I've broken my diet; why not go the whole hog?" they reason.

This means that a bulimic who would accept a slightly higher weight for herself would find the urge to binge dissipating. The problem with this theory is that it doesn't account for bulimia in people who are at or above their biologically set weights—even very obese people binge-eat. Possibly they have a hypothalamic dysfunction or disorder. "There are many, many biochemical questions that are not answered at this point. The complexities are only now being investigated," says Craig Johnson. Another complicating factor is that many bingers have lost the ability to respond to their bodies' natural signs of hunger and need to be reeducated in how to eat. And someone who has spent most of her life regarding her body as an enemy is not likely to relax and trust it to tell her when to eat, when to stop and how much to weigh.

Another possibility is that bulimia is one of a few methods to which people resort in response to biochemical reactions to specific foods. Some people, for example, may have a strong demand for carbohydrates. (That bulimics in particular binge on high-carbohydrate foods implies not just that they like these foods but that their carbohydrate intake ties in with some of their other symptoms.) Judith J. Wurtman and her colleagues at MIT conjecture that eating carbohydrates speeds up the synthesis of brain serotonin. Serotonin is a neurotransmitter—a substance released by an excited nerve cell that transmits messages to target cells. The carbohydrate craving that troubles some people may reflect the body's need to produce more serotonin. The researchers treated a study group of students with fenfluramine, an amphetamine-like appetite suppressant thought to release serotonin into the brain, and with tryptophan, an amino acid that contributes to serotonin synthesis. The fenfluramine, and to a lesser extent the tryptophan, significantly reduced the study group's carbohydrate consumption without affecting other aspects of their appetites. (Dr. Blinder and his associates have also begun clinical trials of fenfluramine, tryptophan and trazodone—another drug that enhances brain serotonin transmission—with initial encouraging results.) These findings are exciting because they show the possibility of central brain control of aspects of appetite and eating.

Wurtman's group also found that some of the students not only overate particular types of foods, they also tended to snack during certain times of the day. This implies that diet planning should include an evaluation of the dieter's eating pattern, allowing him or her to satisfy a craving for a specific food at the appropriate time. Drug treatment could likewise be patterned according to the dieter's eating habits.

Food cravings are no less real in those who are not under medical supervision. They become frightened and anxious about becoming fat and learn to control their craving as they were taught to handle all of life's troubles. Some people give in and become fat; others avoid the problem food(s) and work their way into anorexia nervosa; and still others learn how to vomit.

Yet another research topic is that of bulimia as a disorder confined primarily to women. "Depression, schizophrenia, neurosis and behavioral disorders are found in women of all ages," says John H. Rau of Long Island Jewish–Hillside Medical Center. "But has anybody known a bulimic who was either pre- or post-menstrual? Is bulimia in some way related to female endocrine cycles?" As previously noted, both bulimia and anorexia have been associated with specific hormonal aberrations, but researchers are stumped about the relationship between the hormones and the eating patterns themselves.

A more generalized research subject has to do with eating disorders serving as methods of self-medication against depression, anxiety and other forms of human misery. "We have no proof for this at all," says Dr. Huebner, "but speculatively, at least, we can organize eating disorders along two basic reward systems." One reward system is food; the other is endorphins, a group of hormones that serve as the body's natural painkillers and are part of its system for coping with physical and psychological stress.

According to the endorphin theory, a person who overeats occasionally or is overweight may decide to lose weight. As a result of self-imposed starvation, she experiences food withdrawal signs such as preoccupation with and craving for food. The starvation triggers the release of endorphins, shown in animal studies to be involved in eating behavior, weight regulation, and control of the feast and famine cycles of hibernation. These endorphins make the dieter feel better because they produce a coping effect similar to that of drugs or exercise (a known trigger of endorphins).

Like other painkillers, however, endorphins are addictive, so the dieter continues to move away from food to obtain endorphin effects. If she stops losing weight or actually gains weight again, her endorphin levels decrease, so that she is less able to cope and feels distressed and depressed. Her increased desire to lose weight again is actually a manifestation of her craving for endorphins. As she gains more weight, she may abandon the endorphins and become addicted to food instead. The food and the endorphins are like two delicate balances of a scale, with the unhappy dieter alternating between addictions to one and to the other.

This theory explains how the dieter became overweight to begin with by postulating that food can serve as an antidepressant for distressed and depressed people. Their bodies not only are trying to restore their biologically set weights but also have learned to seek out one of two coping mechanisms. Endorphins could help clarify why many anorectics become obese—perhaps anorexia nervosa and bulimia are part of the same illness at different times.

"It is possible too that vomiting, which like exercise and starvation produces a high, may serve as a powerful endorphin trigger in view of the violent autonomic nervous system shift that occurs with it. The tendency of bulimics to increase the frequency of binge-vomiting cycles suggests that endorphins may mediate this addiction-like behavior as well," says Dr. Huebner.

In observing bulimics, psychiatrists and psychologists must be careful to distinguish true bulimia from other medical and psychiatric disorders known to cause binge-eating. That there are biochemical causes for *any* kind of binge-eating suggests that researchers should continue exploring these possibilities in bulimia, however frustrating the search may seem. Two illnesses in particular that closely resemble bulimia seem likely to have met their magic bullets even though their causes are not well understood. Although rare, they are discussed here because they are sometimes mistaken for bulimia.

Bulimia's Imitators

RUMINATION

One of these illnesses is rumination. Rumination was defined earlier as a disorder of infancy, but out of the hundreds of eating-disorders patients he has treated over the past fifteen years, Dr. Blinder has found a few cases of rumination in adolescents and young adults of both sexes. These older victims can't keep food down; it comes up fifteen to twenty minutes after they eat, fairly consistently. Like bulimics, rumination victims keep their disorder a secret; even when they reveal it to internists or gastrointestinal specialists, the physicians find nothing wrong. The disorder is usually attributed to minor psychological problems, and the victims can suffer from it for years.

Dr. Blinder and his associates are trying to define the rumination pattern. They have found that rumination victims are definitely not bulimic—they may binge, but only because they grow very hungry from their inability to retain food. (Some women ruminators admit to using their illness secondarily to allow themselves to eat whatever they want.) Most victims are well adjusted psychologically; they are leaders in school activities and sports, sociable people who compartmentalize their problem and try not to let it interfere with their lives. "There is a very small incidence of rumination among adults," says Dr. Blinder. "Its importance is that the secondary hunger and overeating, followed by vomiting, may cause it to be mistaken for bulimia. Actually it's almost the reverse of bulimia: the vomiting, rather than the binging, starts off the cycle and must be compensated for."

Although they seem to be less disturbed than bulimics, rumination victims resemble them in being difficult to treat. "Psychotherapy and even hypnosis for rumination have been attempted with no specific improvements," says Dr. Blinder. "I suspect that it's probably a self-limited condition in young adulthood."

Researchers have assumed that rumination in a baby might be related to the mother's behaving inconsistently while feeding it —withdrawing because she feels anxious or depressed. The usual treatment was to switch the baby to a more affectionate caretaker or to instruct the mother and have her feed it under a nurse's supervision. In one study several years ago a researcher successfully counterconditioned a baby by giving it very mild external electrical shocks each time it was about to vomit. "With adults nothing is known," says Dr. Blinder. "Possibly rumination is an extrahypothalamic eating disorder with a muscular (neurotransmission) contraction deficit in the walls of the gut. It may be the one eating disorder that may prove to be not part of the central brain mechanism but rather related to neurotransmission in the gastrointestinal tract itself."

Dr. Blinder and his associates have begun clinical trials with Reglan (metoclopramide), a drug normally prescribed for diabetic paralysis of the gut or vomiting caused by cancer treatments. The drug's mechanism implies that it might counteract rumination: taken an hour before eating, metoclopramide increases stomach contractions, opens the pylorus (the opening through which food passes into the small intestine), and stimulates the stomach to push food down instead of out. Preliminary results have been promising, but long-term outcome is not yet certain. If successful, metoclopramide would suggest that at least one of the eating disorders might have neurochemical rather than solely psychological causes.

NEUROGENIC BINGE-EATING

The one pattern of binge-eating that has been most extensively studied seems to result from a neurological problem. John H. Rau, his colleague Dr. Richard S. Green, and other researchers have speculated about an as yet undefined epileptic equivalent seizure that may cause binging. Because of their research, and because of the ambiguities in the *DSM III* definition of bulimia, Rau believes that bulimia should be subdivided into two categories: psychogenic (psychologically caused) and neurogenic (neurologically caused) binge-eating. Psychogenic and neurogenic binge-eaters behave similarly; their difference is based on their sense of responsibility for binging.

The overwhelming majority of bulimics are psychogenic bingers. They may not like their binging, but they are aware that they themselves are responsible for it. The bulimic who binges to cope with anger and frustration and claims that she "can't help it" may be out of control, but she understands why— she is psychologically dependent on food.

Neurogenic binge-eating is an entirely different experience, one that resembles a sudden possession or an eating seizure. The victim can be going about her business contentedly when suddenly she is overwhelmed by an insatiable desire to eat anything that happens to be around. She feels as if not she herself but rather forces outside her were making her eat—episodically, unpredictably and uncontrollably. She feels disoriented and strangely unlike herself during her binge, as if she were in an altered state of consciousness, and if she sleeps afterward, she is likely to be confused momentarily when she awakens.

Several years ago, Rau and Green (upon whose research this discussion is based) did a pilot study on neurogenic binging. It was picked up by the newspapers, and they received hundreds of letters. Many were from people who were absolutely convinced that some kind of brain problems were causing their eating. And they were right. One of the first patients treated by Rau and Green was a competent nurse on a medical ward. She would be at work, not even thinking about food, when suddenly she would be seized by the urge to eat. She would helplessly eat food off patients' trays even though she knew perfectly well that in so doing she could contract hepatitis, typhus or other diseases. If she had an eating seizure on her way home, she would look around for a restaurant or pick up the lid of the nearest garbage can.

Researchers suspect that this mysterious disorder may be an electrical disturbance in the brain similar to epilepsy, because patients stop binging while taking Dilantin, an anticonvulsant drug. Aside from believing that the disorder involves the hypothalamus, investigators have no clue about its origin. Dilantin complicates the guesswork because physicians don't know precisely how it works; moreover, the drug causes side effects that could relate to eating. Dilantin affects insulin production, for example, and since any alteration in sugar metabolism could affect eating, the drug could be acting not neurophysiologically but rather through the pancreas. One way to help determine this would be to find people with neurogenic disorders who practice compulsions other than binging. "I have no evidence for this, but I'm convinced that there are subpopulations of compulsive gamblers, compulsive drinkers, all kinds of compulsive behavior, who have neurogenic disorders," says Rau. "I would suspect that these people have very different family and development backgrounds that led them to select food or drugs or gambling."

Theoretically, an unfortunate person could have a neurogenic and a psychogenic eating disorder simultaneously, and each aspect of that disorder would need to be treated differently. While a positive attitude and a sense of responsibility for one's illness are important to any treatment, a personal commitment won't stop neurogenic eating any more than it will cure any other neurological illness. Neurogenic eating needs to be identified as such and treated with appropriate medication. Unfortunately, some neurogenic bingers have wasted time, money and energy in undergoing psychotherapy for their problem. "Those futile years of psychotherapy make these people feel like complete failures in both controlling their eating and solving their problems," Rau says. "We saw a number of bright, gifted, talented women who had become convinced that they were bad patients because they just couldn't stop binging. In three weeks, with the proper medication, their problems were solved."

This is a dangerous point to make in a book about bulimia. Bulimics are notorious seekers of magic cures; no doubt many of them will line up in front of a neurological target if that's what the bullet will hit. How can a person determine whether or not her eating is neurogenic? Aside from her feelings about her binging, which are really too subtle to be used in diagnosis, she can show the disorder in specific medical tests. Rau and Green have found that a certain EEG pattern, 14- and 6-per-second positive spikes,* is frequently associated with neurogenic binge-eating, although many neurologists and encephalographers don't consider this pattern abnormal. In normal people the 14/6 pattern begins at puberty, increases in frequency until ages twenty-one to twenty-five, then slowly declines until it becomes very rare after age thirty-five and almost nonexistent after ages forty-five to fifty. This tendency ties it in with sexual endocrine functioning, interestingly enough, which links it with the hypothalamus, where the appetite drive centers. And bingers who show the 14/6 pattern benefit from Dilantin significantly more frequently than those who have either different abnormal patterns or normal patterns.

Along with the 14/6 EEG pattern, Rau and Green look for related symptoms such as rage attacks, headaches, dizziness, stomachaches, nausea, skin tingling or prickling, convulsions, perceptual disturbances like *déjà vu* or hallucinations, other compulsions like stealing or handwashing, and family histories of epilepsy. The presence of both the EEG pattern and these other symptoms predicts that the binger might improve with Dilantin.

Also significant is the victim's weight: if she is either very fat or very thin, she is more likely than normal-weight bingers to respond to the medication. Rau's theory is that the weight deviations measure the severity of the neurological illness—and the worse the illness, the more likely the medication is to work. Someone terrified of her binges may maintain a very low weight

---

* A pattern of brain waves clinically associated with episodic headaches, nausea, dizziness, skin tingling, perceptual disturbances, fainting, temperature dysregulation, impulse-control problems and higher probability of suicide attempts.

as insurance; she knows that at some point she will overeat and gain weight, so she compensates for that. Another binger may not be able to diet that successfully, so her disorder's intensity is instead shown by her resulting obesity. The weight therefore does not necessarily indicate psychological disturbances.

Unlike many psychogenic binge-eaters, neurogenic binge-eaters have no body-image distortion because weight is irrelevant to their illness. But it's interesting to note that researchers have found it very difficult to continue obese patients on Dilantin even when it's obviously successful in curbing their binging. These patients seem to be most disturbed and least able to cope with the social and sexual changes that normal weight would bring to their lives. In general, it's hard to separate the secondary psychological problems resulting from neurogenic binging—depression, anxiety, embarrassment, fear-of-eating seizures—from the primary psychological problems that cause psychogenic binging.

The medical profession is divided about whether the use of anticonvulsants can be extended to treat bulimia. Although open to the possibility of neurological causes for bulimia, many clinicians have looked in vain for EEG abnormalities among their patients. Still others have had the odd result of reducing binges with Dilantin only to have improvement continue long after the medication was stopped. Did the experience of control somehow enable the bingers to take control of themselves? If so, this would be an impressive demonstration of mind over body. But no one is sure, and although research in the neurology of bulimia continues, some investigators disparage the whole idea.

Why Psychotherapy?

If "bulimoid illnesses" like rumination and neurogenic binging may be biochemically based, and if bulimia itself is open to that possibility, why treat it with psychotherapy? Even if bulimia's imitators were not rare, biochemical disorders can't entirely explain why so many women use severe dieting and other drastic measures to reduce. If they exist, biochemical factors in bulimia

are interacting with psychological ones: both seem nec
gredients in the recipe. Craig Johnson explains:

> The group who would get into the most trouble with
> bulimia are those at risk for some kind of general or
> weight disorder. When this *zeitgeist* pushes them to-
> ward weight loss, it probably exacerbates some vulner-
> ability they already have. Speculatively, we can say
> that some biological vulnerability rears its head given
> certain circumstances. Regardless of that, bulimia vic-
> tims develop behavior patterns that become en-
> trenched. They need psychotherapy to help them un-
> derstand how the binging and purging became such a
> central part of their lives.

Yet another possibility is that measures as biologically violent as
vomiting, fasting or using laxatives and diuretics may not only
result from psychological disturbances but also cause psychological changes. This would not surprise anyone familiar with
the observable effects of chronic gorge-purging.

Possible Effects of Bulimia

The consequences of gorge-purging depend on the eating patterns, the amount and type of food retained, the frequency of
the purges, and the activity and constitution (as opposed to the
weight) of the binger. Although not all bulimics become ill, the
list of possible complications is impressive, and professionals
don't know whether the body can restore itself to normal once
the bulimic overcomes her problem.

CONSEQUENCES OF VOMITING AND PURGING

Theoretically, the effects of chronic vomiting can range from
anemia to rupture of the heart or esophagus, resulting in peritonitis. Researchers tentatively report subtle neuroendocrine
changes in their bulimic patients that may affect fertility and

find. that about half of them show disruption of the electrolyte balance—the vital chemical equilibrium in the blood that regulates heart and muscle function. The loss of body fluids and electrolytes through vomiting can cause hypokalemia, an abnormally low potassium concentration in the blood that can produce neuromuscular problems ranging from weakness to paralysis, irregular heart rhythms, gastrointestinal disorders and kidney disease. (One patient in England developed kidney failure and hypertension after eight years of self-induced vomiting and purging. A year later she had a kidney transplant, and although her weight rose, she still had occasional bouts of vomiting.) Bulimics can also show abnormally high levels of liver enzymes. They report vomiting up blood and having chronic sore throats and difficulties in breathing and swallowing. Their periods become irregular. Their parotid glands enlarge in association with abnormally high amounts of amylase (a digestive enzyme), taking a long time to subside once the bulimia has stopped.

Meanwhile bulimics are feeling the more obvious effects of their purging. They report stomach cramps, ulcers and other digestive problems. (Those who stop binge-purging can find themselves constipated; some end up sick in bed as their bodies go through withdrawal symptoms after prolonged abuse.) More fortunate bulimics binge-vomit with no ill effects, while others complain of general ill health and constant physical problems— dizziness, weakness, tremors—as well as tiredness, apathy and irritability. They develop broken blood vessels under their eyes and in their necks and suffer from headaches. Their skin becomes grayish and blotched with acne and other sores that don't heal. Since dieting lowers metabolic rate, their bodies immediately store any food they do retain as fat. Ironically, the bulimic's desire to stay attractively slim by vomiting ruins her appearance in other respects.

Probably the most common effect of self-induced vomiting is irreversible tooth damage caused by the sweet foods that bulimics eat, the acidic vomitus washing over their teeth, and the fruit juices that many of them drink to relieve their excessive thirst. Dehydration and electrolyte imbalances contribute to this process by decreasing and/or altering the pH (acid/alkaline balance) of the saliva, which normally helps to protect the teeth from decay. It is not hard to find bulimic women who have had abscesses, mouth sores and various problems requiring full sets of crowns, several root canals, and other dentistry costing thousands of dollars.

Dentists are in a good position to diagnose bulimia and to confront victims with it. Preliminary studies suggest that the damage caused by vomiting follows a pattern distinguishable from other causes of enamel loss (like brushing or grinding the teeth) if the dentist knows what to look for. Most of the time dental erosion occurs on the outer side of the teeth, but that caused by vomiting affects the palatal (inner) side of the upper teeth, starting with the molars and moving forward to the front teeth, which become most severely damaged. The edges of the front teeth begin to shorten, and after a long time, when the enamel on the back teeth has eroded as well, the damage to biting surfaces produces a faulty bite. With further erosion the bite changes so much that the bulimic's jaw begins to lose its vertical dimension—her lower jaw scrunches up toward her nose as if she had just removed a set of false teeth. This change to a "closed bite" calls for the dentist to reconstruct much of the victim's mouth to restore her original bite and proper facial dimensions. The extent of the damage determines how complex a problem needs to be corrected by crowns. If the bulimic has had her teeth crowned with plastic or gold in the past, these crowns will have eroded also and will need to be replaced by porcelain and metal crowns, which are better able to withstand attack by acids.

Miriam spent several years having her teeth replaced a few at a time, as two entries from her diary note:

August 3, 1965

Went to dentist to get teeth in. Two hours of pure torture. He hammered them out and hammered the new ones in. I wouldn't have minded if I liked them. But one front tooth is set back and shorter than the other. I was so disappointed I could have died. How I regret letting my old teeth be ruined. To smile like I used to. I guess I'm just too vain.

I'm so wrecked, so depressed. All I do is look at other people's teeth.

March 26, 1973

Went to the dentist. He had to put to death two more teeth. Wages of sin are tremendous. All because a silly little girl chooses the sweet life of gum, candy and cookies over the life of a 28-year-old woman with a pretty white smile and no dentist bills, who doesn't live like a pig and spend $300 a month on groceries that go down the drain. Think what that money and your time could go for. THINK!

Although the consequences of vomiting can be more obvious, abuse of laxatives and diuretics can be just as pernicious. Diuretic abuse can damage the kidneys and result in dependency that causes water retention once the diuretics are stopped. Excessive use of laxatives causes a variety of chemical upsets along with pain, disorders and infections; it has also been associated with both benign and malignant bowel tumors. Some laxative abusers complain that their hearts flutter for hours after a laxative purge. Like diuretics and vomiting, laxatives can cause massive dehydration; they also ruin normal bowel functioning, for the body quickly becomes dependent on them. It also becomes resistant, as thirty-seven-year-old Gina, a bulimic anorectic, found out:

The first few times I took sixty Correctols, I became violently ill with both diarrhea and nausea. I couldn't walk and was literally crawling from place to place in my apartment. I kept wanting to give up both that and the vomiting, but as soon as I ate anything, I'd start to round out. I'm five feet seven inches and weighed about ninety pounds then; when you're a stripped skeleton like that, any food shows up right away. I kept saying that this was the last time I'd do it, but it didn't work.

After I recovered from that first terrible episode with the laxatives, I took sixty Correctols again but didn't get as sick, because my body had already started to become resistant. So I took that many laxatives at a time on several occasions.

Besides all these problems caused by their purgative methods, bulimics obviously don't get proper nourishment regardless of whether or not they resort to fasting.

SCARE TACTICS DON'T WORK

Is a list of possible consequences likely to scare people away from gorging and purging? Hardly—people also ignore warnings against smoking, drinking or driving without a seat belt. Anita B. Siegman describes the attitude of one of her patients:

I have a patient who just saw her internist because she's been vomiting blood. She takes laxatives twice a day; she has severe abdominal problems, and she has been sicker in the last few years she's been bulimic than she has ever been in her life. Her physician wants to do an upper GI series on her, so she's even getting some data on her body, and that's not stopping her. And she's bright enough to know that what she's doing is a kind of self-mutilation. Yet it's too difficult for her to stop—first, because there's something about the process of losing weight that's somehow more gratifying than the end result of being the ideal weight; and also because she fears that if she doesn't do this she'll become very fat, and that is more terrifying than vomiting blood.

Siegman's patient is so afraid to stop vomiting that she canceled her scheduled gastrointestinal work-up. How remarkably different our society would be if health rather than appearance were the criterion for prestige.

We have so far seen the problems that can occur in healthy women who take up binging and purging. If a woman has a medical problem to begin with, or if her health is complicated by pregnancy, bulimia can do even greater damage. Yet the

gorge-purging becomes so central to the woman's life that her
other medical considerations simply give way. Twenty-seven-
year-old Grace, a social worker from Washington, D.C., stayed
bulimic for ten years despite a medical situation that became increasingly complex:

I was in college when I was diagnosed as diabetic.
My first thought was, "Did the binging do this?" Doctors have told me since that all my binging on sweets
could have done was perhaps bring on the diabetes
earlier, because essentially it's hereditary. But I
couldn't handle being sick or, for that matter, being
anything other than what I wanted to be. They treated
me as an outpatient, although I wish that they had hospitalized me because I couldn't quit binge-vomiting.

The first time I binged as a diabetic I ate a box of
malted-milk balls, then called my doctor and asked her
hysterically if I was going to die. She told me that I'd
feel lousy for a few days and that I should increase my
insulin to help stabilize the effects. "Hmmn," I thought.
I started increasing my insulin regularly to compensate
for my binging. A diabetic's life has to be consistent for
the treatment to be effective, and mine was anything
but that. Some days I'd fast, and others I'd binge three
times a day and give myself three shots—my self-
prescribed limit. I lived on luck for six years without
seeing a doctor.

I was using the bulimia to deny the diabetes, among
other things. I had expected a bolt of lightning to strike
me the first time I binged as a diabetic. When I found
out that I could play games with the diabetes and still
binge-vomit, then it didn't stop me at all. I binged on
sweets and starches, and my blood sugars eventually
went insane, so I must have done damage. But I stayed
right with it, with the serious consequences way at the
back of my mind. . . .

I cried when I learned that I was pregnant. Pregnancy does not mix with diabetes and bulimia, and I
thought that both were equally incurable. I'm sure that

I cried because of the binging. It wasn't that I wasn't ready for pregnancy; it was that I was terrified to give up the binging. For the first time I had to turn my body over to the medical profession and start seeing a doctor regularly. As soon as the doctor tested my blood sugar levels, he shoved me into the hospital so that they could monitor my diet. I was in a frenzy. I couldn't binge for three weeks, and I thought about food all the time. I sat in that hospital bed and hated the baby and felt an utter loss of control in my life. I was seeing an excellent diabetes specialist who suspected that my eating was amiss but couldn't get me to admit anything. I thought that when I left the hospital I could end the binging. Fat chance. I had found a way to adjust my insulin to keep binge-vomiting as a diabetic, so pregnancy wasn't likely to stop me.

I felt such tremendous guilt when I resumed binging while pregnant—another life depended on what I was eating and vomiting. I would binge because I was worried about what my binging was doing to my body and the baby's. I was sad, very scared and disgusted enough to at least stop eating sweets because of the diabetes, but I kept binging even though it did less to relieve the tension.

The tension didn't last that long, because I miscarried. I thought that now I would really take my illnesses seriously. But now I was eating to avoid even more guilt and unhappiness. I had wanted an abortion because of my crazy eating but had since become attached to the baby. I had started anticipating it, and now it was dead. I was never any good at accepting sympathy, and now I got loads of it. And not a single person knew of my fear that I had killed the baby with my eating. I look for things to feel guilty about, but isn't it reasonable to wonder whether stuffing yourself and vomiting your guts out is harming your unborn child?

After I heard about a bulimia program and finally worked my way into treatment, I had long talks with a

couple of my doctors. They said that the diabetes more
than the bulimia was likely to have caused the miscar-
riage, but that the bulimia might have aggravated the
diabetes enough to be indirectly responsible. How do I
live with that?

Grace's final question relates to her guilt about her baby—like
most bulimics, she cares too little about herself to act on her
fears for her own health. (Another bulimic was once hospitalized for phlebitis—vein inflammation—and ordered to have
complete bed rest and a heparin IV. She pulled out the needle
after every meal to go to the bathroom and vomit.) The point
is not for the bulimic to judge her behavior but rather for her to
try to understand herself better. Unfortunately, Grace is not
alone in finding pregnancy an insufficient reason to give up
binge-vomiting. Many bulimics have vomited throughout pregnancy, perhaps compensating by eating normally after a purge,
and still managed to have what seem to be healthy babies. But
who knows what kinds of congenital weaknesses those babies
may have?

Dr. Blinder and his colleagues plan to study the first year of a
baby expected by one of his bulimic patients. The mother has
managed to cut her binging from twice a day to twice a week
during pregnancy and has been following her vomiting with a
nutritious drink or a snack. The psychiatrists will monitor both
the baby's health and its relationship (especially during feeding) with its mother.

Grace's encounter with a suspicious diabetes specialist raises
another point—how are bulimics who see physicians able to hide
their disorder? Are they experts at manipulating people who
threaten to remove their habit? Are their physicians incompetent
or uninterested? Or are the symptoms too sporadic to be readily
detected? Bulimics' "luck" is probably a combination of the
three. Lab tests run on patients being treated for bulimia come
out negative half the time, and most of them seem to be in good
health. Even though most therapists recommend that their bulimic patients find internists to evaluate them, the medical doctor
often plays a minor role in treatment. Estelle Miller had one pa-

tient who coughed up a cupful of blood while vomiting after a binge. The woman went to a doctor at Columbia University who gave her a complete work-up and found nothing wrong. Physical responses to binge-vomiting seem to be a matter of luck. Some people vomit a few times a week and suffer excruciating stomach spasms; others do it several times a day with no ill effects. Most of the time physicians don't know where to look for symptoms of bulimia—and of course patients don't tell them why they're looking.

BULIMIA CAN KILL

What is the bottom line to all this? Can the bulimic's symptoms, obvious or not, eventually kill her? Certainly stuffing oneself has its dangers. The media have described a twenty-four-year-old London woman who ate herself to death after three days of fasting. She swallowed nearly twenty pounds of food, damaging the walls of her stomach and intestines so badly that peritonitis had set in by the time the doctors were able to operate. A woman was admitted to the University of Minnesota Hospital with acute gastric dilatation—her stomach, swollen by a binge, threatened to burst for twenty-four hours until she was finally able to make herself vomit.

Vomiting can be just as life-threatening. Many bulimics report being haunted by the idea of strangling on their vomit and dying in the bathroom. One woman developed a hiatus hernia from vomiting. A twenty-three-year-old nursing student died of a heart attack while participating in a sleep experiment at the National Institute of Health; the medical examiner ruled that the cause of death was severe vomiting. Dr. Yager heard from a colleague in San Diego about eleven bulimic anorectic girls who died of suspected electrolyte imbalance in one year. Who knows how many women die without the real cause of death being known? Potassium deficiency can cause cardiac arrest, so the sudden death of a young, apparently healthy person might have resulted from bulimia. Dr. Mitchell explains:

Certainly electrolyte imbalance is a cause of death in anorexia nervosa. I think we may begin to see case reports of bulimics as well. I've seen a few women in our clinic who had such a low level of potassium that I was really surprised they were able to get up and walk around. People's electrolytes can change rather dramatically in association with the binge-vomiting, and I think that it's a real cause for concern.

Even if they are not done in by their physical problems, bulimics risk endangering themselves because of their chronic depression. One of the anorexia associations was founded by the father of a bulimic woman who killed herself shortly before her twenty-first birthday.

PSYCHOLOGICAL EFFECTS OF BULIMIA

We have seen that there is a close tie between the biological and psychological causes of bulimia. What, then, are the psychological effects of gorge-purging? Do bulimics undergo the kinds of psychological changes common among acute anorectics? Any changes are probably not as severe, although some victims have noticed spooky results from their practices. "One woman in our group had periods during which she would eat and throw up for eight hours at a time day after day," says William Davis of the Center for the Study of Anorexia and Bulimia in New York City. "If she then attempted to drive, for instance, she would feel confused and shaky, and every once in a while she would report hallucinations. If the bulimia is very intense, it can certainly upset some psychological processes." For twenty-two-year-old Christina, this upset was clearly evident:

For me the worst effects of the bulimia were mental rather than physical. Aside from feeling schizophrenic about the lie I was living, I became paranoid and lost a lot of sleep from all-night binges. While binging I'd often hallucinate—always that people were coming around a corner to catch me—I'd both see and hear them. I was terrified of being caught binging, except for the last year of it, when I wished someone would catch me because it was so out of control.

We have seen that bulimics are often trapped in a vicious cycle in which they binge, fast to compensate for the binging, become depressed from the fasting, binge to ease the depression, and so on. This cycle has its parallels in many types of behavior that psychiatrists and psychologists try to assemble into a model for the bulimic personality. Aside from the obvious disturbances that troubled Christina, there are other factors associated with binge-vomiting that make it difficult to separate the cycle into causes and effects. The illness itself causes great isolation, loneliness and secrecy—it becomes a terrible stigma that destroys its victims' lives. We learned to eat as we learned to use the toilet—both are fundamental processes that adults should not even have to think about. The pressure of having to gorge and purge must weigh heavily upon the bulimic, altering her personality in a way that we all experience when coping with extreme stress.

But no one knows how much of the bulimic's personality led to rather than resulted from her illness, especially if she is quite young. "Bulimics might be somewhat perfectionistic, for example," says Gretchen Goff, "but as a result of becoming bulimics they become extremely so. Because they see themselves as awful people who binge-vomit, their expectations of themselves become more outrageous, and they have to flip into total perfectionism." It's also difficult to analyze the personality of someone whose feelings are constantly being obliterated by binge-vomiting. Nevertheless, we can try.

Chapter 6

ROUGH SKETCH OF A BULIMIC

Bulimics probably don't want to hear that their illness affects their personalities any more than they want to hear other generalizations about themselves. They're tired of it, and they're not pleased by some of the press they've been getting. "When you talk about us," said one woman as she left a group-therapy session, "try to make us out to be human beings. We're always reduced to 'characteristics that can be clinically observed.'" Her discomfort is understandable. But an important difference between the clinician's observations and the interviewer's is that the latter meets only those bulimics who are recovering or abstinent from gorge-purging. Others won't admit to the illness, much less talk about it. While practicing bulimics may be grappling with clinicians, those who share their experiences with interviewers do so in retrospect. Although their narratives are edited by time and memory lapses, it's best to let them speak for themselves.

Bulimics are women whom we know. Every reader of this book has an acquaintance who secretly binges and purges. Bulimics are different in their tendency to reach out to food instead of to other people. As a group, recovered bulimics (like their fellow addicts) are distinguished by the exact opposite—a sense of mission. For some, altruism has merely replaced bulimia as their major compulsion. Most, however, genuinely want to spare other women the anguish of bulimia for a moment longer. Through her interviewer, then, the bulimic woman tries to reassure other bulimics. As she speaks, her façade crumbles to reveal her problems—some of which she recognizes, and others that she has not yet discovered. She describes what she thinks is the most disgusting thing about herself in order to show others how to accept themselves.

Like others who have endured more than their share of human misery, the bulimic has been paradoxically enriched by her unhappy experiences with food, especially in her relationships with other women. Many bulimics do not get along well with other women until they start treatment, when, in a desperate attempt to find other *bulimics,* they discover the special warmth, support and friendship shared by *women.* If bulimics can recover, they will do so probably because of what they can offer each other. They learn to accept themselves by learning to love other women who are much like them. And that knowledge is obvious in them.

But back to what the clinicians, the experts, can tell us. Bulimics are elusive not just because of the circular relationship between their personalities and their illness. They are observed by researchers in private practice or in clinics that inevitably attract homogenous groups of patients—usually those who are most accomplished psychologically and socioeconomically. Certainly this is true of the many eating disorders clinics that dot college campuses across the country. Despite this limitation, however, investigators are finding that bulimia victims represent a cross section of America womanhood.

The media appear to have fastened upon merely a subgroup of bulimics: those oriented toward social recognition, academic achievement and appearance, especially thinness. Michael Strober explains:

> The stereotype refers to this segment of the bulimic population, but many bulimics do not fit this quick sketch. *Some* are successful businesswomen who use bulimia as a secretive means of relinquishing control. But I have done consults on two hundred eating-disorders patients, and we see a very broad spectrum of personality types and socioeconomic and occupational backgrounds.

There is very little known about the factors tying these women together. Quite possibly those women who come for treatment fit a pattern, and those who don't are socioeconomically and demographically quite different.

Other therapists agree that bulimics are a garden-variety population—they run a whole gamut of intelligence, wealth, attractiveness, and ability to function well in life.

Problems in Describing Bulimics

The gamut ranges between two extremes. At one end are the stereotypical "bulimarexics"—attractive, bright, nice, perfectionistic and successful—who *may* tend to be bulimic anorectics. At the other extreme are women who lead chaotic, quite miserable lives, who may have undergone hospitalization for depression, psychosis or chemical dependency, for whom bulimia is one of several symptoms of their problems. (These problems are not their fault and nothing to be ashamed of—unless they allow them to persist by refusing to seek help.) The only legitimate generalization we can make about observed bulimics is that they are Caucasian and able, through either income, prostitution or theft, to support their expensive habit. All we can do here is list isolated characteristics that many bulimics seem to share— together they may not necessarily be a prototype of the bulimic personality.

Another obstacle to finding common denominators for bulimics is that many of them don't show much psychopathology on standard psychiatric rating scales. They don't always seem classically depressed, anxious or afflicted with headaches or nausea, and they are not always stuck in unhealthy relationships. The bulimic woman may be holding down a responsible job, may appear to be, and in fact may actually be, functioning quite well. These factors make it easy to overlook her difficulties or attribute them to transitory problems. Because bulimics have specific disturbances, they require tests specifically designed to detect those patterns, such as the Eating Attitudes Test devised by David Garner and Dr. Paul E. Garfinkel at the Clarke Institute of Psychiatry in Toronto.

As if all this weren't complicated enough, bulimics consciously suppress their feelings, a tendency aggravated when they resort to binge-vomiting to numb themselves. Like the anorectic, the bulimic is basically compliant due to an almost adolescent desire to fit in; she does not express her emotions or frustrations if these mean conflict with the important people in her life. She surrenders her individual rights and powers, especially in relationships with men. She is compliant in therapy also, and that desire to please makes her difficult to treat.

Bulimics who live together, are acquainted, or share the same treatment program can often be identified by their clichés: "I wanted to have my cake and eat it too," "I set myself up for rejection and disappointment," "I had to get away from people to do what I had to do [vomit]," and, for those in Overeaters Anonymous, "My illness is cunning, baffling and powerful." Those who like to read about themselves also parrot the formulas they have learned, regardless of whether or not they apply: "I'm your typical bulimic—perfectionistic, nice and achievement-oriented." Beneath these platitudes can be a high degree of creativity and intelligence being squelched by the binge. There may also be a lot of misery—bulimics delude themselves into thinking they are happy because that's what they're expected to be, and they fear others' opinions of their true feelings. "One of the most important things I've learned about staying abstinent is the importance of talking," says one victim. "Expressing your feelings is important, and your feelings themselves are okay—they're not right or wrong, just valid as honest expressions of yourself. That's true for everyone, not just bulimics, but it's awfully hard for us to learn."

The result is that researchers must wait until a person has stopped binge-vomiting to determine what she is all about or try to peer through the interstices of the bulimia for a glimpse of the woman underneath. "Although bulimics may have predominant personality characteristics, we're finding that, like alcoholism, bulimia can occur in a whole range of personality disorders," says Judith Brisman of the Center for Bulimia in New

York City. "Underneath the bulimia are arrests at all different developmental levels. Bulimics range from alienated to extroverted. Whatever their underlying conflict is, the bulimia is like glue holding it together—remove the glue, and the conflict begins to emerge." When the conflicts do emerge, bulimics turn out to be very much like other women—another reason that the illness is so insidious.

The Bulimic Personality

FOOD AND BODY ATTITUDES

Having acknowledged the problems involved in describing bulimics, we can point out some tentative personality patterns. Predictably, bulimics are obsessed with food and body size. Many of them have uncontrollable appetites and don't know when they're full at the end of normal meals. Despite this problem, most of them feel positive toward food; some enjoy cooking for others, as do their anorectic sisters, or they may take jobs as waitresses or food handlers. But many bulimics lack a clear sense of themselves, their physical boundaries and their bodies' typical behavior. They may be terrified that if they eat something their bodies won't eliminate it. They must learn to trust their bodies to work normally and to recover from laxative abuse and chronic vomiting. Bulimics must also learn to trust when they're tired, lonely, full, or hungry for something other than food, since they are badly out of touch with themselves in these respects. As previously noted, bulimics fear becoming fat and perceive themselves unrealistically as being overweight, although to a lesser extent than do anorectics.

This critical preoccupation with appearance and body image is a symptom of narcissism (in the psychiatric sense of grandiosity, exhibitionism and entitlement that disguise an extremely low sense of self-esteem). Alma, a twenty-three-year-old bulimic, explains some of it:

> When your self-image is low, you think that your body
> is the only thing about you that people can like, and

that puts terrible pressure on it. I used to have no concept of my body except as a sexual body, because sexuality terrified me. I refused to admit my femininity to anyone and wanted desperately to be neuter, not female. I still want my body to be perfect; I don't know how to deal with it, and I'm afraid of how others will react to it.

"In group I ask bulimics what percentage of their days they spend thinking about food, and they say eighty to ninety percent," says Anita B. Siegman. "I will then ask them, 'If you weren't thinking about food, what might you be thinking or worrying about?' They respond that they'd be thinking about their anxiety, low self-esteem and lack of control, and their idea that if only their figures were okay, life would be wonderful."

PERFECTIONISM

This obsession with attractiveness as the solution to all of life's problems is tied in with the perfectionism so often seen in bulimic women. Perfectionistic bulimics usually come from families that emphasized the importance of looks and achievement. A bulimic from this background may well grow into a beautiful woman who succeeds scholastically and professionally, but her expectations of herself remain so unreal and unattainable that she always falls short in her own eyes. Trying always to meet artificial standards, bulimics naturally evolve into very competitive people and sometimes can't see others except in those terms. "Part of my bulimia involved my wanting to get away from people because I believe that they are all superior to me, and I can't handle it. I can't be as good as them, so I escape from them to eat," explains one victim.

Because her standards were imposed on her, the bulimic doesn't know how to reinforce herself when she falls short of her own impossible demands. Hers is purely an all-or-nothing attitude. "One enlightening question I often ask during a consultation is, 'What do you do for fun?'" says Craig Johnson. "It puzzles many of the women I talk to. They have no means of really letting go, enjoying themselves and having fun, without feeling a need to conform or fulfill expectations or do something right." Twenty-two-year-old Fay is a good example:

> The only redeeming thing about perfectionism is that I'm being perfect in abstinence along with everything else. That's ridiculous, but it's also constructive. But I'm still trying to be perfect at every moment. I can't *feel* to be positive; I have to *think* to be positive—I just can't live with my feelings. I'd love to be able to just sit around, relax and do nothing. But I've got to be doing something, and doing it perfectly, all the time. And it's still really easy for me to get depressed about that.

Bulimic women must learn to fill themselves up from the inside through intrinsically satisfying activities rather than always driving toward recognizable accomplishments. Instead, many of them either abandon their perfectionism when they become ill, feeling that they are hopeless, or continue it so that it subtly contributes to the bulimia. Some of them switch to become the best at acting the worst, thereby spiraling down to self-destruction.

DEPRESSION

Fay is correct in saying that the struggle to be perfect contributes to one of the major characteristics of bulimia—depression. Bulimic women tend to exhibit an agitated depression that nevertheless involves some very dreary moods. Their eating is apparently not a symptom of primary depression, however, because although many bulimics respond well to antidepressants or shock therapy, these treatments may not help them stop binging. The depression may be secondary and typical of that which occurs with chronic mental or physical illness; as such it may diminish as the bulimia is treated.

ANGER

Much of what the binge eats away is the pain of unexpressed anger. Bulimics are frightened of any kind of hostility or badness because they are aware of the rage that they themselves suppress. Thirty-two-year-old Glenda, a New York musician, has been furious ever since she can remember:

> I have a brother six years younger than I am; he was the spoiled brat, and I was the problem child. He used to go into my room and pull my closet apart looking for my toys, and I'd get so angry that I'd start beating him and screaming. My mother always took my things away and gave them to my brother; when I complained, she'd tell me that I was selfish. I had no way to compensate for this with other relationships because we lived on the edge of town far from where my classmates lived. I was used to being with adults and was expected to act like one—I was supposed to be "mature" about my brother's behavior—so I never learned how to get along with other kids, and I hated school. I always misbehaved in school and managed to get sick often enough to stay home at least one third of the school year. It got so that I was expected to be sick and naughty. My sickness was my way of taking my anger out on myself; my naughtiness got back at other people, especially because it embarrassed my mother. Later in life I became angry about other things, but always remembering that I had been punished for being angry, I never learned how to face my feeling.

For some bulimics, binging actually makes anger concrete. A binge may even symbolically murder someone; a guilt-induced purge is intended to bring them back to life.

STORMY MOODS

Other emotions agitate bulimics but remain unexpressed. Bulimics are anxious, tense, irritable and afraid of stress because they feel that they can't handle it or anything else. "I felt stuck in a nowhere job and couldn't control my days; I had to go to work and be controlled, so I'd go home at night and control food," one victim explains. They feel desperate and worried—when they have nothing to worry about, they worry that they are not worried. They are impulsive and compulsive, buffeted about by moods that fluctuate extremely, as twenty-seven-year-old Olga explains:

I had always had a real problem with severe mood swings. I didn't realize that it was a problem because I never understood what they were, let alone that something could be done about them. They were aggravated by my experiments with drugs when I was in college.

During my hospitalization for depression, I felt that it was almost a luxury not to be responsible for what I did or felt. I had always stifled my moods, but there it was easy for me to show them. For the first time in my life I was able to show how terribly angry and unhappy I really was.

Like many bulimics, Olga keeps her feelings boxed away in a back closet of her life, unexplored and poorly understood. It takes a measure as extreme as psychiatric hospitalization to help her acknowledge emotions as common as anger and sadness.

RELATIONSHIPS

Their alienation from their own feelings naturally makes it very difficult for bulimics to get along with other people. Afraid of commitments, they tend to be irresponsible, spreading themselves thin in all kinds of activities, then giving them up. Many bulimics can't settle down and concentrate on one source of fulfillment, whether it be an activity or a friendship. Bulimics are alienated and isolated, avoiding people and emotional intimacy, yet paradoxically they are very lonely people chronically trying to please others (especially their parents). Their relationships tend to be short-term and full of problems, and some of them are genuinely puzzled about how to fit other people into their lives. Suzanne, a twenty-nine-year-old systems analyst, had this to say in group therapy:

My life just feels closed off. It's me, and I'm happier with myself, but it's not changing anything else. And I feel very lost, as if I don't know where to go to change things. I want to take risks but don't know where they

are. I don't know what I want. I don't know what
would make me happy. I know I'm very lonely, and I
want somebody else in my life, but I don't know where
to look for him. That's what's really killing me right
now. I feel like I'm alive, but I'm not living. And I want
to live. A year ago I didn't even want that; I wanted no
one to touch me. I feel like I'm still doing it out of
habit. I don't know anything else except pushing people away. I don't know how not to. And I look around
for someone to try with, and there's no one there, and I
wonder if I should walk a little farther and look a little
harder, but I realize that there's nowhere to find relationships.

It's hard for most people, with their interests and social contacts,
to appreciate the emptiness that bulimics complain of and that is
well expressed by Suzanne's statements. She is imprisoned by
her bewilderment and her behavior toward others. Few bulimics
are married, let alone happily married; those who do marry unconsciously choose spouses who show promise of being distant
enough to allow their bulimia to continue. Along with emotional
closeness, sexuality is a big problem for bulimics of both sexes.

All their emotional turmoil of course does not raise the low
self-esteem that afflicts most bulimics. They hate themselves;
they have little self-confidence; they are insecure and greatly
fear rejection. Although they spend thousands of dollars a year
on binge foods, many of them object to treatment for bulimia
because they feel that the cost is more than they deserve.

SENSE OF IDENTITY

Despite their isolation, bulimics depend heavily on others, especially their parents, and fear taking risks that would damage
what little security they do enjoy. They accept the traditional
feminine role of passive compliance at the expense of developing
identities. Emily, whose travels have landed her in Seattle, can
describe herself as a poet for the time being but doesn't value
her talent and has no idea what her career goals are:

In college I majored in biology, women's studies, sociol-
ogy, political science and psychology. But I never grad-

uated. I'm twenty-seven now; I don't have a degree, a husband, a family or a career. I've done a lot but never finished anything and have no idea what I want to do. The things I've done that other people find exciting don't excite me—I always think that *their* lives are much more interesting. It really bugs me to know that I never held down a job for more than a year and have bounced around the country a lot. What does it matter how much poetry I've published if I don't have a job? I have about ten ideas for a career but don't know if any of them are right, so I have to go for skill and personality testing to try to figure it out.

At any particular time, a bulimic's personality is likely to be a collage of what she has picked up from other people, yet somehow the pieces don't fit together into a pleasing whole.

Bulimia as Symptom

The widespread interest in weight control and eating disorders can distort our view of bulimics. Misdirecting our attention to the bulimia itself rather than its sufferers, we think: "This is bulimia; its victims tend to have these personality characteristics." A more accurate way to approach bulimia is by thinking: "Here are people with certain personality disorders; as a result, they can develop several problems, one of which is bulimia." Just as a runny nose and watery, itchy eyes can signal an allergy to any of a number of substances, bulimia can be a symptom of any of a number of disturbances. Dr. Yager explains:

The bulimia is a habit of behavior disturbance or style that somebody got into as a symptom—it's superficial. You can have any kind of personality under the bulimia, any degree of psychosis or ego defect or ego health. Some very healthy people put all their eggs into one neurotic basket like bulimia. Very healthy or very disturbed people can have neurotic symptoms—all the symptom does is bind a certain amount of anxiety. If it

binds only some anxiety, then other symptoms are necessary as well.

There seem to be groups of people at risk of developing
bulimia. One group comes from families that show a high incidence of alcoholism and depression. Another group has great
trouble dealing with tension. Their characters and moral development preclude their regulating tension through alcoholism,
drug abuse, delinquency or promiscuity and instead push them
toward food, which is safer in many ways. Harriet, a twenty-
four-year-old graphic designer from New Orleans, speaks for
many women in explaining this tendency:

> I was in art school and knew that I was good at art and
> was doing very well. But I was on pins and needles all
> the time. I would clutch during classes; my instructors
> would tell me to be more relaxed and expansive in my
> work, and meanwhile I'd be crouched in a corner of my
> canvas trying to make details perfect. There was a lot
> of pressure and constant deadlines, and I met those
> deadlines by eating my way through them. I'd do noth-
> ing but binge-vomit and procrastinate, then hand things
> in at the last minute. I had no confidence in my work
> despite the praise it got, and I was always comparing
> myself unfavorably to others, as if the competition built
> into my situation weren't bad enough.

Harriet's description points out how elements of the bulimic personality tie in with each other: perfectionism combined with
lack of confidence results in unbearable tension.

Borderline Personalities

One suggestion that frequently pops up is that bulimia is a
symptom of an underlying disorder known as the borderline personality, features of which are often seen (in a quieter form)
also in anorexia nervosa. "Borderline personality" is a very popular term in clinical psychiatry but an unclear one: it refers to a

quality in personality characteristics. People with borderline personalities are precariously balanced between neurotic and psychotic behavior (some bulimics have in fact been hospitalized for psychotic episodes), and their parallels with bulimics are striking. Like many bulimics, borderlines are distinguished by their tremendous impulsivity. Unlike anorectics, with their pathological rigidity, borderlines show violently oscillating behavior that they simply can't control. Their instinctual drives break through in various forms—emotional outbursts, food abuse, alcoholism, drug abuse, stealing, promiscuity or self-mutilation. (Some bulimics cut their forearms, pull out their eyelashes, tear off their fingernails, and so on. One bulimia victim reports being terrified of knives—she is worried that she will stab someone.) Bulimics who use food as their single means of letting go are therefore unlikely to be borderlines.

Borderline personalities also tend to have unstable, intense relationships in which they feel very dependent but hostile. With their great need for and fear of closeness, and with the jealousy these emotions give rise to, borderlines guarantee their rejection, which hurts them deeply because of their vulnerability. Borderlines trust no one but themselves, even though they don't understand themselves very well. Their identity disturbances show up in their bewilderment about who they are, how they want to earn a living, what they really believe in. Their moods fluctuate wildly between intense anger, loneliness, severe depression and emptiness. Far from successful, borderlines continue family traditions of personal confusion. They sense conflict between their aggressive impulses and their submissive roles as women. They can work hard but desire instant gratification without the patience to see things through. The perfectionism of some bulimics may actually express their impatient, unrealistic, simplistic attitude toward human limitations—for borderline personalities life is all or nothing, good or bad.

Dr. Katz and his colleagues believe that anorexia nervosa is most likely to occur in women with compulsive personalities, histrionic personalities or borderline personalities. Compulsive personalities have trouble expressing warm and tender emotions; they are perfectionists preoccupied with trivia who insist that others submit to their way of doing things. They are excessively devoted to work and often indecisive. Histrionic personalities behave in a melodramatic, overreactive and intensely expressed manner, especially when angry; in relationships they are shallow, egocentric, demanding, dependent and manipulative. Of the three categories, borderline personalities, with their all-or-nothing attitude and their intense rage and depression, are most likely to binge after a single forbidden bite. Thus, Dr. Katz feels that anorectics with borderline personalities are the best candidates to become bulimic—in fact, the anorexia itself seems to aggravate the borderline characteristics. This group of anorectics has the poorest prognosis for recovery. He also suggests that compulsive anorectics seem the most likely to remain pure restrictor anorectics, while histrionic anorectics fall somewhere in between the other two groups.

This theory means that at least some bulimia victims suffer from major psychological problems as well as their eating disorder. The borderline state can manifest itself in different ways. Some borderlines, for instance, do become addicts rather than bulimics; some make frequent suicide attempts; some drift in and out of bad relationships. While all this is likely to horrify dabblers in binge-vomiting, it might provide much insight into treating victims of severe bulimia. The combination of a very specific symptom like bulimia with a less specific personality disorder means that therapy must be flexible, multidimensional and individualized. It also means that the screening of prospective bulimic patients must be careful and thorough. A social worker, for example, who feels competent to treat mild or intermittent bulimia might want to refer a borderline bulimic to a psychiatrist, and vice versa.

Vocational Bulimics

Probably the best-known bulimics are those who start purging because thinness is important to them vocationally. In this category are models, actresses, athletes and dancers who try vomiting or laxatives as a means of weight control and get hooked on purging. (One might also expect to find high concentrations of male bulimics in these fields.)

As Dr. Vincent explains in *Competing with the Sylph,* dancers are a classic example of women whose appearances help determine their ability to earn a living. Vivian Meehan agrees:

> The weight restrictions on dancers aren't always for the excellence of the dance. I asked one dance coach in San Francisco whether the weight is really important or whether there are some people who would be marvelous dancers anyway. She agreed that weight should be secondary and said that she was feeling a little guilty over something that had occurred that morning. During auditions she saw a girl who was a little heavier than she liked but an absolutely wonderful dancer. She chose a girl who was thinner and had a better line. Who determines that line? I hear all kinds of stories like this, and I think it's incredible. Let them teach these kids to dance. If the dancers want eventually to go onstage and have to be thin, let them be thin then, although it's not right even then.

These women present a special obstacle to treatment, for to treat a woman for bulimia, the therapist has to consider the reality of the culture within which she operates. "It would be unreasonable for me to try to convince a dancer that she doesn't have to weigh ninety pounds," says Craig Johnson. "She's going to leave my office to work in some chorus line, and some dance coach will tell her to lose ten pounds because otherwise she'll look too heavy onstage. And the dance coach will be right, given the current standards for dancers."

Women who purge because their jobs require thinness are certainly easier to categorize—at least initially—than bulimics as a group. We might wonder, though, whether the factors that drive other women into bulimia are any less compelling.

Chapter 7

DAUGHTERS AND LOVERS

Bulimia victims live in very private little hells of self-imposed isolation and loneliness. As they descriptively wend their ways through the years they have been ill, the listener wonders whether other people ever figured in their lives at all. And yet bulimia clearly develops out of a human context—the bulimic's family, friends and lovers hold skeins of the food web in which she has become trapped. Most bulimics are aware that something in their family backgrounds has sadly crippled their ability to become close to other people—has taught them that people will fail them, but food will always be there. It's difficult to pinpoint the "something," because bulimics come from families both large and small, intact or disrupted, involved with or uninterested in food. Like the daughters, the families elude generalization.

Bulimics as Daughters

HOME IS WHERE THE FOOD IS

One aspect of family life that all bulimics (including several studied in England) agree on, however, is that the hardest place in the universe in which to avoid binging is their parents' home. Of course, this particular place holds a jackpot in the form of Mom's cooking, which brings back all the memories of security, protection and pleasure connected with home itself. It would seem natural that once home, the bulimic would head for the refrigerator to enjoy herself and to the bathroom to rid herself of the bloat that her appearance-conscious parents would not approve of. But bulimics themselves talk less in terms of anticipation than they do about home or their parents being like poison to them—triggering the feelings that cause the binge. "I've heard that anorectics have to be removed from their parents to be treated," remarks one bulimic. "I can understand why."

For some bulimics home is not necessarily the place to binge, but it's always the place to vomit. Younger bulimics still living at home may binge-vomit to assert their independence—their parents disapprove of their behavior but don't stop them. Older bulimics may recall that home was the place to binge successfully.

Why does a daughter choose eating as her response to some kind of family disturbance? The obvious answer, that food represents the nurturing parent, is not necessarily the best one. The families of bulimics may or may not have emphasized food, as Michael Strober explains:

> Some families are remarkably rigid and perverse around eating: the family must eat certain foods, must use perfect table manners or follow certain rituals around eating, must share the same likes and dislikes. But that's not the norm for eating-disorders families in my experience. *Some* families do emphasize thinness and physical activity and appearance, and these things —not necessarily all of them—will undoubtedly affect the daughter's body image.

Many bulimics do describe families that aspired to perfection. A daughter fed up with the pressure might at some level of her thinking consider bulimia a good joke on her parents—a thoroughly *im*perfect way of indicating her disgust, her rejection of their idea of nurturance. Or she may simply use the binge to cope with her inability to measure up to her parents' standards for her.

Twenty-eight-year-old Peggy, a bulimic anorectic studying
computer science, distinctly remembers learning that one aspect
of perfectionism is always to behave pleasantly:

> I'm not sure where my family really stands on this, but
> what's important is that I perceived an implied pres-
> sure never to show any of my feelings. You know—big
> girls don't cry; they don't get angry, much less swear;
> they love their families, their friends, their teachers, the
> whole town, and they're always happy. To please ev-
> erybody else, I took care of *their* feelings and left mine
> to the last. Anorexia and bulimia were my means of
> coping with this. All these buried feelings, and all the
> pressure I felt to have a good body, got saved for a
> binge.

Whatever the family ethic, the bulimic may forget her own
wishes and follow it—small wonder that some bulimics become
chronic people-pleasers. One reason bulimics grow up so angry
is that many of them are expected to do well, but they are given
confusing messages and are not properly reinforced for their
achievements. They hide their sadness and fear under a mask of
youthful independence. In many cases their parents use them to
fill their own unsatisfied needs.

An interesting side effect of such family difficulties is that
many bulimics eloquently describe their love of honesty and
marvel that their illness has turned them into chronic liars. Actually, many of these women learn in treatment that they have lied
for most of their lives. "Bulimics have emphasized honesty all
their lives because they were always dishonest in hiding their
anger and other feelings," says Ellen Schor. "Their idea that
honesty is all-high and -powerful is a lie too. Their families were
probably set up to contribute to the bulimia by making them believe that there were no lies, that everything was perfect, even
though there were plenty of deceits in the family, and nothing
was perfect at all." This may be more true of the families of
bulimic anorectics. The parents of "the best little girl in the
world" insist that the family is normal and stable and practice
rigid emotional control. The bulimic's family, on the other hand,

shows a kaleidoscope of shifting conflicts involving distance, overt disagreement and attempts at control.

PARENTS OF BULIMICS

How do these conflicts show up in the bulimic's relationship with her parents? For one thing, the bulimic's father is something of an elusive figure and as such is invested with magical powers by his impressionable daughter. "It strikes me that bulimics have a great deal of trouble with their fathers, disproportionate numbers of early deaths, for instance," says Dr. Atchley. "The father is distant, divorced, or 'too close.' But whether there's more of that than there is with many women is hard to say." Other therapists agree that the fathers of bulimics tend to be emotionally distant and preoccupied with their careers. "Fathers are perceived as critical because they are distant," says Anita B. Siegman. "Many of these women start talking about their mothers and gradually end up talking about their fathers, who, because of their lack of input, become important. Their fathers also become significant in their relationships with men." Often fathers are stellar figures, competent and dynamic, usually very dramatic. But as the fathers of daughters who can afford psychotherapy, they would inevitably fit such a stereotype. It will be interesting to see what happens in bulimic families as more breadwinning women become mothers.

Since the daughter's illness involves food, it seems even more likely that her mother would be involved, especially since most bulimics distrust other women as well as men. Traditionally, mothers are blamed for all our problems; the various theories of how they steered their daughters into bulimia are no exception. In *Fat Is a Feminist Issue,** therapist Susie Orbach explains the complex tie between food and the idea of nurturance associated with the mother. Aware of their own status as second-class citizens in a patriarchal society, mothers are ambivalent about whether they want their daughters to identify with them or to lead independent lives. Mothers are also tense and confused about their roles: although they are the primary caregivers, child "experts" tell them that they are inadequate for the job, so they distrust their reactions to their children's signals and instead

---

* Orbach, Susie, *Fat Is a Feminist Issue* (New York: Berkeley, 1978).

overfeed them. The daughters' manipulation of food is a reaction to this unhappy state of affairs. "I suggest that one of the reasons we find so many women suffering from eating disorders," Orbach writes, "is because the social relationship between feeder and fed, between mother and daughter, fraught as it is with ambivalence and hostility, becomes a suitable mechanism for distortion and rebellion." (As more daughters are raised by members of Weight Watchers and Overeaters Anonymous, the opportunities for testing this hypothesis increase.)

In her attempts to generalize about what causes bulimia, twenty-five-year-old Sue Ann, an architectural engineer from Washington, D.C., has drawn similar conclusions:

> I think that one of the biggest factors in bulimia is the type of mothers we have and the sociological factors we operate in. Most of our mothers are older, protective, oversolicitous and quite limited. I see the illness as an outgrowth of women's transition from the traditional martyr role to that of daughters with both opportunities and pressures. The difference in the two generations has changed the mother/daughter relationship: we get double messages from our mothers to go and compete and succeed and be perfect without breaking our mothers' apron strings or surpassing them. These double messages about becoming someone cause terrible pressures, and meanwhile our mothers are teaching us not to express our feelings, so that we have no outlet for the pressures.
>
> My mother sent me for dance and art lessons, but I always had to go alone, and when I came home really excited about some accomplishment, I'd get no support from her. The frustration from this contributed to my compulsiveness. I was too perfect to get into drugs or liquor at first; the food was always there, and that's what I turned to.
>
> But I know bulimic women whose mothers or other older family members were bulimic, and I don't know how to explain that.

Sue Ann's comments locate her within a particular group of bulimics—some bulimic women don't feel pressures to succeed because they didn't have the opportunities to begin with. Her generalizations are true only up to a point.

There are other ways to think about how women's changing roles are driving them into compulsions. Some experts feel that bulimic women suffer from the psychological dependence that author Colette Dowling has termed "the Cinderella complex." "One thing that I suspect connects these women is a very strong need to be independent and a fear that if they express their equally strong wish to be taken care of, they'll be rejected or criticized for it," says William Davis. A psychoanalyst, Davis attributes this to the mothers of bulimics:

> They appear to be concerned about and interested in their daughters, and they are up to a point, but they have trouble with someone who asks them to show tenderness or kindness. I think these mothers feel anxious and nervous about whether or not they can really show that. They instead leave the field, so to speak, become unavailable or unresponsive to requests for protection or support. Their daughters feel that expressing such requests makes them *personae non gratae*—something happens that's funny and that they don't understand. They translate these situations into the idea that they're bad persons if they want to be this way.

The daughters' response is to turn to food for the comfort, nurturance and good feelings that their mothers don't provide. When the daughters feel guilty for wanting these things, they can just get rid of the food by purging.

Another observed pattern is that the mothers' limitations may show up in the opposite manner, with their showing too many feelings, many of them ambivalent. The daughters may not be prepared for such openness from their mothers, as Anita B. Siegman explains:

> The mother is somewhat fragile and does not see herself as having maternal authority. The boundary be-

tween mother and daughter is not clear; the mother is overprotective, and there is some role reversal. The daughter takes care of her and panics when the time comes to leave her mother and go off to college. Some bulimic women have told me that they feel responsible for keeping their mother and father together. There may also be some competition between the parents that causes the mother to cling to the children.

These generalized theories suggest an unintentional, unconscious attitude that victimizes the mother as much as the daughter. Other therapists attribute more conscious control to the mothers, saying, for instance, that their frustrations at having to give up careers for motherhood have made them manipulative and domineering.

PATTERNS IN BULIMIC FAMILIES

Although provocative, these hypotheses about the parents of bulimics are less useful than more definite patterns that have appeared in studies of bulimic families. Different researchers have pointed out noticeable incidences of alcoholism, depression and weight problems in these families. Since these same problems show up in many bulimics themselves, there may be hereditary as well as environmental ingredients in bulimia.

Michael Strober and his colleagues at UCLA have carried out extensive studies of the families of their anorectic patients. Comparing the families of restrictor anorectics to those of bulimic anorectics, they found some important distinctions. Although the researchers have not studied pure bulimics, the bulimia itself may be associated with these differences. The two groups of families are distinguished less by superficial patterns of eating than they are by deeper and more generalized problems in feelings and behavior. Unlike the families of restrictor anorectics, which tend to be conforming and conventional, families of bulimic anorectics suffer from intense conflicts and mutual disapproval. The bulimic families are not set up to offer mutual support and concern or a clear behavioral and emotional structure in which each member feels at home. The parents of bulimic anorectics show more marital disharmony, unrest and separation than do those of restrictor anorectics. The bulimic is more distant from both her parents, especially her father, than is the restrictor.

Compared to the fathers of restrictors, fathers of bulimics are more maladjusted, immature, impulsive and intolerant of frustration. They find it hard to control their feelings, especially anger, hostility and excitement, and they are slightly more moody and self-deprecating than their counterparts. The mothers of bulimic anorectics are more preoccupied with their bodies and more depressed than those of restrictor anorectics, although they seem to have fewer neurotic fears and anxieties. Both parents are less sensitive, passive, submissive and withdrawn than are the parents of restrictors. Not surprisingly, they express more dissatisfaction with the states their families are in.

The parents of bulimics more often suffered from severe illness while their daughters were young. (The incidence of illness in the parents of these anorectics is interesting. Is their observation of it one reason that anorectics feel alienated from and mistrustful of their own bodies by the time they reach puberty?) Psychiatric disturbances, especially in mood (depression) and impulse (alcoholism), are more common among bulimic than among restrictor families. The severity of the daughter's bulimia is associated with more pronounced depression in both parents and more impulsivity in the father. It seems as if the bulimic has the cards stacked against her from the start, but there are no data to suggest how her parents' impulsivity and character disturbances are transmitted to her.

These related factors are not limited to the bulimic's parents. Strober's research has also revealed that the incidence of depression in other relatives of bulimic anorectics is not only greater than that in the relatives of restrictors—at 15 percent, it is more than twice that of the general population. The relatives of bulimic anorectics also have a higher incidence of alcoholism and drug abuse than do the relatives of restrictors. Needless to say, preliminary studies of family patterns in bulimic anorexia can't be said to prove that they are related to bulimia. But perhaps, as more bulimics and their families agree to be studied, the significance of these patterns will become clear.

MY SISTER, MY SELF

Bulimics can encounter difficulties and pressures from their brothers and sisters as well as their parents, as twenty-eight-year-old Rebecca, an administrative assistant from Ohio, explains:

> I'm the middle child of three girls. We're close in age, and both my sisters are beautiful, sensual women who grew up to have great figures and lots of boyfriends. I was overweight and had no boyfriends, so I compensated by having lots of girlfriends, playing the violin a lot and doing well academically. I looked at my sisters constantly and was insanely jealous of their attractiveness; by going to the other extreme, I pretended that I didn't care about being inferior when actually I cared a lot.
>
> By the time I reached high school, my older sister had turned into a wild type with a bad drinking problem. She was a real grief to my parents, which of course gave me the opportunity to look even more perfect by comparison. We complemented each other in our behavior extremes. My sister had a hot temper; I was terrified of her anger and learned to stifle mine because I couldn't handle it. Between my sister's drinking and peer pressure to be the goody-goody plain-Jane superstudent, I couldn't turn to liquor to help me unwind. I wasn't good enough at any hobby to really enjoy it, so I had no method of relaxing. I always enjoyed food, and no one criticized me for eating unless I gained weight, so I started using food to relax.
>
> One night I stuffed myself during a meal in a restaurant. I felt very uncomfortable, and making myself vomit seemed a commonsensical way of removing the discomfort. I had never known anyone who did that, but there seemed to be nothing wrong with it—until I found myself doing it more and more often. I went from stuffing and vomiting at holiday meals to doing it

for no real reason except to relieve tension. I did that for ten years.

My older sister heard me vomiting in the bathroom a few times, figured out what was going on, and took up binge-vomiting herself. So did my younger sister. The younger sister got a promotion not long after she started, and between not having been bulimic that long, being very satisfied with her career and hearing me talk about my treatment, she somehow managed to stop on her own. She's the only bulimic I know who has been able to do that. My older sister is still bulimic and refuses treatment. I know that she had a predisposition for it, but I still feel badly about having started her on her way.

Rebecca's older sister was not available for an interview, but we can imagine her thinking: "My younger sister is so good-looking [Rebecca underestimates herself] and so accomplished! She's a real brain; she plays the violin; she always has her act together; she's Mom and Dad's favorite—she even has lots of girlfriends, while all my girlfriends are jealous of me, and I'm afraid of them taking my boyfriend away. I could never measure up to my little sister, so . . ." Who can tell whether the three sisters became bulimic because of heredity, environment (including peer or job pressures) or bad example?

UNSEEN AND UNMENTIONABLE

The fact that some bulimics take up vomiting in imitation of other family members contrasts with a more common pattern. One of the most pointed commentaries on the family lives of bulimics is that some have indulged in their gorge-purging for as long as twenty or thirty years without their families finding out. Sometimes this is a measure of the alienation between family members. "My parents found out about it," says one bulimic, "and my father is nervous about it because he works for a fast-food chain and is afraid that my eating disorder will jeopardize his status with the company. I told him that was his problem, not mine." Some bulimics recognize in retrospect that their families knew about their problem but didn't confront them. Thirty-three-year-old Ann Marie was aware of this in her family:

> My mother must have known about my vomiting but would never admit that she did. She loved feeding me too much to worry terribly about what I was doing with the food. I remember once that my aunt was complaining about how much her son ate, and I overheard my mother say, "I know how you feel; I have an overeater too." I recall the impression that my mother was embarrassed by my overeating in front of the family and was apologizing for me, but she never confronted me. Without confrontation I never took responsibility for my behavior and stayed bulimic.
>
> My husband was the same way. Our toilet kept backing up because of my vomiting, and one day he got really angry at me and said, "You'll have to stop throwing up." That really hurt me; I screamed at him, "You never told me to stop for myself; you just want me to stop for the sake of the goddamn toilet!" He had known all along, but never cared enough to say anything.

Bulimics often feel that someone—husband, physician, boss, whoever—should have rescued them from their illness. Instead of being relieved that her husband faced her bulimia after all, Ann Marie lashes out at him for not confronting her sooner or for better reasons.

Sometimes the family of a bulimic tries to help her but doesn't know what to do. Twenty-six-year-old Terry recognized her family's helplessness:

> My mother cleaned the bathroom while I lived at home, and on a few occasions I was careless about cleaning up after myself when I vomited, so that's how she found out I was doing it. She tried to talk to me about it and wanted desperately to help but didn't know how. Of course I tried to deny the problem as much as possible, because at first I had no motivation

to stop. I love my mother very much, and it's hard for me to think about the agony I must have put her through.

Family members just don't know how to deal with bulimia. I finally told my husband about it, and he was helpless. He loves me a lot, but he can't understand it and really doesn't want to know about it. He never knew that I vomited, but he had noticed that I was strange around food and pretended not to pay attention.

Unlike many bulimics who would interpret a husband's lack of confrontation as a lack of love, Terry accepts her husband's inability to understand her disorder. Her comments imply an important point: almost every bulimic thinks that she is the only person in the world who gorge-purges. If she herself can't believe that other people also gorge and purge, how does she expect a family member who suspects her behavior to believe it, let alone accuse her of it? We've seen that even experienced therapists who encounter bulimia in their patients have trouble accepting it at first—how then can a loved one be expected to voice his or her suspicions?

Much of the time this problem is avoided entirely, because the bulimic has cleverly hidden her habit. Here are the testimonies of three husbands who were completely unaware that their wives were bulimics. Harry, age twenty-nine, is an industrial engineer:

We had been married four years, and I never knew about my wife's bulimia until she told me. She was a mystery in general, and we didn't communicate very well. Sometimes I'd find candy that she had hidden, but I didn't consider that unusual—I come from a large family that was rather poor, and if any of us had been able to get some candy or some other treat, we'd tend to keep quiet about it. Even if I knew that there was a disease called bulimia and knew what it was, I wouldn't have connected it with her behavior. She often suggested that we eat out; she seemed to enjoy the meal, and when she went to the ladies' room afterwards, I always figured that she wanted to wash her hands.

Grant, age twenty-five, is a store owner:

I was not aware that my wife spent a lot on food. She was not expected to budget; I did that for both of us. And she didn't binge on that much—five cookies was enough to make her vomit, as I found out later. She told me eventually that she was sneaking money for food; like she'd eat in a restaurant, write a check for a greater amount than the meal, and pocket the change. Or she'd cash her paycheck and use the cash to buy groceries. I also remember in retrospect that if I snacked on certain foods we had around, she'd get very upset. I thought she was complaining about my bad habits, when actually she considered those foods her binge foods.

Donald, age thirty, is an architect:

When my wife told me she had bulimia, I was stunned. I had heard about it but didn't really know anything about it as an illness. My first reaction was to wonder whether there was anything I could do. Then I decided that the best thing to do would be to encourage her to investigate it and learn about it from her. I knew from marriage counseling that she had to learn to handle things on her own. When our counselor suggested that she enter a bulimia intensive group, she turned to me and asked for my support. I realized that I could really get roped into solving her problem for her, so I avoided her question, worded my response carefully, and didn't give her the answer she wanted. That was the response she needed. Sometimes I'm tempted to take the food away from her or help her somehow, but I know that I have to step back, painful as it is, and give her space in which to struggle and grow.

Donald's wife is lucky. Many bulimic women unconsciously marry men who they know will allow the bulimia to continue. "I have a fifty-eight-year-old patient who has been binge-vomiting for forty years, who married a man she knew would ignore any telltale signs of the illness," says Estelle Miller. The person a bulimic chooses while ill is not the sort she would choose after she has recovered, and bulimics are the first to admit that once they stop binge-vomiting, their husbands or boyfriends immediately begin to look less suitable to them. This is another dangerous point to make, for some bulimics are afraid to begin treatment because they believe that recovery from bulimia will end a relationship or lead to divorce.

Bulimics as Lovers

MEN

Contempt. Anger. Fear. Longing. All these emotions color the attitudes of bulimic women toward men. The feelings strengthen each other—these women are angry that they can't get men off their minds, for instance, and the anger makes them think about men even more. "We bulimic women are all different, but we're all working our ways out of the same kind of relationship with the same kind of man," says one victim. "We overreact to men. We pick men who are insecure and dependent, not people we can grow with but people who hurt us. And yet it's very important to bulimic women to have nice relationships." This is a perceptive summary, even though some bulimics are too afraid of relationships even to allow themselves to reach the point of getting hurt. One of them had this to say in a group session:

THERAPIST: What does a sexual relationship mean to you?
JANINE: Mistrust.
THERAPIST: Where did you get that idea? From your parents?
JANINE: Their relationship is really shitty.
THERAPIST: Are you going to have shitty relationships because they did?

JANINE: I guess that's why I've never really gotten close with anyone, because no relationship is better than a shitty one. And everyone I see has shitty relationships. I know intellectually that if things don't work out with a guy, then he's not the right one for me. But there's a spot in me that just hopes that things will work out because I'm so tired of feeling lonely. And I can't trust anyone. I always choose guys that are fucked up, and I don't know why or how to make better choices.

Terribly insecure, committed to pleasing others at their own expense, many bulimic women allow themselves to be dominated by men they clearly perceive to be wrong for them. A woman who marries before becoming bulimic often latches on to the first man who pays any attention to her, hoping to learn to love him. Very few bulimics have healthy relationships with men, as Beverly, a senior executive, explains:

Out of my twenty-three years of bulimia, I did stop for about a year. This happened because I was leading a very sheltered, controlled existence, especially as far as men were concerned. I was not dating, just working and enjoying my interests and my friends. I was stabilized in my eating until I started dating again, and then the bulimia escalated.

My psychiatrist says that although I'm thirty-nine years old, emotionally I'm about eighteen because I had no social life as a teen-ager. I know that right now I could just stop seeing men and work on my therapy and my eating instead. But also I know that I want a relationship desperately, and unless I confront the potential problems of dating men, I'll just regress. I can't keep running away from men. It's hard to control my eating and my emotions at the same time, but I have to learn not to base my self-esteem and my eating habits on what a man thinks of me. I have to accept the fact that not every man is going to be attracted to me and that this fact has nothing to do with me and is no ex-

cuse to go and eat ten donuts. If I had dated for several
years and had concluded that I didn't want to be involved with a man, that would be different. In that
case, my not seeing men would not be a step backward,
denying my need for a man.

Despite my immaturity, I don't think that my emotions are far removed from what other women feel. I
have a very attractive girlfriend who takes her phone
into the bathroom when she showers so that she won't
miss a man's call.

Like other bulimics, Beverly uses her eating to help her cope
with the problems inherent in relationships. Among its other
effects, binge-vomiting acts as a narcotic that befuddles the
woman's thinking and precludes her becoming aware that a love
affair has gone sour. Twenty-four-year-old Tina explains:

I attract men with low self-esteem and with problems,
so I always feel that it's my job to straighten them out,
meanwhile avoiding my own problems. This one guy
had really great potential and made me think that
when I fixed him, he'd be perfect, except that he was
thinking the same way about me. I corrected his behavior all the time, and he pressured me, and it was a real
problem.

During the bulimia it was hard for me to sort out any
of my feelings about him: did I love him, hate him,
want to marry him? Abstinence helps you figure out
what you feel. After three months' abstinence I could
see the relationship clearly and realized how little I was
getting out of it. This was partly in contrast to the
women I had met in my bulimia group. They were my
friends, and I grew to love them and to figure out for
the first time what friends really are. My boyfriend
gave me no positive feedback at all, and my relationships with these women helped me recognize that
he wasn't worth all the hurt I was getting.

It's still hard for me to think about him today. I keep

thinking that if only I had tried longer and harder with him, it might have worked.

Tina and Beverly indicate the kind of maturing process that many bulimic women must face as they try to recover. Both have come to recognize that their own interests and their women friends are just as pleasurable and important to them as men are; both have to keep themselves from using men as a way to avoid working on their own problems. Yet both of them also feel strong needs for relationships with men and are unable to let go of their dependencies.

BULIMIA AND SEXUALITY

An especially big issue in bulimics' relationships with men is sexuality. It doesn't matter whether the bulimic is a classic good girl or an impulsively promiscuous borderline—she is still likely to insist that sex is a problem for her and that it is somehow tied in with her bulimia. Some bulimics easily achieve orgasm; in describing sex as a problem they may be mistaking physical for emotional intimacy, which they can't tolerate.

Other bulimics don't enjoy sex or have orgasms; they may use binge-vomiting to ease sexual tension. On some level they may hope that the perfect lover will come along to teach them how to be happy and sexually fulfilled. Or they may simply feel trapped in bodies to which they are not reconciled. It's hard to relax in a body that must be disciplined for gaining an ounce— to the appearance-conscious bulimic, an orgasm may seem even better than an extra pound at making her look less than perfect. Roberta, a legal secretary, can't let go of her self-consciousness during sex:

> I have a distant fantasy view of relationships. I date around but have never been able to be intimate in any way other than friendship. Sexuality is a real biggie for me. I know that one reason I want to lose my body awareness is that I'm scared to death to enjoy myself sexually. I'm twenty-three years old and have never had an orgasm. I sleep with men, and intellectually I know

that sex is okay, but emotionally I can't let go. I think that it's a final thing in growing up—becoming comfortable with your body in all its aspects, including acknowledging your sexuality. I need to learn to feel safe even with just physical affection. And I need to develop the courage to date men that I'm attracted to without setting myself up for rejection to avoid dealing with that attraction.

Twenty-nine-year-old Sally sees more of her own doing in her bad experiences with sex:

In college I was very competitive on all counts. I wanted to do well both academically and socially. There were many more women than men enrolled in our school, so we really had to give out to get a boyfriend. I started drinking at parties—reluctantly, but I needed liquor to be clever and witty and attractive. I had not dated in high school and wasn't used to men, and I became very promiscuous and really into bar scenes and parties. I became bitter about one-night stands and scarred by a lot of negative experiences. I didn't really enjoy sex and tried to work that out with a counselor. I became convinced that all men are bastards. I cheated myself of good, healthy relationships with men. And all this time I repeatedly dove into food to ease my unhappiness.

Sexuality in bulimia seems like an obvious topic to be explored from a strictly feminist point of view. But that troublesome minority of male bulimics speaks up in agreement from an enemy standpoint. Thirty-one-year-old Stan is a salesman:

I think that sex is really tied up with bulimia. All during high school I always had a steady girlfriend and was never afraid of heavy petting, but I was always afraid of intercourse. I used common sense to defend my fear—"We'd better cut it out; you might get pregnant." I got very close, but I never actually did it. Then

I met a girl that I really liked who seemed eager to make out, and one night when we were parked I thought, "Hell, why not? Let's go through with it." I tried to, and I was impotent. She was comfortable and reassuring about it and said it was okay, but it wasn't okay for me, and I absolutely refused to discuss it. In fact, I dropped her to avoid dealing with the memory. It's been a hangup ever since.

I associate binge-vomiting with the fact that it's lowered my sex drive and I use it to sidestep what's really bothering me. What bothers me with sex is that I feel incomplete. I can't honestly say that I've ever had a really good sexual experience. I've had sex, but it never was fulfilling. I'm too old to be this inexperienced. It limits me because I can't meet people or ask them out. I can't deal with it myself, so how do I make other people understand?

A woman tries to sleep with a man who obviously isn't excited by the prospect; after the incident he drops her. Naturally, she will think of him as a bastard who made her feel unattractive. While we can't condone Stan's behavior, his comments explain that he was embarrassed and miserable about a major problem. Male and female bulimics are convinced that sexuality figures powerfully in their illness, although they are hard put to explain how. Stan tries to associate his binge-vomiting with his lowered sex drive and with his attempt to escape from his problems, explanations that would hold true for women also. Sex also forces bulimics to face their own naked bodies under the most obvious and vulnerable conditions. For some bulimics, letting go during sex may, like overeating, imply some vaguely undesirable consequences. For those bulimics who enjoy sex, the indulgence is harmless because their feelings stay locked up safe.

THE JEALOUS LOVER

Although we talk here about bulimics "controlling" themselves and "using" gorge-purging in certain ways, in the end it's the bulimia, not its victim, that has control. This becomes clearly evident in relationships, in which bulimia becomes almost a tangible presence to be accommodated. Bulimics often refer to their illness as a substitute lover or friend—it provides them with all the needs that other people can't reasonably be expected to meet. It turns a marriage into a *ménage à trois* in which one marriage partner is unaware of the third party. This is illustrated by the narrative of thirty-one-year-old Bridget, a librarian; her husband Jeff, thirty-three, is a technician. Bridget has recovered from bulimia; her marriage seems to have survived it, although she and Jeff are in counseling together:

> I had dated Jeff for five years. He sort of knew that I was weird about food, but I tried not to overeat in front of him so I wouldn't have to escape to the bathroom to vomit, so he didn't know the full extent of the problem. Food was a fairly large part of our relationship, and he had no idea. When I got engaged, I finally realized that I had to do something. At first I refused to marry him, telling him vaguely that I had a problem with food that was affecting our relationship. He didn't understand what I meant, and I couldn't tell him the truth, so I let myself get talked into marriage, because we really do love each other. I thought, "Marriage will end the bulimia; I will be so in love, so swept off my feet; I won't have the time, and Jeff will be there and always entertain me," and so on. I was in a dream world even though I knew he wasn't Prince Charming.
>
> I really thought this was it. I had my last binge the night before the wedding. And when I said my vows I wasn't thinking about what I was saying. I was thinking, "God, I can't binge-vomit anymore." I was panic-stricken about the food. I ate almost nothing at the reception, thinking, "It's over; I can't vomit up this food."
>
> I can stop binge-vomiting for short periods when circumstances make it impossible. Our honeymoon was a month-long cross-country trip. Toward the end I was tense and bitchy from abstinence. Here was the honeymoon, supposed to be the best time of my life, and I just wanted to binge. We finally stopped to stay with

Jeff's old roommate and his wife, who took us out to dinner and let us stay in their guest room with a private bath. I ate like a horse, and it felt good, but I was devastated because I was married and supposed to be abstinent. "Well," I thought, "it's just this once." For a bulimic, there's no such thing as "just once." We reach a point where there's always just one more time—over and over.

I started telling Jeff that there was no reason for us to be together all the time just because we were married—that he would want to be off with his friends. Actually, I wanted to get rid of him so I could resume binging.

We moved into an apartment that I must have picked out unconsciously despite my resolve not to binge after marriage. It had the bathroom at one end off the bedroom, then the kitchen, then the hallway with a dining area, study and living room. Our bulimia group leader told us that family members usually have a trade-off with a bulimic—that they'll pursue their own addictions while ignoring the bulimia. For Jeff it was sports. He spent hours watching sports on TV in the living room while I spent hours at the other end of the apartment in the kitchen and bathroom. I binged all night, and I spent what little money we had on food, which didn't help our sex life or our budget. I was comfortably alienated from my husband within months of marrying him because of my addiction. I was bored when I wasn't at my job, and I was disappointed that my husband wasn't dashing and romantic. I had studied dancing and art, but all I was interested in anymore was binging and vomiting, which took up all my time.

Later we moved into an apartment in a building in which we were the caretakers. I didn't like the apartment because the bathroom was more centrally located, but my husband insisted we take it because we got free rent. One thing that happens when you're bulimic is that you think that a situation will rule out binging, and then you figure out ways to get around it to work binging into any living situation. We had the master keys to the building, and I found a small bathroom in the basement used by the janitor or somebody, so I'd make an excuse to step out after meals and go down there to vomit. I even worked binging into pregnancy.

Bulimia is almost like a fickle lover in a fragile affair—the woman knows that if she slips up just once and her obsession is discovered, she will lose her major source of pleasure and comfort. Meanwhile she shuts out people and opportunities to fill her life genuinely—for bulimia is a jealous lover as well.

One of the bulimic's most difficult tasks is to shove food back into its proper place and get on with more important things in life. Until she can do this, bulimia remains a personal problem that cripples her social life. It is also a social problem that interferes with each victim's personal life.

Chapter 8

STEREOTYPE VS. SUPERWOMAN:
THE SOCIAL CONTEXT OF BULIMIA

Part of the reason that bulimia hasn't received the professional attention it deserves may be that many people see it as just another fad diet. It's true that modern society attaches symbolic significance to the thin female figure and that women are influenced by its enormous importance. But since anorexia nervosa and bulimia are often attributed *strictly* to social pressures on women to be thin, we should note that this point of view disregards several important facts. As previously noted, biochemistry could well be the most important among several factors determining who develops an eating disorder. Men as well as women can turn to or from food and become obese, bulimic or anorectic, while not all women exposed to identical cultural pressures develop bulimia. Anorexia nervosa (and bulimic anorexia) has a long history, as do anorectic and bulimic personalities. We don't even know whether there are more women with bulimia today or just more psychiatrists and psychologists looking for them. Although we'll probably see books devoted to bulimia as a cultural phenomenon, social pressures are its intensifier, not its cause.

The Social Context

THE EMPTY ARENA

Despite these qualifications, social factors are powerful forces pushing susceptible people toward food. It has long been known that culture creates, shapes and influences psychopathology of all kinds. Hundreds of years ago possession and witchcraft were fads; in the Victorian Age hysteria was in vogue (and as we have seen, "consumption" might have given would-be anorectics a socially sanctioned excuse for emaciation). There is very little classic hysteria now; it has been bumped by eating disorders, which may well be the psychopathology of the twentieth century. "I don't think women are inherently fueled toward self-induced vomiting or laxative abuse; bulimia is not a natural state. In some ways the culture is responsible for it," says Craig Johnson. But many writers on eating disorders fail to recognize that we must determine the *degree* of cultural influence as well as the *kind*.

The very prevalence of eating disorders suggests some kind of mass movement, a social problem for which medicine does not have all the answers. Anorectic and bulimic women are both crying for help and protesting, but their illnesses muffle their cries. Some of them must be saying that women should be free to eat, love, dance, wear clothes, go naked, and just be themselves without having to worry constantly about being the wrong size. They must be asking why their expectations of success, their self-esteem, their sense of power and control, their positive feedback from families, friends and society in general should all be determined by their ability to deny themselves food.

The bulimic personality, nebulous as it is, seems the most vulnerable to the kinds of pressures all women experience. Men disturbed by their social roles can act out their aggressions and antisocial tendencies; they have outlets for competition among themselves and areas that they can control. Women have fewer opportunities to act out their distress socially. Their major means of gaining approval is that of owning attractively thin bodies. Women's attitudes toward their bodies indicate the scarcity and superficiality of their chances to win at something in today's society. Craig Johnson explains:

> I think that body and appearance become a way in which many women have learned to compete. I'm not sure that the prize is male approval—it could be, but I think it's deeper than that. That's like saying that men

want to win football games so that women will love
them. Men want to win football games so that they'll
feel better than the team across the line from them—so
that they can enjoy a sense of mastery and confidence.
What do women have available to provide them with
those feelings?

The competition Johnson refers to is theoretically healthy and
natural—a means of establishing self-esteem. But while men
may compete on the basis of what they can do, women traditionally have competed only in terms of what they look like. Instead of being able to act *out*, to test themselves against others
and actively win at something, women have instead resorted to
acting *in*, hurting only themselves in their desperation and self-
defeat. Their competitive arenas expand only when their waist-
lines contract; the woman who remains defiantly plump finds
that she has few options left for coaxing back society's approval.

No wonder women take out their frustrations on their bodies
—eating is the most dangerous game to play, the final resort of
those determined once and for all to win or lose. In *Fat Is a
Feminist Issue* Susie Orbach offers an interesting comparison of
anorectics and compulsive overeaters showing that their very
different ways of handling food express similar social conflicts
about their roles as women—their ambivalence about their
mothers, their femininity, their sexuality. Kim Chernin suggests
in *The Obsession** that a woman's trivial preoccupation with
food is really a spiritual hunger for a state of being, a unified
condition of the self. Therapists talk about a continuum of eating
disorders as if a woman could, by selecting a point, arbitrarily
select her manifestation of despair.

NARCISSISM

We have seen that many bulimics are perfectionistic and
narcissistic. Regardless of how else she may demonstrate these
qualities, the bulimic woman is always obsessed with her appearance. It would take more than individual personality characteristics to make bulimics as aware as they are of microscopic

* Chernin, Kim, *The Obsession: Reflections on the Tyranny of Slenderness* (New York: Harper & Row, 1981).

differences in their figures. A few pounds gained or lost literally transform them.

Miriam was on the tenth day of a fast on August 18, 1968, when she wrote:

> *103 POUNDS.* UP at 5:30, showered and shampooed, got everything shipshape. House is neat and orderly—like me. NOW DON'T MESS THINGS UP. I feel great. My energy came back. Ten days I'm not weak. I'm lean and mean. 34½–23–34 and I'm not hungry. My face isn't bloated. My high-cheeked bone structure is beginning to show. My eyes aren't puffy. I don't have a double chin. I feel so feminine and pure. I feel happy-go-lucky. No terrible depression that I'd been living in so long. It's a fantastic feeling. I'm as good as anybody. In different ways, of course. And I'm learning and progressing and getting it together. Looking forward to trip, planning and making lists. I'm praying I won't mess it up like I did last year. I WON'T, I WON'T.

This unfortunate narcissism has its reverse side—a few extra pounds make Miriam feel ugly, worthless, self-conscious, trapped in a prison of tight-fitting clothes. How many women have attributed their "femininity" and "purity" to a few notches on the scale? How many of them feel "as good as anybody" only when they're thin?

Some bulimics take the implications of thinness even further. Olivia, a twenty-six-year-old dental technician, explains what it means to her:

> When I lose weight I lose control of myself and spend all my money on clothes because I'm so high on my new figure. It's always just five to ten pounds that make the difference in how I feel about myself. A little extra weight makes me feel fat and ugly, and I stop taking care of myself. The change in my attitude is a horror to me. I can recall being late for work on several occasions because I'd spent an hour or so almost hypno-

tized, trying on different uniform tops to find the one that would make me look thinnest. Thin means being pretty—and being sane.

Olivia makes no value judgment about the loss of control that leads to her spending spree—it's a socially sanctioned gesture of triumph. The loss of a few dollars is nothing compared to the gain of a few pounds.

Of course, all these women are following socially acceptable norms in staring at, weighing and measuring their bodies. Women's bodies were supposedly made to be looked at. It wouldn't occur to many of them to turn their bodies inside out and use them as a means of self-expression rather than setting them up as targets for the world's opinions. Craig Johnson encounters this distorted thinking frequently:

> In consultation I often ask the women if I can make a deal with them: if I could relieve them of the binge-vomiting in exchange for their gaining ten pounds, would they do that? A sizable portion of the women I see tell me no. They'd rather be dead than gain ten pounds. And they would be—it would be a type of psychological death to them. The women I hear that from usually have been overweight in their lifetimes and have experienced a transformation as a result of losing weight. In their experience they have gone from darkness to lightness. Women who can get into designer jeans for the first time in their lives suddenly feel much better about themselves. They suddenly find themselves attractive to men. It's a life that they've never known before.

HOW TO LOOK AND WHO TO BE

There's really no area of her life or consciousness to which a modern woman can withdraw to escape this kind of thinking. It's ironic that bulimia is considered shameful and disgusting, for in a sense the disorder, although abnormal, is a creative response to an impossible situation. Society offers women an inappropriate norm of how they look as ideal reflections of femininity.

Women are expected to be nurturers who fit into junior sizes. Any copy of a women's magazine will probably contain diets, advertisements featuring skinny models and dessert recipes. This kind of craziness is so perpetuated by the media that few women can help being obsessed with food.

As Dr. Bruch has pointed out, our society is flexible about every aspect of individual life-styles except body build. We associate maturity with plumpness and cheerfulness. We also emphasize the sexually attractive woman, who is very thin, and admire her at the expense of the dowdy, unfeminine, maternal woman. Women must therefore choose between two stereotypes—motherhood and sexiness. And they respond to the same dilemma in different ways—by avoiding motherhood, by becoming obese during and after pregnancy, by rejecting their children, by striving to maintain an adolescent boy's body, either because it's childlike or because it's masculine.

The conflicts women face about what they should look like are paralleled by the questions they must ask about what to do with their lives. The maternal-looking woman becomes a housewife and mother. The thin, sexy woman can adopt these roles if she wants to, but she is also expected to build an exciting career for herself. The proper figure seems to represent reserves of tremendous energy that transform the average woman with a bit of ambition into a superwoman. Dorothy, a twenty-four-year-old bulimic anorectic, explains why she is uneasy about her role in life:

> The women's movement greatly increased my expectations of myself. It was no longer okay just to be a housewife, have kids and just live. I had to not only have, but also be very successful in, a career and be aware of all the current issues and insist on my rights. The superwoman thing really took its toll on me.
>
> Expecting to be top woman, I naturally modeled myself after those in the limelight. Whether they're models or executives, they're always shown in the media as thin, tall, fine-featured, high-cheekboned, rich-lipped, beautiful women with Esquire-type men at their sides. For me this appearance thing had a lot to do with my eating disorders.

The commercials teach us what perfect women should look and act like. It's assumed that the unliberated woman is still a dull, chubby housewife cleaning house and having kids and panicking if she's out of Clorox. The liberated woman may not be in business, but she holds her own in a household. She's married, has 2.5 kids, still keeps up a career and a good body and wears the right makeup.

Even the women who emphasize the women's movement, at least the ones I've seen most often in the media, are all good-looking, attractive, thin women. There are more women speaking out now who don't have the bodies I want, but the first ones I was exposed to were Gloria Steinem, Ellen Goodman, the forerunners.

Like many people, Dorothy confuses the ideals of the women's movement with those of the fashion industry. The movement doesn't pressure women to be liberated—rather, it tries hard to reeducate people into recognizing that women have been denied opportunities they deserve. Threatened by a mass movement arguing that women are intelligent, independent human beings, and not just glamorous clothes horses, the fashion industry and media simply appropriated its goals, suggesting that traditional beauty standards were appropriate for women succeeding in new roles. Thanks to this joining of forces, the beautiful woman can now expect to land the right job as well as the right man.

Thinness has come to rival food in terms of how many connotations it calls to mind. While food entices us with memories of home, warmth, security, childhood and mother, thinness beckons to us with promises of success, admiration, power and prestige, adult independence and self-sufficiency. In other times and cultures fatness symbolized these attributes; the point is not how thinness achieved its status but how to free women from the physical and psychological agony involved in maintaining it. The point is, as Dorothy sees, that in fighting to provide women with opportunities to succeed, the women's movement has not yet had the chance to insist upon their right to weigh what their bodies damn well please.

The Women's Movement

THE FEAR OF LIBERATION

Traditionally women have been expected to marry and raise families, to be fulfilled not because of individual accomplishments but as reflections of their husbands and children. They have been bombarded with ideals of beauty and behavior designed to catch a man and make possible the approved life-style. Since they strive for feminine perfection, many bulimic women have aspired to this role with a vengeance. Relying on appearance rather than personality, measuring themselves against external rather than individual standards for happiness and fulfillment, bulimics use food in part to fight off their devastating, inevitable sense of failure.

Some bulimic women are successful because they are hardnosed, ambitious people whose traditionalism is confined to their relationships with men. A career and a boyfriend will gain them society's approval because these are standard criteria for the status of superwoman. And a disturbing number of bulimic women talk as if their careers are just time they put in to please society, while their boyfriends, unsuitable as they may be, are people they are involved with to fulfill themselves. Their illness ties in with this need in that many of them work to stay thin because they think that men want them to look that way. Whether most men would actually prefer a Cheryl Tiegs to a Raquel Welch is beside the point, at least to the bulimic's way of thinking. If fashion dictates that women be thin, the bulimic will play it safe and go along with the crowd, regardless of how her individuality and assertiveness may suffer in the process.

This is the only explanation that some bulimic women have for their illness. Twenty-eight-year-old Beryl has been an alcoholic, a drug addict and a thief, yet she attributes her bulimia to her need for a boyfriend:

For me bulimia is tied up in the whole business of keeping a slim figure to attract men. I want to be an independent career woman in the hope of attracting the right kind of man, and I'm really angry about being dependent on men. My feminism gets lost along the way. I get into bad relationships because nice men bore me and because I tend to go for exciting bad men or unattainable fatherly types. I want to be taken care of, and I'm too insecure to live without men. But I can't live with one until I'm whole and in touch with myself, able to grow more and hold my own in that kind of situation. They say to stay away from men while you're recovering, but I find that impossible. I don't want more sick relationships, but there are some guys I'd do anything for.

There are obviously two kinds of problems underlying Beryl's remarks—the social problem of why women depend on men rather than deriving satisfaction from their own accomplishments, and the personal one of why Beryl herself is not only dependent on men but also prone to get involved in sick relationships. Foisting too many of the bulimic woman's problems off on society gives her an excuse to avoid solving those she has brought upon herself. It invites procrastination and eventual despair. Few of us can change society—bulimics must instead learn that they can change themselves.

Bulimics often speak of the tremendous conflicts they feel between traditionalism and liberation. One of the major issues in this conflict is not that the two terms are mutually exclusive but that the family backgrounds of many bulimics have taught them that they can't have both. Twenty-four-year-old Ellen, a postal employee, explains:

I feel really in the middle: I want to be attractive and I want to have kids, but I don't know if I can emotionally. I was brought up with a nice little image of a nice little *un*healthy family life. Every guy I've dated has been sick, mixed up, horrible! I wonder if I can get married, take care of a husband and stay healthy myself instead of getting trapped in more sickness. I'd have to work and wouldn't be home to care for kids if I had them; that would have to be shared. What kind of man will do that? I want to meet a perfect man, and that's impossible. And I've heard that the happiest people are single women and married men. It's all so confusing!

Like Beryl, Ellen can't conceptualize a happy married life because she can't imagine having a healthy relationship with a man—even the possibility of her staying healthy in marriage involves her "taking care of a husband." The equality that the women's movement is fighting for presupposes that in marriage, for instance, both partners are healthy and self-sufficient. Ellen thinks that a man willing to share child care is "a perfect man," an impossible ideal, just because he's so distant from her own experience. Small wonder that many bulimic women hesitate to embrace the ideals of women's liberation. They have yet to liberate themselves as people.

For twenty-nine-year-old Brenda, a marketing manager, part of the problem is that she uses her job as a means of bolstering her self-esteem, which she feels would be sapped by motherhood and family life:

People have always told me that I'm independent and stubborn. I *am* stubborn. I never felt independent, although I don't know who I'm dependent on, and I never felt strong at all, but I think of those qualities as being positive ones. I want to be independent, self-sufficient, self-supporting, living alone. My salary gives me status. Can I handle the executive position I want? Can I be a good wife and mother? Another part of me wants a simple family life, but I keep thinking that marriage and kids will be a weakness that will ruin my career. It's hard for me to realize that I can have both, and I've felt confused for a long time. Just thinking about all this makes me feel exhausted. To make matters worse, I want to leave my mark on society, yet be liked as well. I want people to say of me, "Wasn't she something?" and "Wasn't she *nice?*" I still have to be liked as well as successful.

I feel I grew up at a bad time, with the women's

movement coming out and making me look at my mother, for example, and compare her to new standards. Women are under terrible pressure today just to decide what we want. I have no idea what I want.

The women's movement is attractive to bulimics even though they recognize that it's not a viable alternative for them. The movement presupposes specific ambitions and desires in women that have been squelched by a patriarchal society. Bulimic women must first figure out what their ambitions and desires are.

KEEPING UP WITH THE FEMINISTS

Seeking to demolish feminine stereotypes while encouraging women to explore individual options, the women's movement might have been expected indirectly to decrease the incidence of bulimia. Instead, it began by addressing the major issues, especially economic ones, that have prevented women from developing their full potential. Because it has concentrated on basic significant social matters, the movement hasn't yet explored the more personal elements of women's oppression that affect bulimics. Some bulimics, like Dorothy and Brenda, have misunderstood or felt pressured by liberation; others aren't in a psychological or emotional position to take advantage of the progress that has been made toward equality. They look for feminist ideals pertinent to them and instead find that the movement applies to strong, healthy women they would like to imitate. They find few references to slimness as an unreasonable ideal of beauty. And the movement's position that women must change not only society's arbitrary standards but also their own habits of complying with these standards is a hard lesson for the insecure bulimic to learn.

The incidence of bulimia among professional women may be due in part to the increased stress that goes with a career. Many bulimic women are above average in intelligence and well educated; some are lawyers, doctors or executives with or without families to complete their lives. Others feel pressured because they don't have careers and worry that they should be superwomen juggling several roles at once. Because women have mistaken opportunity for obligation, the women's movement has caused pain and confusion for those unsure of what course to pursue—how then does this perceived pressure to act liberated affect women with tendencies toward bulimia? Describing anorectics in *The Golden Cage*,† Dr. Bruch writes, "Many of my patients have expressed the feelings that they are overwhelmed by the vast number of potential opportunities available to them which they 'ought' to fulfill, that there were too many choices and they had been afraid of not choosing correctly." Opportunities that are presented rather than made offer no meaningful challenge. The factors that predispose a woman to bulimia make her especially vulnerable to the conflicts that women face today, conflicts that she attempts to resolve with her binges. Nor are these problems peculiar to eating-disorders victims—a lack of identity is for many women a reality caused by all kinds of social and cultural as well as psychological influences.

The problems that women face today are different from those they faced a generation ago. If bulimia is a product of social factors, perhaps its increased incidence parallels the rise of the women's movement itself. Bulimia may be prevalent because liberation is ubiquitous, and some women don't recognize liberation as a means to greater happiness and fulfillment. Instead, they find it a source of more confusion and helplessness. They work only to earn a living, or they cling to their jobs, as Brenda does, as symbols of prestige. Even those who are very successful seem disinclined to discuss their work. The marriage alternative just reminds them of their past hurts and humiliations from men. Trying to avoid the pressures of liberation, bulimic women have succumbed to an illness that, at least part of the time, traps them back in women's traditional place—the kitchen.

The women's movement has met resistance not only from men but also from women who refuse to accept the ideals of liberation. Among eating-disorders victims, however, the movement has potential allies who haven't reached the point of personal development where they can benefit from its goals. Proponents of women's liberation would do well to recognize eating disorders as symptoms of women's difficulties that have yet to be

† Bruch, Hilde, M.D., *The Golden Cage: The Enigma of Anorexia Nervosa* (Cambridge: Harvard University Press, 1978).

worked out, and eventually to address them seriously as such. Although it's not a solution to bulimia, the women's movement, like group therapy for bulimics, can serve as a social medium within which to deal with a social problem. Therapy for bulimics must, after all, help them work around the impossible role that society has asked them to play.

Psychotherapy for Women

As it is with women's liberation, however, the relationship between bulimia and psychotherapy is ambivalent. For many years dogmatic in approach, psychotherapy for women has changed tremendously, thanks to the women's movement. More women Ph.D.s and M.D.s mean more women in professional organizations and more programs dealing with women's issues. More men have come to women's programs and asked whether they should be treating women for problems like bulimia. Male therapists are in a position to provide insight to women concerned about intimacy with men. And the individualistic approach emphasized in bulimia treatment helps to reinforce the greater flexibility that has developed in women's therapy.

But therapy for women is at a disadvantage with bulimia, which many people find repulsive. "An illness that seems to be the legacy of women tends to stereotpye them," says Dr. Rudnick. "It becomes a vicious cycle: weight consciousness has been the burden of women; this spawns illnesses that are the burden of women, which in turn further stereotype women as weight-conscious. I don't find it an advantageous development for women that bulimia has popped onto the scene." We can hope that this problem will be corrected as therapists further explore *all* of the factors—medical and psychological as well as social—that contribute to bulimia. It needs to be recognized as an illness more deeply rooted than is the desire to be thin.

Twenty-two-year-old Jonelle, a beautician, is well on her way to "liberation" from the bulimic mind-set as a result of her therapy:

At times I still think that if I were thinner my personality would be better or I'd be more "well-rounded," for want of a better word. I try not to nurse these feelings. I still want to hide while I'm losing enough weight to have a comfortable margin of skinniness. I don't like my body all the time now. Being normal weight is like living in a new house. I know that at my favorite weight I don't menstruate, so it's not a healthy weight for me, but I want to have my cake and eat it too.

But I can honestly say that I now depend on feedback from people in general, not just men. If a man doesn't like my body now, TOUGH. Before, I'd be up in arms about it. I'd prefer that people I care about appreciate my body, but that's not all I have or all I am. The most important things now are my feelings, personality, involvement with people, goodness as a person, not just a body.

Society wouldn't agree with Jonelle. It would either remind her that since she's in a business to make people look good, she should look good herself, or it might disregard her developing attitude as being strange or sick. Her illness would get her into further trouble, since society doesn't view bulimia seriously or objectively. No woman is happy to admit that her world is bounded by the kitchen and the bathroom. Most people react to descriptions of bulimia with horrified laughter or disgust. Unfortunately, such reactions don't discourage self-conscious young women from beginning the "ideal diet."

Yet bulimia is not that different from (or for that matter, more "disgusting" than) alcoholism, drug abuse or other understandable, prevalent addictions. And as more victims come forward in hopes of recovery, bulimia will come into its own.

Chapter 9

MALE BULIMICS

Like male anorectics, male bulimics form a puzzling minority in disorders whose hypothetical explanations depend largely on their being confined to women. Yet both anorexia and bulimia begin superficially because of a concern about weight, and men share with women the pressure to be attractive and athletic that might cause them to experiment with fasting or purging. Sportsmen have to watch their weight: jockeys, for instance, want to weigh as little as possible, and wrestlers want to compete in lower weight classes in which their strength gives them an advantage. Men also get into body building, and although that's not the equivalent of an eating disorder, it does suggest a preoccupation with body image that may eventually center around weight. Appearance may play a central role in a man's personality just as it may in a woman's, but the implications of appearance don't seem consistent among the male eating-disorders victims seen to date. "The several adolescent male anorectics I've seen have all been preoccupied with body building," says Michael Strober. Estelle Miller has seen the opposite. "Like thin women, thin men don't want muscles or any kind of masculine form," she says. "Thinness makes them look like children."

Incidence of Bulimia in Men

If the incidence of bulimia in women is difficult to guess, that in men is practically impossible. Men are more secretive than women about psychological problems and may worry about weight more quietly. Because fewer of them have been observed, men are the subjects of more contradictory reports. "We have seen only two men but have received so many letters from them that we'll be putting together groups for males," says Ellen Schor. "I would say that only about 5 percent of bulimics are men, but they do write to us a lot. I feel that they aren't as common as female bulimics for several reasons, primarily societal norms: men are reinforced for being big, while women are reinforced for being little."

The 5 percent incidence is that referred to most often, possibly because it matches that of men in anorexia nervosa. About 7 percent of the bulimic patients treated at the University of Minnesota have been male, but Gretchen Goff feels that the incidence of bulimia in men is much higher than people have been seeing—more like 20 percent. The author's experience in uncovering male vomiters corroborates this, as do statements from bulimics of both sexes. Richard, a twenty-eight-year-old recovered bulimic, reports having known but lost touch with several men who gorge-purged. "One was a friend who moved to another state," he says. "We'd scarf down half a gallon of ice cream apiece, then race to the bathroom—or we'd feel so guilty after a quart or so that we'd pour the rest down the sink. Any food that was around, we'd eat." Betty, a twenty-two-year-old recovered alcoholic and bulimic, feels that male bulimics aren't obvious because they are even more adamant than women about keeping their illness a secret:

> My neighbor's son, who was a wrestler, died of bulimia. Most of the men I know are in Alcoholics Anonymous, and many of them are bulimics. One is an R.N. I've talked to them about it, but they don't like being approached and asked about their problem. They think of it as a women's disease and won't admit to it for that reason—as if it were a period or a yeast infection or something.

Twenty-five-year-old Joel, an accountant, admits to the feelings that Betty describes and adds that he is embarrassed about being a male lost among women:

I'm convinced that a lot of other men have bulimia. There's getting to be so much emphasis on weight that guys are talking about it all the time. Sooner or later they'll start experimenting with purging.

I'm really embarrassed to go to my AA and bulimia groups and talk about being bulimic. The most repulsive thing I can think of is throwing up, and I have to tell people that I do that. I'm amazed that people are so understanding. It's hard to feel worthwhile or masculine or attractive. I wonder what they think of me, knowing that I do this. If I saw them on the street, I'd wonder if they thought I was attractive, but in groups I don't get that far—I wonder if they think I'm human. I forget that they're bulimic too.

I can relate very easily to what the women say. The disorder is person-to-person, not divided by the sexes. I think the only possible difference between male and female bulimics is that in women it makes their periods irregular, and in men it lowers the sex drive.

Joel's attitude is not chauvinistic; rather he does exactly what bulimic women do—he bases his self-esteem on the opinions of the opposite sex. His discomfort arises from admitting that he vomits and having to confront that among people with whom he can "relate" but not identify. Since identification with fellow bulimics is an important factor in a victim's recovery, the obvious implication is that male bulimics need to be treated in groups of their own.

Male and Female Bulimics

It's unfortunate that more male bulimics haven't been treated, not only for their own sakes, but also for the insight they could offer into bulimia as a "women's disorder." "All they talk about in group is how difficult it is for them to be there, how unmacho it is," says Gretchen Goff. "Those we've seen have been through chemical-dependency treatment, which makes them more prone to accept treatment for bulimia, but apparently many men are not coming forward." The preliminary conclusions about male

bulimics emerging from the medical world sound even more hes-
itant than those about women. Therapists report that male
bulimics tend to stick to vomiting rather than relying heavily
upon laxatives and that they have personalities similar to those
of female bulimics. Both men and women seem afraid of intimacy and relationships and are socially handicapped by their
lack of assertiveness.

Until more men come forward, we must infer comparisons between male and female bulimics from what we know of the food
habits of normal men and women. The University of Minnesota
survey of college campuses questioned both male and female
students about their eating behavior. The researchers learned
that more women binge-vomited once a week or more, while
more men binge-vomited daily or more for at least a month. The
same pattern was true of stealing in each group. (*If* this holds
true for male bulimics as well, they may be more severely ill
than female bulimics because, as in anorexia nervosa, only the
most vulnerable men may be prone to a "women's disorder.") In
the Minnesota study, more women students were found to use
some form of weight control, and four times as many women as
men felt depressed and disgusted with themselves after gorge-
purging. Male and female students shared a fear of becoming
fat, and both groups ate high-calorie, easy-to-ingest food;
women outnumbered men two to one on the other *DSM III* criteria for bulimia.

One difference between male and female bulimics suggested
in interviews is that while women are diverted by their quest for
the "ideal diet," men seem more aware from the start that
bulimia involves issues having nothing to do with food and
weight. Even men who do mention their love of food and fear of
fat nevertheless connect their gorge-purging with other addictions or attribute it to other causes. Some men who use bulimia
to cope with tension, for instance, make little or no reference to
weight control. Twenty-six-year-old Norm, a government employee, remembers why he used to binge-vomit but can't recall
his attitude toward his weight at the time:

> I've always been able to vomit easily, ever since I was a
> kid. Maybe I did it when I was a kid. Like we're sitting
> here having lunch, and I could just vomit what I've

eaten all over the floor before you could finish your sentence. Anyway, when I was in ninth and tenth grades, I was binging and vomiting a lot. I can't remember whether I was worried about my weight, but I know I did it to relieve tension. It was like alimentary masturbation.

Twenty-three-year-old Gerry, an editorial assistant from Chicago, doesn't even associate binging with food—he associates it with his job:

I want to binge while I'm at work. I work in a really hectic office where I'm always under pressure, and people keep asking me questions, and the phone keeps ringing. I have a lot more to do in one time than I'm physically capable of doing. I have three editors that I work under, and each treats me as if I were working for him alone. I resent it—I feel like a little toy at their whims. I don't feel in control; I feel like I'm being used. "Gerry, do this; Gerry, do that; Gerry, I need you to do this." And they all need these things done right away.

At times I'm highly critical of myself and think I can keep handling it better and getting more done. And I have. But it can never be enough because it's always too much work. I've done this for over two years now—it's my first job, and it gives me a sense of security.

Doing the work at my own pace means staying late. I've told them I need another person to help, but they don't see it. My particular boss can do ten things at once and always works well under pressure and thinks that I can too and that it will help me grow. So I feel anxious and frustrated and angry and helpless. When things get out of hand, I start to think, "Gerry's going to feed." And I go to the deli or somewhere and start eating. But once I start eating, I'm more helpless than ever.

Gerry suffers anxiety, frustration, anger, helplessness, lack of control, insecurity and implied unassertiveness—all feelings that are food for bulimia.

Generic Bulimia

The experiences of male bulimics can at least help us single out aspects of the disorder that may be central because they are shared with women. Jason, age twenty-seven, is a recovering bulimic anorectic looking for a job in Los Angeles while still having great difficulty holding his life together:

> I read about the "typical bulimarexic woman" all the time, and I think, "But what about me?" For a while I guess I fit that stereotype as much as a man could. I was an overachiever and a real winner: the best athlete in my high school, strong, tough, attractive, popular— I've always had girlfriends ever since I was a kid. Somewhere along the line I lost all that.
>
> The summer before I started college I was working in a factory. For some reason I got attracted to the idea of being empty and hungry, so I started eating less and less. I justified it by saying that I was saving money. I got into trouble because my job required lots of lifting, and I became too weak to do much.
>
> One day I developed terrible pains in my stomach and was sent to the hospital for exploratory surgery. They found out that I had a bowel obstruction. After that I felt as if I never fully regained my health, and I got very interested in good health and nutrition. I read a lot about nutrition and decided that we eat more than our bodies need, so I started eating even less. I must have gotten into anorexia nervosa, because I went from 220 to 140 pounds and eventually down to 124. I'm six feet tall. Of course, whenever I came home from college my family would notice and encourage me to eat. Well, I'm very rigid about standards I set for myself, and once I violated my standards of not eating so much, that was it. To this day, if I eat one M&M, I vomit.
>
> I don't really know how or when the binge-vomiting started. All I remember is that it was a real high—it

felt great to throw up, and I'd feel wonderful for a
long time after I did it. I'd do it once a week and felt
really comfortable with it, but it became very habitual.
It ended up blacking out eight years of my life. I find it
really hard to recall much of what went on. I would eat
from fifty to a hundred dollars' worth of food in one
day and vomit from thirty to fifty times a day, as long
as it took me to get all the food out, and I'd do this for
weeks at a time. Needless to say, this helped me lose a
lot of the weight. I was starting to drink and use speed
more heavily too. I really started to go berserk.

My uncle owns his own business, and after college I
went into partnership with him, still drinking, binging
and vomiting. Finally I started feeling so sick that I
went to our family physician for a checkup. He found a
tremendous imbalance of electrolytes and adrenal hormones and had me hospitalized. I got extra food from
the cafeteria, ate everything I was brought, and vomited all the time I was hospitalized, but no one noticed. They gave me a potassium supplement and let
me go.

I started seeing a psychiatrist but didn't tell him
that I binge-vomited; I just mentioned that I couldn't
hold down food. He had me hospitalized in a psychiatric
ward, I think to scare me into admitting that I was
binging. It didn't work. I just became very bitter and
left the hospital after five days. Shortly after that I was
charged with drunk driving, which scared me enough
to make me check into a ward at a different hospital.
But I claimed that I was nervous and said nothing
about my drinking or binge-vomiting. I *was* nervous—
there was a girl in the ward being treated for anorexia
nervosa, and she insisted that I had it. I was there for
five weeks. We got passes to go out every day, and I
went to a bar on every pass. I kept up drinking after I
got out of there and still binge-vomited, although I was
really getting into fitness and health foods.

I made up my mind that I had to quit my bad habits
and start getting my life together. I moved out of my

hometown to a larger city and took the first job I could get—selling business insurance. It was a good job; I was treated well, and I could make two thousand dollars a week just by closing one sale. And that's all I did —I'd travel off somewhere, make a sale and spend the rest of the week in a motel room, eating a twenty-four-piece bucket of chicken, tacos, or anything else I could get, drinking, vomiting and watching soap operas. The better the job went, the worse I would be. I got on an overachievement kick for a period and earned ten thousand dollars a week for six consecutive weeks, won a Caribbean cruise and a car—stuff the company used for incentives. Finally I got burned out. I had the chance to close what would have been the largest sale the company had ever made, and instead of going to the appointment, I headed for a motel room with my supplies. I ate and vomited and drank and passed out. When I woke up I showered, got dressed, drove to the company, wrote out a letter of resignation and just left. I said something in the letter about career conflicts, and I don't think I fooled anybody.

The next day I went to a chemical-dependency treatment center. They refused to take me because I was bulimic. I didn't even know what bulimia was—I thought that I was crazy and that I was the only person who binged and vomited. I'm bitter that they sent me away. But I found another treatment center that got me off the booze and was willing to try to help me deal with the food. I've been sober for nine months, but I can't kick the food habit.

I can attribute everything to the eating: until I kick that, nothing else is going to turn around for me. It's just destroying me: I want help so badly, but I push people away when they try to help me, and that scares me because, what if they don't try anymore? Everything scares me—I can't pinpoint the feelings; it's just something I can't face or don't want to experience. When I'm scared I binge-vomit, and that makes me feel better, and it's obvious that that's what I'm using it for.

I want to work on this so badly, but I don't know where
I'm at or where I'm going. I've been feeling suicidal.

I try to resolve to be better, but I know that I can't
take my own word for things anymore. I used to be a
moral person, and during the past few days I've started
stealing. There are two parts to me: the part that
binges and vomits is the ugly, weak, repulsive, crybaby,
self-pitying part. When I think of what I've done in
bathrooms—if I could sit and watch myself do it, I
don't know what I would think. The other part of me
would just say, "That's not me," and I'd turn my back
on it. That's the part that wants so much to get well. I
value myself so much to a degree—I have so much potential that I can't use. Part of me is screaming to come
out, but it's scared of the things it wants so badly.

So much has been taken away from me. When I was
in insurance I had one hundred thousand dollars net
worth. I can't account for that money now—I can't
even pay my bills. The bulimia made me feel completely worthless—that's the only emotion it's left me
with. I've violated every standard I ever had. Knowing
all this doesn't seem to help. It's such an uncontrollable,
insidious, compulsive thing, and it's so tied in with alcoholism. With everything. I want to get into primary
treatment because I have so much to talk out, but I'm
scared. Scared out of my mind.

Jason recognizes that his old life was close to that of the "typical bulimarexic woman," although now he feels that the stereotype is meaningless (no doubt many bulimic women do also).
He follows a common pattern of not being able to recall the
onset or experiences of his bulimia; it has blacked out a section of
his life and still controls an area of his thinking that he feels is
unlike his real self. Like many women, Jason finds that the
tiniest bite starts a binge, and that a new job in a new home
does not help him control himself. His binging is tied in with his
alcohol and drug abuse—"with everything." He believed himself
unique in his binge-vomiting, kept it from his therapist and had
some bitter experiences with the medical profession both when

avoiding and seeking help. Jason is ambivalent about reaching out to other people. Having turned his back on a tremendous professional challenge, he is obviously ambivalent about success as well—is the terror that haunts him actually a fear of recovery?

Some eating-disorders therapists feel it crucial to take a feminist perspective on anorexia nervosa and bulimia. One can hardly imagine an area of study that would not benefit from a feminist perspective; within this field, however, there seems to be a disturbing tendency to eliminate men because they form a minority. Male bulimics are victims of discrimination, second-class citizens within the context of their disorder. It's much easier to generalize that all women want to look like fashion models or that bulimia in men represents a conflict about homosexuality than it is to make a point of rounding up male bulimics and studying them with an open mind. After all, theories about bulimia are shaky enough without men coming along to kick their foundations. The evidence that bulimia is much more than an outcome of social pressures suggests that bulimics of both sexes are alike, but some therapists disagree, and no one knows for sure.

In a sense, male bulimics are maintaining the *status quo;* they have an obligation, as do female bulimics, to come forward and seek help. Until they do, researchers can only hope that their findings about women are valid for men as well.

Chapter 10

THE LOST WEEKENDS

An excerpt from Miriam's diary, February 27, 1976:

Please, God, forgive me for giving in to my sickness
again. The guilt and remorse are unbearable—the
money, dishonesty . . . No more. I'm so ashamed of
the example I'm setting for my children. Please, God,
forgive. Only you can straighten my warped mind out.

My urge to binge is a cancer in my life that's ruining
every part of it. I feel so depressed, forsaken, bound by
this evil. I feel inferior in my work and everything else.
My life is a mess. I can't sleep, and when I do I have
terrible nightmares. I want to die.

Yvette, a twenty-two-year-old keypunch operator:

I could spend a few days restaurant-hopping. I'd go in,
have some food, go to the bathroom to vomit, and walk
out on the bill. Or I'd use my parents' credit cards. I'd
get the restaurant to accept a check that I knew would
bounce, because I couldn't see far enough into the fu-
ture to imagine making good the amount. Usually I'd
manage to pick up some guy on my food hunts. Or I'd

somehow find myself in a motel room two days later, with grocery bags and candy wrappers all around me.

Karen, a twenty-nine-year-old editor:

Bulimia is so crippling and so insidious; it affects every area of your life. It's not just overeating and vomiting; ironically, it's a starving yourself of all things in life. It builds up walls around you, cuts off intimacy, numbs you. Even the bad feelings are better than that kind of insanity, although we need support just to deal with feelings the rest of the world takes for granted. Twelve years of my life were on hold, absolutely nowhere. It removed the highs and the lows because I couldn't take anything—anger, rejection—I'd deal with it later by going home to eat. I thought I was the only person who binge-vomited. I wanted a miracle cure, and there are none. I just wanted to die; I was so alone.

Robin, a twenty-four-year-old waitress:

I was my high school valedictorian and got a small scholarship to a local college. But I couldn't imagine living in a dorm. "Where will I throw up?" I thought. "What if I don't fast perfectly while I'm in college? What if I eat up my tuition money?" I couldn't trust myself not to spend any money I had on food. I wanted desperately to go to school; instead, I took a job in a cafeteria where I could binge and vomit without anybody really noticing. They thought that I went to the bathroom so often to touch up my makeup because I was vain.

For three years I could not do anything until I had binged first. I was always late because that had top priority. I felt as if I'd never amount to anything because the bulimia was always in the way.

A large part of my life has been wasted on bulimia: my family, the money, the misery I went through, the misfortune, the pain.

Multiple Addictions

If we substituted references to liquor, drinking and bars for those to food, binge-vomiting and restaurants in these accounts, the four women could easily be mistaken for alcoholics. As a matter of fact, three of them *are* alcoholics—Miriam was addicted to diet pills. Because of the nature of bulimia itself, and because 25 to 40 percent of bulimics abuse alcohol or drugs (compared to a 10 percent alcoholism rate, for example, in the general population), some psychiatrists and psychologists view bulimia as an addiction. Although this hasn't been proven, researchers able to study different populations of bulimics notice that they show a gamut of addictions and the behaviors that are part of them. A sizable number of bulimics have not only experimented with, but also abused, just about every substance, including food.

Twenty-seven-year-old Greta can offer a catalog of all the related addictions and activities that bulimics get into—liquor, men, cigarettes, drugs, stealing, lying:

> I went wild in college. I hooked up with a crazy crowd and started much too much drinking, smoking cigarettes and pot, and partying. We had an all-you-can-eat meal plan at the cafeteria, and I think that's the point at which I started binging before vomiting. I was abusing diet pills too around this time. I also hid bags of candy in my dorm room and stole the cookies my roommate's mother had sent her. I was always hitting the vending machines for candy bars or shoplifting from local stores. Often I'd make messes in the bathroom from my vomiting, and along with the other girls I'd talk about it and say, "Isn't it awful that someone is doing that?" without ever letting on it was me. I tried to stop but couldn't get past a grocery store without buying bags of candy and junk. If I knew that my roommate had a date, I'd stay home that night and sit alone in our room eating, smoking pot and feeling sorry

for myself. If I wasn't doing that, it was because I was
addicted to some guy.

It should be clear by now that it's very difficult to recover from
bulimia alone; these victims of multiple addictions are even
harder to help. A woman who has abused only food is forced to
confront reality once she stops binge-vomiting, but if the problems underlying multiple addictions are not dealt with, the addict is likely to just switch to a different substance. Multiple addicts also find it more difficult to tolerate the working-through
stages of therapy.

Bulimics with other addictions may share a basic problem
with their fellow addicts. "Some people may be unable to identify their internal states, so they express their feelings by acting
them out," says Craig Johnson. "This is speculative, but there
may be people who cut across alcoholism, substance abuse, what
have you, who don't have the usual ability to articulate their
feelings." (This disadvantage is obvious in bulimic "good girls,"
who restrain their behavior in so many respects that they leave
themselves no means of letting go.) "To talk about an addictive
personality is simplistic but has some merit," says Dr. Rudnick.
"It's amazing how many polyaddictions one can see in an individual addicted to any one thing."

Addictive Behavior

LYING

Certainly bulimics behave like other addicts. They deny the
addiction when confronted with it, for instance, and lie to maintain it. As previously noted, bulimics may have spent much of
their childhoods living lies in the sense of not recognizing problems in their families. The bulimia suddenly unleashes a talent
for make-believe that protects it from interference from the outside world. Thirty-two-year-old Sarah explains:

> I was really honest as a kid, but that absolutely died
> out when I became bulimic. I lied constantly, and in

order to lie I'd have to believe the lie myself, so I completely lost touch with reality. I denied it so much that rather than go out to buy binge foods like other bulimics, I just binged on what we had around, even if it was potato chips or peanut butter or something else painful to throw up. I'd steal food from my college roommate's care packages, then I'd fantasize that someone had come into our room and stolen the food, and when I believed it I could suggest that to her convincingly.

One weekend I was afraid that someone would hear me vomiting in the sorority bathroom, so I vomited into a dishpan and hid it in the back of our closet until I could clean it out. My roommate came back, started digging in the closet for something, and stepped in the dishpan. What could I say? We become so adept at lying—I invented a story that someone had gotten drunk, vomited and hid the dishpan in the closet for a bad joke. I even nagged my roommate to find out who had done it and make them buy her new shoes.

Later on when I was married, I tried to hide the bulimia from my husband. I was throwing garbage into an old chest in the basement until I could sneak it out. For some reason my husband opened the chest and found all these food containers—empty vanilla wafer boxes, graham cracker boxes, donut boxes, cereal boxes. When he confronted me with that, I panicked and couldn't think of a lie, so I just ran out to the car and drove off. I had just binged and was desperate to vomit, which made it worse. I drove out of town, stopped the car near a field, went out into the field to vomit, then sat there crying for hours before returning home. I didn't know how to tell the truth on this one occasion without my whole life's fabric of lies coming apart.

When I got into treatment, my support group gave me a love of honesty that has become obsessive. I can't lie any more—I can't even exaggerate to tell a funny

story. At first I'd want to lie even about ordinary
things; in therapy was the first time I realized that my
first response in any conversation was to lie. It was a
surprise to me that it's been easy for me once again to
become honest most of the time. It's such a relief to go
to bed instead of binging all night, without wondering
if my husband would find hidden food, wondering
what lies I had to keep track of. Honesty was not one
of the things I recognized I had lost, and it's a relief to
have it back.

Sarah has swung back to her original extreme—from obsessive
lying to obsessive truthfulness. Like many bulimics, she will say
anything that makes it possible to vomit—to "do what I have to
do," as they say—without being discovered. And as Sarah points
out, the lies of bulimics aren't limited to the illness itself but
rather encompass all aspects of their lives.

STEALING

Binge-vomiting can easily cost its victim from fifty to a hundred dollars a day; laxatives for some bulimics cost hundreds of
dollars a month. Bulimics get food or money from their parents;
they get grants or loans; they work a second job, especially one
that allows them access to food, to earn money. Many resort to
more unsavory and drastic measures to finance their habit—they
take up prostitution or stealing.

Stealing is especially common among bulimics and may be an
aspect of the impulse-control problem that plagues them. Like
the bulimia itself, stealing lets them relinquish control and gives
them a high. Bulimics can start by stealing food, and some of
them who abhor the idea never get beyond that point—food is
necessary for a binge, they reason; other stealing is wrong. But
others become addicted to the thrill of getting away with the
theft; that, along with their sense of entitlement, prompts them
to start stealing other items like clothes or jewelry. Perhaps this
is part of the bulimic dynamic: their needs had never been
readily asked for and met, so they steal food and money as a
symbolic way of stealing love. Or the stealing may be just a

practical matter, as it was for Jocelyn, an ex-high school Home-
coming Queen:

> I worked as a volunteer in a hospital, but instead of
> doing my assignments I'd prowl around looking for
> food to steal from the nurses' station or from patients'
> trays. I'd hide in a linen closet and eat it in a frenzy,
> then vomit. I stole money that patients left in their
> rooms. I also had a part-time job in a superette, where
> it was so easy to shoplift Twinkies and candy that I'd
> have a pocketful of food all the time. I knew where the
> employees kept their purses and could steal money
> from them. And if someone bought a carton of ciga-
> rettes or something and was in too much of a hurry to
> get a receipt, I'd just pocket the money. Once they
> missed some money and accused another cashier of tak-
> ing it, since I looked so clean-cut and normal. I kept
> quiet.

Margot, a twenty-seven-year-old secretary, put a bit more
variety into her theft:

> If I were visiting relatives, I'd go into their kitchens,
> sift through the cupboards, and pocket whatever I
> thought wouldn't be missed. I'd think to myself, "What
> the hell; they're family; they'd give it to me if I asked
> for it." Then I started stealing money. The women in
> my office would leave their purses inside their desks
> when they stepped outside for a minute, and I'd take
> money out of them—very small amounts, so the owners
> wouldn't miss it. I always spent every cent of that
> money on food—God, was it a high to binge on food I
> bought with stolen money! I think at first it was the
> food that was all-important in the stealing. Then I
> found myself wanting to take other things. I'd go into a
> clothing store with a plan all mapped out for stealing
> something, and I really used to relish the experience. I
> remember two things in particular—I'd always feel

very brave and excited about what I was doing, and I'd
pretend that I was Robin Hood and deserved what I
stole. Once I stole four identical bracelets. I never wear
bracelets!

Stealing could also be an expression of the bulimic's narcissism
and low self-esteem: she wants something and feels entitled to
it, while another part of her feels too unworthy to deserve it.
Margot graduates from stealing from relatives, who would give
her food anyway, to stealing from strangers, who would not.
Whatever the reason, the stealing, like the lying, becomes a way
of life *per se*. And this shoplifting may serve as a blessing in disguise—the bulimic is caught; the confrontation blows away her
highly valued cover, and she comes in for treatment.

Related Addictions

ALCOHOLISM

Probably the most common related addiction that bulimics get
into is alcoholism. Other investigators have corroborated Michael Strober's findings on the incidence of alcoholism in the
families of bulimics. Dr. Eckert, at the University of Minnesota,
and her associates at the University of Iowa Hospital and the Illinois State Psychiatric Institute have studied the incidence of
alcoholism in anorexia nervosa. They found that alcoholic anorectics were likely to be bulimic and that bulimic anorectics,
like pure bulimics, show a high incidence of family alcoholism.
Although there's no strong, clearly proven correlation between
bulimia and alcoholism, most researchers feel that the two addictions are linked. Some of them are pursuing the hunch that
alcoholism is an affective disorder like depression and manic-
depressive psychosis and that it involves the same neurochemical
problems that may make certain people biologically vulnerable
to these illnesses. Bulimia can't be categorized as an affective
disorder for sure, but its obvious link with alcoholism and
depression is intriguing. Could affective disorders be the key to
the addictive personality?

Some bulimics start using alcohol in a conscious attempt to stave off their binging by stifling their appetites. But true to their fashion, they lose control of the drinking as well. Twenty-five-year-old Marge found that her drinking complemented rather than squelched her binging:

> It was as if I were two people. One was on scholarships, excelling in school. The other was a cocktail waitress. I started drinking because drinking took the place of when I couldn't binge. Then they'd work hand in hand. I'd get drunk enough to binge, or binge while I was drinking. I was always binging, vomiting, drinking, taking laxatives, or all of the above.
>
> I found that I never had to worry about the calories in the alcohol or the prospect of getting a hangover. I'd get drunk, come home, and binge all night. I guess that food absorbs the alcohol and brings it back up again, because when I binged and vomited afterwards I'd grow sober and wake up the next day with no hangover.

Once this information gets around, we may see alcoholics who have taken up binging to avoid getting sick.

It's hard to determine which of the two addictions is more difficult to treat. Alcoholism has been recognized far longer than has bulimia; many psychiatrists, for instance, are medically sophisticated about it. Bulimia not only is less well known but also involves less pressure on the victim to get help, since she keeps it a secret. Its effects are not as obvious as those of drinking, so it becomes more deeply ingrained. "I have more optimism for a bulimic than for someone who has been a really bad alcoholic for the same amount of time," says Dr. Rudnick. "That's different from talking about someone who is both bulimic and alcoholic. The bulimia may start before the alcoholism and be harder to treat for that reason."

Bulimic alcoholics unanimously agree that bulimia is much harder to recover from, not because of the length of time they have been ill but because of the difference between alcohol and food. Obviously, treatment for bulimia can't involve the total-abstinence model that is so effective with alcoholism. Bulimics must handle food both for themselves and often for their families, several times a day. They must learn to control and live with a terrifying substance and to experience the normal hunger that signals their lack of control. Food addiction is devastating to their sense of self-control and to their trust in their own judgment. And the addict's outlook on alcoholism and bulimia must be quite different: drinking is an adult activity; stealing candy bars and stuffing them down is the behavior of a naughty child.

DRUG ABUSE

Like alcoholism, drug abuse can form a symbiotic relationship with bulimia. Appropriately enough, some bulimics are introduced to drugs in the form of diet pills. Thirty-six-year-old Irene, who was bulimic for fifteen years, explains how she got hooked:

I've been obsessed with food and dieting since I was nine years old. When I was fifteen I spent a summer visiting some cousins and found that one of them had boxes of diet pills. I started taking them to lose weight. I have a terrible appetite, and once I discovered that the pills curbed it, I became addicted to them for the next twelve years, until I ran out of doctors to supply them. Twelve years ago amphetamines were okay; they weren't a street drug, and my cousin and her sister-in-law were both nurses and got them for me easily. The pills were a crutch for my appetite. I'd take one and fast all day, then binge and vomit all night. I was controlled during the day and freaking out at night. I'd get a month's supply from my doctor and ration them out to myself. I was terrified to have a day without my pill; if I so much as ate breakfast, the entire day would be a binge. It was fast or nothing.

I had a really crazy life because of those drugs. I acted like a fool because I was spaced out on a high with raging emotions all the time. I got divorced and had two affairs. And the pills did not completely control my appetite, so I stayed bulimic.

I could not get off the pills myself because I was too frightened of gaining weight. When my doctor refused to give me more, I thought my appetite would become completely hopeless, but I didn't gain that much weight. I missed the jolt of instant energy from the pills; I had a full-time job, three kids and no husband, and I didn't feel I could cope without it.

Irene's remarks are a good example of how concentration on eating can hide the real problems: she is actually psychologically dependent on pills that don't even control her appetite.

ADDICTION TO SUGAR AND CARBOHYDRATES

An interesting report, one promulgated by Overeaters Anonymous, is that starches and especially sugars can become addictive substances for some people. Whether this is due to their own metabolisms or to some kind of biochemical shift caused by binging is not known. "We get stories of very peculiar idiosyncratic responses to sugar or to carbohydrates," says Dr. Katz. "Long-standing bizarre dieting can actually cause a person to develop such reactions to sugars and starches, but I don't really see this problem as a causative or even a predisposing factor, at least in the majority of bulimics." Despite Judith J. Wurtman's findings that carbohydrate craving may result from a shortage of brain serotonin, such reactions would not explain binging entirely. But regardless of when or how the problem started, it is a severe one for some people.

Thirty-three-year-old Ethel, for example, spent a month in Europe, where the change in diet caused her to relapse into binge-vomiting:

I found myself having to eat a small amount of bread made with white flour each day. That lowered my resistance, and by the end of the trip I was eating small servings of ice cream. Circumstances did the rest. The plane home was late, and I was waiting in a German airport with a fistful of European coins and some time to kill, so I went into the duty-free shop. I had been sober for eight years and wouldn't buy booze, and I hadn't enough money for perfume, and there was all this chocolate . . .

On the plane flight I had plenty of time to think about my normal abstinence from sugars and starches and what I was doing. But four times I got up from my seat, locked myself in the stinking little biffy, ate chocolate until I was sick and threw up. And by the time I got off the plane I really, really believed that there is a chemical factor to bulimia.

Like a first sip of alcohol, a first bite of sugar can throw an abstinent addict off the wagon, even if she has eaten nourishing meals and is comfortably full.

Like alcohol too, sugar can unleash uncontrollable emotions in some people or make them feel either sleepy or high. Cheryl, a twenty-six-year-old research assistant, gave up sugar and starches to avoid such reactions:

Sugar and refined starches always caused me to binge. The sugar also made me sleepy and incoherent. Sometimes binges made me high; in fact, once I went to an appointment with my counselor after I had binged, and he thought I was high and made me go get a drug test. The binges also caused me to black out, and eventually I developed hypoglycemia.

It's ironic, because I didn't grow up with sweets. My father hated them and allowed only fresh fruit and things like that in the house. When I was a kid and wanted a snack, I always bought sunflower seeds or nuts rather than candy.

I know a lot of people in Alcoholics Anonymous who never really recovered, because they've started eating lots of sugar instead of drinking. I went through a treatment program that taught people to avoid both liquor and sugar because they're so alike.

People with food allergies crave the foods to which they are allergic. Sugars and starches may have strange effects upon the body's neurochemistry. Ideas like these sound ominous, for they mean our facing the possibility that food, our basic source of life, is a legitimate addictive substance.

Addiction to Food

Some bulimics recognize that their attraction to food resulted largely from accident. At the opposite extreme from polyaddictive bulimics are those who take up food because of social proscriptions against liquor or drugs. "It wasn't socially acceptable in my town to drink, smoke or use drugs, and food was all I could control," explains one victim. "It was really all I had. People could make me say or do anything, but they couldn't feed me. Food was what I had that nobody else could take away; it was as if I had created it." The dependence here is clearly psychological rather than physical. Most women are naturally preoccupied with food—for those who covet a pair of designer jeans, practically all food is forbidden fruit.

Is food merely a low-priority choice for those who would rather drink or smoke, or is it an addictive substance in its own right? Most addictive substances clearly have some biological effects upon the central nervous system: certain drugs cause a high, for instance, and alcohol dampens down feelings of distress. Although some foods are likely to affect the central nervous system, the relationship between such effects and the eating disorders is not as clear as it is for the more classical addictions. Nevertheless, bulimia acts very much as if it were an addiction. Bulimics describe their illness much as other addicts describe theirs: "I can't help myself"; "the urge comes out of the blue"; "I'm completely lost"; "I'm in a totally different state"; "I'm unaware of what's going on at the time." The binging frequently ends in exhaustion or sleep. The victim resolves not to binge again, but within a short period of time she's back at it, apparently out of her conscious control.

Some psychiatrists and psychologists have always seen bulimia in this way and have proceeded on that basis, as Dr. Huebner explains:

> In German medicine, out of all the psychological entities, the best-known eating problems are referred to as

addictions. The German for obesity is "fat addiction";
that for anorexia nervosa is "puberty-meager-addiction"
or "addiction to thinness in puberty." When these terms
were invented, the medical profession did not think of
eating disorders as true addictions, because there was
no evidence of a substrate in the body. Clinicians described them intuitively that way.

We're back to wondering whether food takes on the disturbing
role of triggering a substrate.

The testimonies of bulimics show that they think of food
differently from the way most people think of it. To the chronic
bulimic, food and the consequences of eating have lost much of
their heavy symbolic significance. The weight issue becomes secondary to the power of the binge-vomiting itself, even though
the bulimia may have started as a diet. Food becomes fuel for a
whole psychophysiological cycle—it's preferred; it's more acceptable or it's just more readily available than other substances.
It's not really tasted or thought about during a binge—just shov-
eled down. It's transformed from food into something else.

This process of change is implied in the narrative of Betsy, a
secretary in Chicago, who was bulimic for twenty years:

> Every time I go back to visit family on the farm, I
> want to binge-vomit again. There were my parents and
> my four brothers and sisters until I was nine, when my
> father died. He was a huge man who weighed over
> three hundred pounds; my mother is a big woman, but
> she never had any food problems that I noticed. But
> she loves to cook. When my father died she started
> cooking constantly because that was her way of show-
> ing love for us. My family is German, and they tend to
> be very reserved and have trouble showing their feel-
> ings. I was never close to my mother, and she never ex-
> pressed love for me except by feeding me. We were
> very poor, so we lived on the kind of starchy stuff and
> cheap baked goods that poor families can afford. We
> were hearty farm people, and all of my brothers and
> sisters grew up with weight problems. I'm five feet four

inches and weighed a hundred and eighty pounds by
the time I was fifteen, when I started vomiting up most
of the huge meals I ate. I guess I picked up my
mother's idea that food equals love, and I was so lonely
and unhappy out on the farm that I started eating everything in sight. I think that bulimia is a person's attempt to make up for something she's missing in life,
but nothing balances out when you're bulimic: you're
always causing some disruption in your family, and the
money situation becomes ungodly. You eat and you eat,
but you get nothing out of it but a sense of hope-
lessness and despair.

On a binge I would eat so much that I'd be bent over
and could barely make it to the bathroom. I was sure
that I would eat myself to death like the sheep we used
to have. They'd get out into the alfalfa field and just
keep eating and eating until the gasses would build up
inside them and they'd bloat themselves to death. I always thought of them when I ate.

Hideous things happen when you're bulimic. Our old
sewer would freeze in winter from my vomiting, so I'd
go outside in subzero weather to throw up. The vomit
would freeze out there in the snow until spring thaw.
Years later, after I was married, I was still a curse to
sewer systems. We would have the sewer man out
every year to pump out our fifteen-hundred-gallon sep-
tic tank. I'd always get a different sewer company to do
it, because each time the man came out, he'd say: "It
must have been years since you had this tank pumped;
I've never seen such sludge." And of course I'd lie to
him. How do you explain that hundreds of pounds of
caramel and chocolate don't break down like other
sewage? Nothing fits or makes sense in the life of a
bulimic; you're always lying. I made sense of this horrible situation by lying to the sewer man. It seemed like
a small price to pay for the privilege of binge-vomiting.

Betsy originally thinks of food as mother love and comfort for
what's missing from her life. As her addiction progresses, food

becomes distorted into frozen vomit and sludge. Lying to get the sludge pumped is easier for her than giving up binging, even though the food itself means nothing to her anymore.

A similar change occurs when the course of the bulimia itself diverts from the goal of the perfect body image. Fat women binge and vomit. Women who gain weight while bulimic still binge and vomit. "The thing that finally got me in for treatment was that, while I had initially lost twenty-five pounds binge-vomiting, I had gained twenty of them back," says one victim. "Now I *knew* I was out of control. And I still delight in the fact that I weigh less now than I did for at least part of the time I was bulimic." Somewhere in the back of her mind the bulimic is still terrified to gain weight, but while she is severely ill, the binge-vomiting overrides all other considerations.

Bulimia in Control

The bulimia, in short, takes on a life of its own. A woman may be biochemically prone to bulimia; she may have psychological difficulties that start her on gorge-purging, but eventually these explanations for her behavior become obscured. Bulimia consumes the lives of its victims; planned ahead in detail, the binges provide a structure for otherwise unstructured lives. Bulimics drop out of school activities, cut classes to head for the cafeteria, fail or drop courses, stay home from work to binge or lose their jobs because of their addiction, and bounce checks. "My life may be totally fucked up," they think, "but at least I'm thin." They believe that the bulimia is unique to them, that it gives them the specialness that they crave. They reduce their identities to being bulimic.

Bulimics close themselves off from relationships except with people like their parents who provide food. "I get pissed at bulimia sometimes because it's a fucking selfish disease—it's self-centered, selfish, me, me, me, and yes I love you but can you please leave my apartment now so I can gorge my face," says one victim. Having withdrawn from their friends, many bulimics instead begin hanging out with weird people who abuse them, or they become promiscuous for the first time in their lives. They count calories as though they were dollars. Nothing is as important to them as vomiting, as twenty-five-year-old Joan explains:

> I wish I could give you some idea of how incredibly urgent it becomes for you to get to a bathroom and vomit after you've eaten. I didn't always overeat when out with my boyfriend, but if I did, I refused to go to a movie or do anything after we had dinner except make up some bizarre excuse to go home and vomit. While I was in college I got this reputation for being compulsively clean, because as soon as I ate I'd feel this incredible desire to get into the bathroom and vomit, with the shower running to cover up the sound.

Bulimics who can no longer vomit for one reason or another are devastated because they can't stop binging. They choose occasions on which to begin abstinence—a birthday, graduation, the start of a new year, the anniversary of the first time they binge-vomited—but the occasions fail them just as they fail themselves. Even though they claim that they had to bottom-out before recovering, they regret that no one ever confronted them with their addiction, and they urge people who know bulimics to do just that.

Bulimia is ironic: food, our source of life, becomes twisted into a pernicious "substance." Even more remarkably, recovered bulimics tend to idealize their addiction once it's over, and even miss it. Jeanette, a thirty-three-year-old management consultant, complains about her ten-year addiction to bulimia and her inability to let it go:

> Bulimia ruined my life and stopped me from growing for ten years, but it was also my comforter. It was even my god—I had become a born-again Christian while I was bulimic and had this bizarre struggle with my religious beliefs because bulimia was my god, and I couldn't worship two gods at once. My life went nowhere; I did nothing but wait for something to happen.
> It involves all facets of your life, stopping growth

completely. It controls your life in a way that only people with other dependencies can understand. It's progressive and makes you feel totally unworthy. Eventually it will kill you.

But sometimes I still miss my bulimia as I would an old friend who has died.

This is a measure of bulimia's power over its victim: recovering bulimics mourn the loss of their binge-vomiting so consistently that therapists allow for these feelings in treatment. Judith Brisman explains:

> Many women are baffled about the depression that follows when they give up binge-purging. It's like giving up a lover; you think about him often, and there are dangerous times about missing binge-purging just as there are dangerous times about missing a lover. We view this as a natural process of mourning and specify to people what will be dangerous times for them. Generally they are high for the first month after the therapy workshop; then suddenly they recognize that they now have to face the rest of their lives and all the issues they've been hiding.

Therapy has the challenging task of convincing the bulimic that the rest of her life is something she should look forward to.

Chapter 11

THE ROAD TO RECOVERY:
PROBLEMS, METHODS AND PROGNOSES

Many bulimics have spent years taking therapy for other problems but kept their bulimia a secret from their therapists out of shame, guilt, and self-hatred. Others have broached the subject to their therapists only to have it dismissed. Neither case is a total loss: bulimic women report that they have benefited from therapy by learning much about themselves, but they have not been able to stop binge-vomiting. Eating-disorders specialists agree that therapy for bulimia must include a program aimed specifically at stopping the gorge-purging, *followed* or *complemented* by insight-oriented psychotherapy to help solve the problems that started it. Some women with severe, chronic bulimia may require long-term hospitalization in a unit that specifically treats eating disorders and knows how to cope with crafty bulimics determined to stay sick in spite of themselves. Most bulimics aren't ill enough to require such drastic measures, so they come for outpatient treatment that usually involves concurrent individual and group therapy. Such programs are still quite experimental. "Everybody wants to hear something dramatic about treatment, and I think we don't know anything dramatic about treating bulimia," says Dr. Herzog. And therapists do know that bulimia treatment is beset with various kinds of problems. To alert prospective therapists and patients about what to expect, these need to be described.

Problems

WHAT IS RECOVERY?

Treatment for bulimia is a difficult process because of the problems caused by bulimics themselves, the experimental nature of the therapy, and the lack of follow-up studies to pinpoint methods that are and are not successful. Underlying all this is the difficulty of defining a "cure" for bulimia; everyone agrees that recovery is possible, but no one knows exactly what it involves. "We see all different kinds of things," says Dr. Yager. "Some people stop gorge-purging completely with treatment, and it lasts; some need very little treatment before they stop. Others stop temporarily. The majority at least cut down. Some can't stop. Very few can't be helped at all."

Recovery certainly means changing the binge-vomiting pattern itself, but that alone is not recovery. The bulimic must also learn to handle the problems framing her symptom. It's a toss-up as to which aspect of recovery is more difficult for her. "I've seen patients who stopped the symptoms and clearly indicated that they became more miserable than ever," says Dr. Herzog. "Others found that they could participate in relationships they weren't otherwise able to have and described an improved mood, yet continued to binge-vomit. I'm not sure which is preferable, but I see it as involving a number of factors."

Some therapists feel that stopping the bulimia before starting psychotherapy is as important as normalizing weight before starting psychotherapy with the anorectic. Others feel that cutting down on the bulimia will do for the time being, because as the gorge-purging decreases, self-esteem increases, thereby expediting the therapy. "The problems with food decrease as body-image distortion does," says Michael Strober. "The food issues are related to other interconnected things in people's personalities and lives. The women feel better about themselves, so they are less concerned about their appearances and less anxious about weight; this makes them less rigid and fanatical about food and more relaxed, which in turn makes them feel better about themselves." A constructive cycle is set up that counteracts the destructive cycle of bulimia.

Bulimia victims are sometimes able to modify rather than stop their binging in a way that satisfies both themselves and their therapists. Judith Brisman gives an example:

> We have a patient who awakens every two or three hours each night and craves food. She would go and eat instead of recognizing that she felt lonely, afraid to be alone at night, angry. If she was traveling and sleeping in a motel room where food was not available, she would sleep through the night. We contracted with her to wash her face and brush her teeth before starting to eat so that she would at least be awake when she decided to do it. She still eats, but now she has what she calls her "safe" foods—an apple, some yogurt—and then goes back to bed. Formerly she would just binge herself to exhaustion.

Like an alcoholic, the bulimic who finds more constructive ways to cope with her life can learn to control her addiction. Craig Johnson explains:

> I don't know how to define a cure for bulimia. If by cure we mean that women come out of treatment and will never again think or worry about food or about their weight, then I don't think we can cure everyone. If we mean that we can help the women decrease the size and frequency of their binges and find alternative ways of dealing with their lives, I think we're quite successful at doing that.

The management of food involves confronting the bulimia and working on a normal, structured eating pattern, avoiding fasts or binge triggers. At first this requires rigidity about food—the bulimic merely substitutes compulsive control for compulsive eating. "Bulimics must expect to develop compulsivity toward their diets at first," says Michael Strober. "They must resolve to have certain calories, eat at certain times, break meals up in certain ways. Eventually they learn to deal with the food naturally. And ultimately they feel greater spontaneity: no rigid, self-imposed limits on what is tolerable."

The rigidity that bulimics can expect to practice raises an important question: how close is the analogy between bulimia and alcoholism? Can bulimics maintain "abstinence" from binge-vomiting? Overeaters Anonymous and some bulimia therapy programs ask their members to be abstinent or "clean"; they follow structured meal plans with no binge-eating, no vomiting or laxative/diuretic use, no skipping meals, no chewing food and spitting it out. For some programs abstinence extends even further into defining what kinds of foods can or can't be eaten. Even though bulimics can't literally abstain from food, their having specific eating rules to follow seems helpful to them.

Some therapists feel that alcoholism is the most effective model to use for bulimia. The fact is that some bulimics stop binge-vomiting just as other people stop biting their nails. These bulimics will not have solved their problems in living and may react to stress by becoming depressed or developing other symptoms. But abstinence is possible, although it is better to think in terms of managing the bulimia than it is to think of curing it. "Once you're bulimic, you may always have a tendency toward bulimia, so you must abstain from binges and keep your eating under strict control," says Dr. Eckert. "It becomes easier the longer you do it. A year of abstinence is probably a fair estimate of success, although I have one patient who relapsed even after that long a period of abstinence." Bulimia is like cancer or tuberculosis in that it can be arrested and seem "cured" after a specified period of remission, but the danger of relapse always remains.

Bulimics themselves seem to resent the implication that recovery can involve less than complete abstinence. Many of those who first came forward for treatment were terribly discouraged by therapists who told them that the best they could expect would be to cut down rather than stop gorge-purging. Some took their prognoses literally and made no effort to stop. Others maintained an all-or-nothing attitude. "If I let myself binge once a year, I would save emotions for that one binge, and I can't handle that sensation. Anything less than abstinence is bullshit. Stay away from professionals who tell you otherwise," says one victim.

Academically we can inquire whether the view of bulimia as learned behavior is applicable here. If bulima is learned behavior, then recovery would mean "unlearning" it and restoring the original state of not binge-vomiting. Unfortunately, bulimics can't erase all that's been learned along with the illness that easily. The point is that a bulimic who wants to stop gorge-purging had better not engage a therapist who feels that her goal is unrealistic, just as a bulimic who wants to cut down should not try to work with someone who will ask her to stop.

The other aspect of recovery is that of restoring the personality factors that bulima has destroyed, hidden or distorted in its victim. Therapy needs to patch up a lot and to rebuild the patient's self-value, control and integrity while helping her develop a sense of identity. This is not an easy task, especially early on in therapy—some bulimics have described giving up binge-vomiting as entering a dark tunnel or falling into an abyss. They need to cope with all the bad feelings that come bubbling up once the bulimia is taken away. The changes in mood and everyday stress that most of us take for granted are terrifying to bulimics. They describe recovery as having to learn to live all over again.

Sooner or later they learn that they *can* get through a day without binge-vomiting—and not only that, they can feel better about facing life than they did about escaping from it. As the bulimic feels happier with and more in control of herself, as she looks within herself for good feelings and starts to value what she thinks and feels, as she recognizes that other people can disagree with her without demolishing her, it becomes easier for her to live without abusing food. Some recovered bulimics find that for the first time in their lives they can feel good about themselves, form relationships, hold down jobs, attend school, discuss and express their feelings (especially anger), act assertively and win most battles in our lifelong war against stress. Until these good things happen, the bulimic can't really think of herself as recovered.

BULIMICS IN TREATMENT

Another difficulty that therapists must overcome is that caused by bulimics themselves, who rival their anorectic sisters in being difficult to treat. Some of them continue to gorge and purge despite their awareness of available help. Many are horrified at the expense of therapy—an especially weird response, since they waste thousands of dollars each year on a destructive habit when they could invest the money in helping themselves. Other bulimics fear that therapy will strip them of their one source of enjoyment. Even Miriam was able to idealize her bulimia in retrospect. "I loved eating," she says. "I was *free* while I did it; it was my hobby, my love, my enjoyment, my outlet." The prospect of losing the binge-vomiting is even worse than that of continuing it, as twenty-seven-year-old Anita explains:

> Once I tried to go and get information on a new bulimia group that had started. I never made it to the hospital—I stopped to eat at a pizzeria and a grocery store on the way instead. I don't know what was wrong with me. Maybe I just figured that I was going to give in and get help and was having a final fling at binging before then. I had my last binge one hour before starting with the group that cured me.

The farewell binge is a common occurrence—just "get me to the group on time."

Getting the bulimic into therapy is one problem. Once she has started treatment, her personality disorders can cause problems in both individual and group settings. In individual therapy, for instance, the bulimic can have difficulty in revealing herself (or can be downright dishonest); she can be either manipulative or excessively compliant and dependent on her therapist. Deep down she may worry that the silent, neutral therapist is not caring about her or is even secretly criticizing her.

These problems should not seriously interfere with therapy if the therapist understands that the bulimic is frightened and out of control. Her defense structure has betrayed her; she is in therapy because in some sense she recognizes that she must let that structure be pulled out from under her and replaced with a healthier system. Bulimics don't lie or manipulate in any morally wrong sense; rather, they fall back on these methods because they know no better way of staying whole. They are compliant because they are genuinely confused about who they are. Therapists often report that they all look and sound alike; over time the uniqueness that was missing or hidden slowly emerges. All of these problems dissipate as therapy proceeds.

The fun really starts when several bulimics are gathered together for group therapy. Therapists quickly discover, first of all, that they must make rules about regular attendance and prompt arrival and that the group members will test these rules out. Any kind of therapy group can fail because its members refuse to face their problems or are not compatible. Besides these potential complications, bulimia groups are still experimental, and of course the bulimics themselves can make the group sessions difficult.

In many ways bulimics act like chemical-dependency patients; if required to stop binge-vomiting they have a hard time sticking with therapy. Bulimics show tremendous entitlement, resistance and unreality about treatment. They may refuse to keep records of their food intake and vomiting, for example. They can have ridiculously high expectations of themselves: one woman was signed up to begin treatment as soon as she returned from her honeymoon, as if getting married and recovering from bulimia were both easy adjustments. Others search for instant cures for their illness; they want help today or never and imagine having their bulimia cured in a week when a year is a more realistic estimate. Gretchen Goff recalls the attitude that kept her from getting well:

> I wasted a lot of time trying to find information about bulimia because I wanted to believe that there was some kind of magic cure for it. I wanted to go to some doctor and say, "Here is my mind; fix it and return it to me." I even went to New York to a conference sponsored by the American Anorexia Nervosa Association. I had to check it out just to make sure that even they had

no magic answers. Then I entered a therapy program that really wasn't that much different from others I had tried. The difference was that I accepted the fact that I had to take responsibility for quitting the behavior. I stopped the minute I started the program and haven't binged for two years.

The search for the magic cure represents the passive desperation expressed by many bulimics; they want to be told what to do when actually their active participation in therapy could help them stop gorge-purging very quickly. Instead, they become furious with therapists for not curing them and resentful about having to work at their treatment.

Other bulimics recognize that therapy is helping them but become impatient with its short-term results. Two bulimics expressed these feelings in a group session:

> SIOBHAN: I dreamed the other night that I came to this group after two new people had joined and you had said that a writer would be observing. When I got here, there were about two hundred people. It was like a lecture series from a podium, and I sat here and thought, "Isn't this getting off the track?" It sounds funny, but I feel that getting off the track is bothering me. I walked out of the lecture and said, "I'm not coming back here." We're here to get better, and it was more like a party, a huge gathering with no focus. I went into this dingy bathroom; I wasn't throwing up, but I felt really uncomfortable because there were all these men in the bathroom. I think that may be because last week in individual therapy I had this session that felt heavy to me, and I was reminded how uncomfortable I am with my sexuality. I had never talked about it—it was like opening Pandora's box.
> THERAPIST: What does the dream mean about your feelings about the group?
> SIOBHAN: I really like coming here and get a lot of helpful feedback. And I try to give the same. But I feel

self-indulgent—when I talk with my friends about how fucked up our lives are, I think, "I don't want my life to be like this."

LOUISE: I feel the same way, and I want to leave the group. I think a lot of times people just want to hang on to their shit, and I don't want to hang on to mine anymore. It goes away when I stop thinking about myself and get busy and do other things. I don't have any trouble about eating unless I sit around thinking about myself.

LADA: But is eating the problem or the symptom?

THERAPIST: I don't think eating and throwing up or not eating and throwing up is the problem.

LOUISE: Yeah, it may be just a symptom, but in the course of the last year a lot of things in my life have changed, have gone well, and I don't think I need to be here. I don't want to be here.

It's common for patients in therapy to feel at times as if they're staring at their own navels rather than making progress. This often means that they have hit a plateau prior to having a whole new set of insights. But bulimics in particular start to feel uncomfortable with plateaus and try to use them as an excuse to quit treatment.

Those who stick with their group cause and encounter other problems. Bulimics do a lot of credentialing: they scrutinize each other, size each other up, and inquire of their groupmates exactly why they think they belong in treatment. This can become a stumbling block for someone in the group who looks as if she has her act together—if so identified, she may try to live up to the first impression she has created rather than letting down her defenses and being honest with the group.

Another common feature is competition. The group begins by concentrating on the worst binge-vomiter, then switches attention to the best abstinent member, each person aiming toward either extreme and tending to feel either guilty or dragged down. Rita, a biweekly binge-vomiter who was able to recover for months at a time over a thirteen-year period, had this experience:

> The first group I was in was a disaster. I was the best in the group, and the others latched on to me. Meanwhile I was getting ideas—listening to them describe the days they'd stay home from work to binge, the lies they'd tell their families and friends, and all that. I confronted the group with my feeling that I was being sucked in and dragged down. The therapists agreed that I should leave the group, which fell apart shortly after anyway.
>
> I went back to very occasional binge-vomiting for the next several months until the clinic contacted me about joining a group with abstinent members. Now *that* interested me! I did better in that group, although I recall feeling hostile toward members who were only borderline abstinent. I'd tell them to make up their minds to quit, and do it! Of course they didn't appreciate that!

Those bulimics stuck in between the group's best and worst stars can usually compete anyway by describing their pasts and complaining of how circumstances made them into tragic victims. They feel as if they must constantly measure themselves against others because their sense of self and control is so blurred. Because they always look elsewhere for cues on how to feel or behave, everyday interactions cause drastic fluctuations in the severity of their bulimia. For this reason, too, they cling to any kind of fantasy, situation or behavior that makes them feel special.

Some bulimics start binge-vomiting when their groupmates become abstinent, just to help themselves feel unique. Bulimics suffer such low self-esteem that specialness is their only way of compensating for it. This subverts the group's purpose of providing them with other bulimics with whom to identify. To try to counteract this, Ellen Schor assigns her bulimic patients to groups that are as homogenous in weight as possible to help them understand that their uniqueness has little to do with weight or binge-vomiting:

> They have used the bulimia to make themselves feel awful but special, carrying on what they used to do in their families: they wanted special attention or had needs that were special or so overwhelming that nobody could meet them. In treatment they hold out; they're very elusive and don't want to bridge to someone else, so we work on that right away. We indicate to them that they are unique but that in holding themselves special they are just alienating themselves from others. One of the terrible psychological damages bulimics suffer is that they cannot be intimate with others and therefore have poor relationships.

This inability to enjoy relationships also interferes with group therapy. Bulimics tend to distrust people, especially other women, and most of all bulimic women. After all, they themselves became chronic liars as a result of the bulimia—aren't their groupmates liars too?

Yet another aspect of the bulimic's personality that sabotages her therapy is the common trait of perfectionism. Groupmates are supposed to help each other, and that can be very difficult, as twenty-five-year-old Ginger found out:

> Helping others is frustrating for recovering bulimics —I want to change the people who are still binge-vomiting rather than letting them help themselves. I should just express my feelings and let go rather than trying to mend people. I've always been a care-giver and nurturer, and I'm still learning how much (and how little) I'm entitled to help others.
>
> I want everyone to be better, because I'm a perfectionist. I recognize that some bulimics, like some alcoholics, just won't recover. That was a shocker; it's hard for me to know that, because it could happen to me too. But it also makes me feel stronger to see that I'm

not that way right now. I'm making it possible for me
to be completely abstinent, and I feel good about that.

Ginger illustrates the bulimic's all-or-nothing attitude: having
become "completely abstinent," she has lost sight of how hard it
is to reach that state and becomes impatient with people who
are still struggling.

EXPERIMENTAL THERAPY

Bulimics don't just bring difficulties into therapy—they encounter them as well. Most bulimia groups under way across the
country are relatively new, and therapists must use trial and
error to determine the best procedures and even decide such
simple matters as group size.

One controversial issue is that of whether group members
should discuss the bulimia itself or their feelings from the past,
as they would in individual psychotherapy. There is a consensus
that the bulimia needs to be confronted immediately and
directly and that overcoming it means enlisting continued group
support. On the other hand, when important issues are raised in
a group, many bulimics avoid them by talking about their food
problems instead—using a verbal binge as they would a food
binge to escape from feelings. In this sense, discussing food and
keeping food diaries may just aggravate their already troublesome preoccupation with food. Part of the purpose of mutual
support is, after all, to teach bulimics to face their emotions with
a little help from other people.

Other aspects of group therapy that still need to be worked
out include whether or not the group should have a strong
leader and what kinds of therapy techniques to use. Therapists
have tried behavioral groups, supportive groups, experiential
groups (which have members learn, then experience, specific
things), insight groups, and so on. Groups are also varied in
their makeup. Anorexia societies, Overeaters Anonymous groups
and some private therapy groups combine anorectics, bulimics
and obese people of both sexes, while others adhere strictly to
homogenous groups. Some therapists have found that male
bulimics tend to dominate groups while the women passively
hide their anger and resentment, that obese members resent the

thinner ones and that anorectics band together and on the whole
require a treatment approach different from one that is appropriate for bulimia.

Probably the greatest problem with bulimia therapy to date is
that it desperately needs long-term follow-up—without it, professionals have no way of determining how well their treatment
methods are working. There are all sorts of therapists treating
bulimia in different ways. Some are absolutely opposed to the
treatment methods of others; all cite certain percentages of success, but bulimia is far too new a phenomenon in psychiatric
medicine for anybody to make any claims. Some therapists go so
far as to boast almost perfect cure rates because none of their
bulimic patients returns for more treatment. Apparently it hasn't
occurred to these people that their patients may have gone right
back to binge-vomiting after treatment, become discouraged and
humiliated, and given up.

Methods

I really think that the best therapy for bulimia is the
chemical-dependency treatment disease concept. In
most treatment centers around here, inpatient treatment is basically the same as AA and OA in that the
disease is believed to have equal physical, mental and
spiritual factors. They teach that the disease is progressive and that you have options for managing it. I can't
cure my bulimia any more than I can cure my alcoholism. I can always go back to it, and if I did, it would be
worse than ever and I'd never make it; I was so sick before that this time I'd die.

Therapy should emphasize that as a disease bulimia
is not just a psychiatric disorder or a mental problem.
If therapists view it as just a mental problem they may
do more harm than good to patients. There is a place
for psychiatry and counseling for many women only
after they have stopped vomiting. Then they can work

out personal problems, because they have to change
their life-styles to keep from returning to addiction, just
as alcoholics do.

More people will recover from bulimia once psychiatrists stop offering theories about it and patients stop
asking why it's happening and get to work on abstain-
ing from it.

So speaks a recovered bulimic who has started her own self-help
group for the disorder. The chemical-dependency treatment concept is heard often in discussions about bulimia. Psychiatrists
and psychologists abide by it at least in believing that severe,
chronic bulimia is too fixed a symptom to be treated effectively
by any single technique. Even with mild to moderate bulimia,
the associated symptoms, ranging as they do from occasional pilfering of a candy bar to multiple addictions, make it hard to decide which treatment methods might be best.

The happy result is that treatment for bulimia has become
highly individualized, patients being assigned to particular
forms of therapy only after exhaustive screening. "To say that a
certain treatment will work for everybody ignores the uniqueness of human behavior. Effective treatment requires a very
complete, accurate assessment of the physiological, psychological and cultural dimensions of the individual," says Craig
Johnson. The most appropriate treatment will depend on both
the patient and the therapist. To begin with, not everyone can
afford private therapy. Some people won't enter groups; some
won't enter individual therapy; and some have been in individual therapy for several years already. Some bulimics have improved in either group or individual therapy, others in neither.
And who knows how many sessions—or months, or years—it
takes to decide whether the treatment is working? Fortunately,
more and more professionals are tackling these kinds of complexities.

In most cases, psychiatrists and psychologists are using a multidisciplinary approach that includes individual, group and behavioral therapy, hypnosis, pharmacotherapy, family therapy
and nutritional counseling. The last three are used as necessary
—if the patient is depressed or anxious, she can be helped with

appropriate medication, and some psychiatrists are trying other medications that may suppress the desire to binge. If the patient still lives at home, the therapist might recommend family therapy. If she is terrified that giving up vomiting will cause her to gain weight, she can learn to design meal plans and count calories to prevent it. The major emphasis, however, is on individual and group therapy, neither of which is better than the other— they just do different things.

INDIVIDUAL THERAPY

Individual therapy offers the advantage of helping the bulimic fulfill her badly needed desire for special attention, special caring, a sense that she is important for *herself* without distracting competition or criticism from a group. It addresses her most central, immediate needs in a way that is important, especially if she is depressed, suicidal or just unable to speak up in a group. Almost all bulimics have severe secondary psychological problems that require this treatment method.

In individual therapy a bulimic can explore her own feelings and figure out her behavior in a way she never has before. She can learn ways to feel secure, reinforced, relaxed and controlled without having to gorge and purge. She can explore the lack of credibility she gives to the value of her own thoughts and feelings and can review her passivity, the impact of events on how she feels about herself. During this process, it is paramount that the bulimic be able to trust her therapist. By giving her the chance to trust someone, to feel that she is cared about, therapy helps the bulimic, in a sense, to redo her relationship with her parents and experience what often was missing there. To have a solid therapeutic relationship, the bulimic must find a person to whom she can tell her darkest secrets without fear that he or she will become disgusted. Without that trust, no therapeutic technique will work; with it, almost any technique will work. Some people undergo therapy unsuccessfully for years until they finally find the one therapist who can help them, so the bulimic who doesn't hit it off with a few therapists right away should not become discouraged but keep looking.

Some bulimics seek out therapists acquainted with their eating disorder, regardless of whether or not they are simultaneously in group therapy. This gives them the option of discussing either their feelings or the bulimia. Of course, these two topics are not mutually exclusive. But others prefer saving the food problems for group discussion while seeing a private therapist who is totally removed from them. Tania, a thirty-two-year-old biologist, has her program set up in this way:

> The bulimia group I'm in has been very helpful and has touched on some of my feelings, but I have so many other issues that I never dealt with and that are not appropriate for the group that I need individual therapy as well. Some of my groupmates use psychiatrists involved with our group. That would not work for me. My doctor has nothing to do with the bulimia program, which is good for me because I don't spend all my time talking about bulimia. He's there for my problems with inadequacy, low self-worth, stuff I was never totally honest about, like my fears. He knows everything about me. In chemical-dependency treatment I was always on guard to make sure that I didn't slip in telling something. Now I'm totally honest about all aspects of my life.

A structure like this helps some people focus more easily on the different aspects of their therapy. Tania has not allowed herself the option of avoiding her feelings by talking about food.

But some of the issues appropriate for individual therapy are really secondary to the bulimia. One difficulty with individual therapy is that by relieving the pain it can make abstinence from gorge-purging seem less urgent. By attending group therapy, the bulimic satisfies her therapist that her food problem is being treated.

GROUP THERAPY

Group therapy has several advantages. Many bulimics were extroverted and had well-developed social skills before the start of their illness, which made them very reclusive. Those more severely ill may never have developed good social skills at all. The bulimia has kept all of them prisoners in their anguish, shame and isolation. Group therapy enables them to meet others who, often to their mutual amazement, share the same illness and the same feelings about it. This demystifies the bulimia and gives them the security of knowing that other women experience the same peculiar, perverse habits. It also minimizes the "specialness" of the bulimia that can slow their progress in individual therapy.

Group support becomes a strong basis for them as they learn other ways to adjust to stress. Twenty-six-year-old Flora explains:

> I was helped the most by the people in my group. Our leader was a role model, and many of the therapists were helpful and sympathetic, with good techniques and constructive criticism. And there is an incredible bond between group members, an intimacy I had never known before. Most of us had never been close to others, especially to other women. But you start sharing gruesome details about how you would vomit into plastic garbage bags when a bathroom wasn't readily available. Your experience with other bulimics goes much deeper than most friendships. You cry together; you start getting to know each other at gut level, then you work up to everyday things like, "What sports do you like?" Each group gets the phone numbers of all its members, so you always have support, any hour of the night or day. It's one of the tools they give us to fight the bulimia.

Being psychologically personal with several other people is very helpful to bulimics, for they learn that opening themselves up to others does not necessarily mean being squelched by criticism. By making friends and growing to like other bulimics, they work toward the difficult goal of liking themselves. Their sense of emptiness and worthlessness is addressed in group therapy in a way that is quite difficult for individual therapy because of the professional/patient dichotomy. These positive effects continue after group meetings are over in the networking that goes on in both socializing and support.

In group therapy bulimics can offer hope to each other by setting good examples. Even if they aren't doing well in life, their abstinence is an inspiration to their groupmates. They develop enormous altruism toward each other. Often the members of a bulimia group will begin with each other gingerly, avoiding criticism because they want to care for, not hurt. The other side of this delicacy is the beneficent confrontation that a group can provide. A bulimic will find it very difficult to fool other bulimics with a lie, and they won't let her get away with it. An individual therapist might not know bulimia as well as its victims do; he or she might assuage the bulimic's guilt and be sympathetic enough to lower her motivation to recover. And of course therapists have been known to tell bulimics that they can never get better.

Finally, the social psychology of groups, the mass spirit itself, helps carry the bulimic into change. Groups can be very powerful, especially if they are based on a similar belief, as the Army, the Communists, and various religious leaders have long known. Bulimics sometimes tend to have difficulty in making decisions and look for gurus, for structure. If a bulimic is seeking a positive cult, a bulimia group with a strong leader can make a world of difference in her life.

BEHAVIORAL THERAPY

Many therapists like to use behavioral techniques in bulimia groups. These include analyzing the binges to see what triggers them, figuring out ways to block these triggers and setting up priorities to reach specific goals. Group members may be asked to set time limits on their binges, to binge only at certain times on certain days and to plan the binges beforehand and write them out. These strategies help control and direct the binges so that the victims can eventually stop them instead of remaining passive victims. A related technique is paradoxical intention, in which a binge is permitted after an agreed-upon activity such as spending ten minutes writing out feelings. Many bulimics report that recording this self-analysis helps relax them and in some cases keeps them from binging. Some therapists have bulimics keep diaries of their emotions, their stress, their hunger and their sense of fullness along with events that are associated with the binges and that cause mood changes.

Having learned to monitor themselves and their binges, bulimics can then learn how to eat properly. Initially this means developing a normalized diet program specifying the number of calories—and introducing forbidden foods to reassure the bulimics that they can enjoy them in moderation without gaining weight. They can also be kept from weighing themselves—the numbers game rules their lives, and many of them mistakenly believe that a few pounds determine what the world thinks of them. Actually, the scale determines how they project to the world, and if they lose a few pounds, what others notice is their elation, not the weight loss.

HYPNOTHERAPY

Behavioral therapy is used as part of a multidisciplinary approach applied to all the feelings and experience within which the bulimia develops. The same is true of hypnotherapy, also useful in treating bulimics. Dr. Meir Gross of the Cleveland Clinic Foundation has treated fifty bulimic patients with hypnosis and feels that its results might be comparable or equal to those of other therapies:

> It's hard to tell because I never use hypnosis as an isolated method. It's part of the whole process of psychotherapy, used occasionally when appropriate. Hypnosis does not create miracles. It can, however, shorten the time required for psychotherapy from, say, two years to a few months, with the rest of the psychotherapy supplementing and reinforcing its effects.

Dr. Gross takes referrals for hypnotherapy and suggests it to patients who might benefit from it. The crucial factor in pinpointing a bulimic candidate for hypnotherapy is her motivation to use hypnosis. She must recognize hypnosis as a method that might help her and not be afraid of it, for fear will preclude her attaining a trance or using it effectively.

Dr. Gross educates each patient about the benefits of hyp-

notherapy so that she will know what to expect. Together they
also set up a contract similar to that established in regular psychotherapy, discussing expectations, goals and methods of achieving them. Once the patient is prepared to begin, Dr. Gross
teaches her self-hypnosis. "I suggest that the patient practice
self-hypnosis daily at home so that she participates and becomes
active in her therapy," he says. "That's part of its benefit—her
activity helps the patient recognize that therapy has to do with
some motivation and change in her, that the therapist doesn't
change her; she must change herself." This idea, of course, is one
that bulimics have to learn not just about therapy but about life
in general.

In hypnosis Dr. Gross treats both the bulimia itself and the
accompanying problems. "At first the patients are very interested
in talking about the symptom," he says, "but gradually I start to
point out to them that it's not the bulimia that's the problem—
it's only a symptom, and there are many conflicts behind it that
they have to resolve." The patients must learn assertiveness and
better coping skills, techniques that Dr. Gross reinforces in regular psychotherapy.

Other hypnotherapists use similar techniques. Anita B. Siegman has a patient being treated in group therapy by a certified
hypnoanalyst. "It's been a very provocative experience for her,"
she says. "He has her recall certain images and memories of
when she was very young, feelings that led to a sense of incom-
petence or self-loathing. For her it's been an opportunity to
remember some very painful experiences that she's pushed down
and pushed aside, so that his work with her in therapy has been
very helpful in my work."

Twenty-three-year-old Kim proved a good subject for hypnotherapy and was astonished by the results:

> I can't say enough about how the hypnosis dispelled
> the anxiety that caused the bulimia and helped me face
> stressful situations for the first time in my life. After I
> had five or six sessions with the hypnotist, the problem
> just went away. The fascinating thing was that he
> never dealt with the bulimia directly—instead, he
> brought out grief I had never dealt with, and I cried

terribly during some of the sessions. Now that I no longer have the bulimia to use as a crutch, I actually feel fear, sadness, insecurity, horror—and I'm amazed that I'm able to cope with those feelings. Another great change is that for the first time in my life my appetite tells me that I'm full.

I'm not through, though. The hypnosis has solved the problem for the time being, but I'm continuing psychotherapy. I want to find out what caused this damn bulimia.

Prognoses

Sharon, a twenty-four-year-old artist from California, has not gorge-purged for seven months:

Recovery from bulimia means that for the first time you must learn to handle physical pain and the chemicals that you put into your body. You can make stupid mistakes by not knowing what your body can take. Part of being bulimic is that you don't know what pain should feel like. There's so much emotional pain and physical weakness that you don't know the difference between feeling good and not feeling good.

I did not anticipate the amount of tension and the wild feelings I'd have to endure once I became abstinent. Abstinence is hard for me if I'm tired or down, or if I have a bad day that makes me angry. I used to handle all that by eating, and food is everywhere. Sometimes I feel that stopping the gorging and purging has made me worse instead of better.

Thirty-one-year-old Naomi has recovered from both alcoholism and bulimia:

Our group leader says that after a period of abstinence the food is less of an issue than your compulsions. I have a real problem with time and activities: I don't know what to do with myself at home. After work I have to go to OA or AA or somewhere constructive for most of the evening, have a late dinner, and come home only when I'm exhausted and can sleep.

I do feel lonely a lot, but at least now I can get high on having responsibility, being independent and doing work. Even during a bad day I can always console myself by saying, "Thank God—at least I'm abstinent."

Twenty-five-year-old Barbara, an economist from Indiana, has been recovering from bulimia for eighteen months:

My therapy has been a major change from my previous life. There's hope now, and there was none before. But I do have some major disappointments in my recovery. It should go faster. I'm still working as a bookkeeper because a real career would be too stressful at this point. I'm still totally unassertive—a puddle on the floor. I still can't deal with stress or anger. I'm still afraid to get pregnant because I'd gain weight and have to sign my life away for nine months. I had wanted sex to improve right away because I felt better about myself, but it's still not a really good area of my life. I feel deprived; I want a key to unlock me. I don't know how much to expect from the bulimia program I'm in, but I'm surprised that some things haven't changed.

There is every reason to be optimistic about recovery from bulimia. The bottom line is that bulimia victims do recover and that their illness and recovery are both tremendous learning experiences that they can put to good use. But it would be unfair to bulimics to suggest that recovery takes place speedily, without much pain or difficulty. Bulimia victims put up with the horrors of their disorder partly because the alternative—giving up binge-vomiting—seems so much worse. Having had an anesthetic for any and all problems, they must suddenly jump into a void that is deep, dark and just plain scary—the reality and the selves that they have been hiding from for years. They experience emotional (and often physical) withdrawal symptoms that can be devastating.

As Sharon points out, abstinence means learning all over again what the body and mind can take. Abstinence sometimes makes life worse instead of better, at least temporarily; for other people, abstinence replaces bulimia as the only source of comfort in an otherwise unhappy life. While bulimics may console themselves by thinking, "Thank God—at least I'm thin," Naomi has progressed to thinking, "Thank God—at least I'm abstinent." She also recognizes that she can't expect abstinence to be the magic wand that transforms her life into something wonderful. Other bulimics must be prepared for the difficulties of recovery so that they won't take them personally, be unduly frightened of them or, like Barbara, become discouraged.

THE TIME FACTOR

The difficulties of abstinence are the major reason that time is considered an important factor in the prognosis for recovery from bulimia. Except for University of Minnesota therapists, who recently overhauled their treatment program, most therapists feel that bulimics should expect to stay with a support group for at least a year. Unfortunately, only 10 to 20 percent of them make that long a time commitment; many leave groups only to return to binging and vomiting. But there is another side to support groups—that of being weakly dependent on others rather than able to stand on one's own. That bulimics have turned to food indicates their need to reach out for help somehow, and they should not be perfectionists trying to recover alone. But they must learn when to seek positive, necessary support and when to let go.

THE SEVERITY FACTOR

The usual statistics of psychiatry seem to apply to bulimia therapy: one third of patients do very well, one third do moderately well, and one third do poorly. The time it takes to stop binge-vomiting varies tremendously, depending on the degree of disturbance in the patient and her family. Generally the earlier the treatment begins and the younger the patient, the better the prognosis, although this seems to hold true for bulimic anorectics more so than for pure bulimics. The reasoning here is that a young girl develops anorexia nervosa as an acute adjustment reaction to puberty. The anorexia is therefore a clear-cut response to a clear-cut precipitant—a simple result rather than a symptom of a deep-seated character problem developing slowly and insidiously later on in life. At the risk of infuriating some bulimics and driving others to despair, we must note that chronic bulimics *may* not recover, although the severity of their symptoms may be alleviated. Among older women with chronic bulimia it's impossible to predict who will do moderately well in therapy and who will not respond at all.

PERSONAL RESPONSIBILITY

The crucial factor in recovery from bulimia is the victim's willingness to accept responsibility for getting well. If a bulimic is motivated, almost any competent, substantial therapy will work for her; if she is not, her therapist could be doing handsprings without getting any results. Emotional readiness for change is very important. So is the bulimic's ability to believe in herself, to determine what she wants out of life and to set up a realistic plan for obtaining it. "These people need to drop their perfectionism; they need to recognize stress and how to deal with it; most of all, they need to communicate their needs and desires," says Vivian Meehan. "We are not self-sufficient; we need other people and can express this need only if we learn to communicate well. I suspect we'll find that eating disorders have a lot to do with the types of relationships that people form with one another."

Over and over again bulimics describe recovery as a complete change of thinking, a rebirth into a different life. Jeannie, a twenty-eight-year-old high school teacher, offers some insights:

> It's terrifying to me to recall how horrible it was to have my head in the toilet much of the time. I strongly feel that you have to bottom-out before you can be helped. If you're in therapy because your family wants you to be, or because you want attention and feel sorry for yourself and want to dwell longer on your sickness, you won't be helped. You have to want to get well.

Some people in my group are comfortable only feeling bad, not good. Life isn't supposed to be like that; it's not what I expected it to be. I've said in group, "I don't want to be in this group because you people are so sick!" That may not be nice, but it's a healthy thing for me to say.

No therapy that doesn't force you to face the behavior and be responsible for it will help you. It's easy to give up responsibility in therapy because your therapist is helping to free you from guilt. That's very liberating, but you can abuse it. You have to be desperate enough to change and smart enough to recognize that it's your responsibility alone to do it.

I can't emphasize enough the importance of changing your attitude. My life-style eating-wise is exactly the same as it was before I became bulimic—it's the feelings that accompanied the life-style that are different. For the first time I'm not running away from a problem. I have hope now, not fear. I never thought that I could be responsible for myself; the idea that nobody can do it for you still makes me very afraid. For the first time I'm starting to live, to take risks, to change! I'm still afraid of change and lack of control. Helen Keller once said something like, "Not taking a risk is like being dead." At least now I'm trying different things.

Jeannie points out another important aspect of therapy: it's not for people who want attention so that they can feel even sorrier for themselves, although many people in general blunder into therapy with this attitude.

Therapy is not an end in itself; it's just a means that the patient uses to heal herself. And bulimics will find that baring their souls to therapists will not by itself help them to recover. Twenty-six-year-old Dolores explains that therapy and abstinence complement each other in her progress:

Therapy helped me become abstinent because of the prevalent ideas that came across. One was the idea that I was not a bad, rotten person because of the bulimia.

Another was that people could stop binge-vomiting and survive. I also got feedback on issues in my life. Maybe it's my family that's crazy and not me. Maybe things aren't always my fault. Maybe I do have control over my life and don't have to let people manipulate me. With that in mind, I don't have to do this to myself anymore. Basically, I helped improve the way I looked at myself by working out these issues.

And I can turn this around—abstinence helped me in therapy. It's the first time I've gotten real help out of therapy, primarily because I'm ready to change.

Dolores is one of many bulimics studying for a certificate in counseling so that she can work with others who need help. Ellen Schor is able to help other bulimics both as a professional and as a victim who has been through the long, involved process of recovery:

I had to go through a phase when it became absolutely repulsive to me to vomit. It was a turning point in my life. I saw that no person or activity was as important to me as binge-purging. That was a real breakthrough. From that point on in my personal therapy, I've seen how I've used food, and I had to let myself gain twenty pounds, which is pretty difficult for a woman in this world. I've always had an eating problem, but I can now say—always holding on in a way—that I can eat a piece of cake and that it won't start a binge. I'm now safe with cookies in my house and with having a normal meal and knowing that it won't put on five pounds so I won't have to throw it up. I can sit down and plan a normal meal and be relaxed about food because I've made peace with it. Not to say that under stress the thought might not come up, but now I know what situations are likely to be troublesome.

I don't know if we can talk in terms of total recovery, but we can talk about personality reorganization and getting to the real feelings. For me, and for other women, bulimia has served to hide all other feelings. It was an umbrella over loneliness, happiness, rage, all sorts of needs. When I started to get back in touch with those needs, the food stopped working—the binge itself was eliminated because it just didn't work. I think it has to be emphasized that this takes a long time and a lot of therapeutic growth.

It is this peace with the "drug of choice" and this level of self-understanding to which all bulimia victims can aspire.

Chapter 12

SAMPLE THERAPY PROGRAMS

The bulimia victim ready to seek help may not be aware of the options available to her. This chapter describes a few different bulimia programs to give the prospective patient some general guidelines. The qualifications that anorexia associations make about their referral lists hold true here as well—these are merely descriptions, not endorsements, of some representative programs. It's up to the bulimic to find the type of program that best suits her needs. It's also up to her to act quickly, since privately run programs generally have long waiting lists. But self-help groups run by the anorexia associations and organizations like Overeaters Anonymous are always happy to expand and welcome new members.

Self-help Groups

Therapy groups and self-help groups generally differ in that therapy groups are directed by therapists and involve a fee, while self-help groups are run by members and are often free. Self-help groups are almost always led by a volunteer who has recovered from either anorexia or bulimia, since the groups are often mixed; sometimes a therapist is involved as well. There are usually no limits to group size.

One function of self-help groups is to serve as a bridge for people who are discouraged by their therapy or who have never had therapy and are not quite ready to try it. As such, the groups provide a forum in which people can exchange ideas and hopes. Because the groups are free, some people denigrate them; actually, there's no law saying that someone must pay for therapy to benefit from it (although many therapists like their patients to think so). The help they receive can encourage bulimia victims to find a mode of therapy appropriate for them and begin treatment.

Self-help groups also benefit people who are in private treatment but have no way of dealing with their eating problems directly. Estelle Miller reports that 90 percent of those people attending groups run by the American Anorexia Nervosa Association are in private therapy, a status not required but definitely encouraged. Often the groups are simply come-if-you-want, with no pressure to continue attending or to contribute to discussions. Anorexia and bulimia victims talk about their feelings and exchange ideas for coping with and overcoming their illnesses.

This kind of format has its limitations, and the anorexia associations recognize this and do the best they can. The American Anorexia Nervosa Association, for instance, runs groups for parents of anorectics and bulimics as well as for the victims themselves. "The parents find their meetings very useful," says Estelle Miller, "because most of them don't want private counseling. They just want to learn how to cope with children who are driving them up walls."

Although they are helpful and serve a definite purpose, these groups are intended only as supplements to professional medical and psychiatric care.

Overeaters Anonymous

Overeaters Anonymous is a nonprofit, self-help organization patterned after Alcoholics Anonymous. It was founded in 1960, has thousands of groups around the world and is used as a resource by some of the established eating disorders clinics. The basic premise of OA is that compulsive overeating, like alcoholism, is a disease that affects its victims on physical, spiritual and emotional levels. Like alcoholics, OA members believe that they can't permanently control their overeating by willpower, not because of personal failure, but because it's an illness. Most people who join the organization have bottomed-out and interpret their lack of control over food to mean that they have no personal control at all. In OA they regain their self-respect by learning new ways to manage their illness in an atmosphere of cooperation and affection.

At meetings OA members show their great sense of mutual support and love and constantly attest to their human imperfections and humility. Members talk to the group about their experiences as compulsive overeaters and the changes that OA has made in their lives. The meetings include specific rituals: members read the twelve steps to recovery, chant the Lord's Prayer and the Serenity Prayer (to better understand one's limitations and capabilities), and distribute pins for one, three, nine, twelve, eighteen and twenty-four months of abstinence to resounding applause. There are no dues or fees; OA operates on voluntary contributions. Anonymity is guaranteed its members.

The purpose of OA is to help its members stop compulsive overeating. Although stressed, abstinence is not strictly defined. Many members follow low-carbohydrate diets consisting of three meals a day with only sugarless drinks or fruit snacks in between. They avoid refined sugars and carbohydrates because of the previously described idea that these foods are guaranteed to cause binges. Others follow diets founded on the basic food groups or prescribed by their doctors. OA reinforces the idea of a balanced diet and offers a philosophical and psychological structure that helps members follow one.

Abstinence from overeating is reinforced by sponsorship. Each newcomer asks a recovered group member to be her food sponsor. The two maintain daily contact by phone calls, which are an important part of the program.

OA members follow twelve steps to recovery, taken from those of AA with "food" and "compulsive overeater" substituted for "alcohol" and "alcoholics." Members who take the steps admit that they can't control their eating, surrender themselves to a "higher power," analyze their wrongdoings, try to improve their characters, make amends to others, engage in prayer and meditation, and communicate the OA principles.

The twelve steps reinforce the concept of overeating as an illness to be managed. Part of this involves seeing food-related lies,
thefts, withdrawal and so on in the context of the illness and recognizing them as "wrongdoings." Members must come to terms
with their guilt about their behavior and absolve themselves
constructively by "making amends" whenever possible. They
must also recognize the difference between what they can and
cannot control in their lives.

Rationalizing the consequences of overeating is part of the denial that must be overcome when a new member joins OA. Their
illness has made many newcomers strong-willed and individualistic. They hope to "have their cake and eat it too" in that
they want to get well without giving up their old bad habits. OA
asks them to accept that they are overeaters who are powerless
over food, to surrender their old way of life and to follow a more
constructive one.

Members' acceptance of their food problem is more than intel-
lectual; one benefit of OA is its emphasis upon the spiritual aspect of addiction as well. New members must have faith that
they can confront the unknown, that they can change and that a
new way of life will work for them. The "higher power" that
permeates OA is a power within or beyond the individual that
enables recovery to occur. Some members understand it to be
God, while others see it as the self's ability to regain control. The
definition of the higher power is less important than the fact that
accepting it has helped thousands of people to recover.

A problem in joining OA is that individual groups may interpret the philosophy and goals of the parent organization in
different ways. There's always the chance that a new member
might not fit in with a particular group. Officially OA addresses
only compulsive overeating; as such it doesn't encourage anorectics and bulimics to join. Without the chance to own up to their
purging in a supportive atmosphere, some bulimics might not be
able to recover. Some OA groups may not have abstinent
members, or their members may follow their diets so literally
that they lose their sense of purpose. Many members persist in
believing that overeating is bad, abstinence is good, and there's
no compromise between the two; some change from compulsive
overeaters to compulsive OA members.

There are no means to evaluate OA membership to determine how successful the organization really is. Members hear upbeat talks at meetings and are encouraged to give the same talks themselves. Recovered members do feel that they have gained control over their lives as well as their eating and have experienced significant personal improvement in the process. While recovery does change their lives in terms of *control,* some members resemble bulimics in mistakenly believing that it will make them completely *happy* as well.

But OA has several advantages to offer bulimics, and some therapists recommend it as a complementary support system or even model their own groups on the OA format. OA offers unconditional acceptance, a quality crucial to the bulimic's development of self-esteem. All the organization asks is that its members "keep coming back"; bulimics who face lonely evenings without binges yet hesitate to begin social involvement can enjoy company and support just by going to meetings. This is helpful to those who can't afford or don't want long-term therapy. And OA offers members a chance to feel successful in at least one area of their lives; even a badly struggling member is not a failure at OA.

Many bulimics feel that OA has helped them. Lisa, a twenty-nine-year-old personnel supervisor, implies that OA is serving her as a bridge to other people:

> I had been in an experimental bulimia group that didn't work out because not enough people were abstinent. I joined a second bulimia group and also joined OA. OA was better for me. You could sense the groupness about it. The group was my spiritual support; I could be open, honest and close to people for the first time. I was able to build and grow into that group as if it were my surrogate family. All those people understood me; I could call them when I had problems.
>
> I love OA and AA because you can see the serenity and peace of mind that their members have achieved. I want that. It's just one day at a time. I read their litera-

ture all the time, and I spend my time now with people from those groups.

In a sense, I'm at a loss when dealing with normal people. I can't go out with a guy who just wants to go dancing or something without getting depressed. I want to be able to talk on a feelings level, because that's what's easiest for me right now.

At some point, of course, Lisa will have to break away from OA and face "normal people" again.

For thirty-four-year-old Harriet OA is not a place to hide but one in which she can find inspirational health and sanity:

Like alcoholism, bulimia creeps up on you and becomes life-consuming. When you don't have a recovering life-style to contrast it with, you have no way of perceiving how sick you're becoming and how many years can be wasted building up bad feelings about yourself. It's crazy behavior in that your priorities become askew, but you need it as a coping mechanism and just get deeper into it. You need to be put in touch with health for the contrast. That's what OA did for me—they gave me an immediate experience of a life-style very different from the one I had led for fifteen years, an abstinent life-style of one day at a time. It was really hard for me to stop binge-vomiting, but I could clearly see benefits of quitting that I had completely forgotten about.

Harriet echoes bulimics who feel that joining bulimia groups with abstinent members was the main reason they were able to recover.

Speaking at an open OA meeting, Joan, a twenty-five-year-old guidance counselor, had this to say about being abstinent:

It felt like a gift when I became abstinent. It was so easy; it's God's power to control it. I gave God food, and He gives me so much in return: why would I want to change that? I like what has happened to my life now that I no longer use food as a pleasure. I could let go of a lot and still be fine, and I'd go to any length to be abstinent. On other diets I was always giving up something. OA does ask a lot, but you also get something back that's so much better. You don't know what you'll get back, so you have to put your faith in it. I got a healing from a loneliness that I didn't even know I felt. The higher power fills you up; my first few months were euphoric. The good things that come from abstinence are not coincidences but God's love. The relationship with that love and with serenity provides the incentive not to slip. God gives you only what you can handle.

For Joan the higher power is "God," and OA is a joyous way of life. Each bulimic must judge what OA would be for her.

Workshop Programs

As more therapists in private practice set up treatment programs for bulimia, we will probably see more of the convenient workshop format. Workshops are intensive programs, often crammed into a weekend, that confront the bulimia so that its victims can take control over it. One such program is offered by the Center for Bulimia in New York City, run by Judith Brisman and Ellen Schor. These therapists base their treatment program on the philosophy that bulimia recovery can't be maintained without long-term treatment (a philosophy that the prospective patient should clarify with her therapist before she signs up; some therapists offer only an intensive program and leave the patient to fend for herself from then on). They feel, however, that direct and immediate intervention of the bulimia is necessary before longer-term care can begin. Brisman and Schor approach bulimia directly through education, behavioral intervention, exploration of emotional denial and extensive follow-up planning. Patients are accepted into their weekend program and follow-up meetings after a screening interview.

The therapists spend Friday evening of the weekend educating the group about the psychological and physiological aspects

of bulimia. On Saturday they do a functional analysis of bulimia
for each patient, exploring situations and feelings that cause
binges, and setting up alternative coping skills for both binging
and purging. Lunch and the evenings following the workshops
are integrated into the program to help patients explore their
attitudes and feelings about eating. Throughout the weekend the
group learns assertiveness skills and uses behavioral techniques
like cognitive restructuring (finding new ways of thinking about
behavior to change it), delays to postpone the binge-purge, and
self-monitoring techniques to evaluate their progress. They also
set up support systems for follow-up.

On Sunday morning the therapists reinforce the work of the
previous two days. The group also learns relaxation techniques,
plans and shares binge-control contracts, and sets up social net-
works and a buddy system for telephone support. Patients are
encouraged to turn to their group leaders, groupmates and other
people for support rather than relying on food.

Within this general framework, Brisman and Schor incorporate specific therapy techniques. Patients are given *carte blanche*
to binge, but only after they have called someone. This rule
helps them delay their impulses, take responsibility for their
binging, and bridge to another person rather than to food. The
therapists themselves serve as transitions to get the bulimics to
trust other people again. Much time is spent setting up goals
and contracts, then analyzing whether they are too modest or
too perfectionistic.

Because the bulimics sometimes set unrealistic goals for themselves, Brisman and Schor use a simple metaphor to help them
keep their ambitions in line. The therapists set examples of how
to be good parents, who are patient with and allow for a child's
experience and mistakes rather than expecting the child to be
perfect. Ellen Schor explains:

> A bulimic woman has within her a raging, screaming
> child that had to steal love because her emotions
> weren't readily acceptable and her needs weren't really
> heard. We role-model good parents for them. They
> need to set limits for themselves, like a parent taking a
> child's hand and asking, "What are you feeling? Are

you tired?" They've learned the persecuting parent so well that they see two extremes—perfect and lowest of the low. We try to show them the middle ground. Very often they're tired, overworked, perfectionistic women who need sleep or a phone call or to be able to say no. We train them to let their feelings emerge, as a parent would do with a child. An angry or crying child shouldn't be stuffed with food to keep him or her quiet, and this is what they've been doing.

On the face of it this sounds like a childish and regressive way in which to approach the problem, but the principle behind Schor's metaphor is sound and disturbingly accurate. A bulimic forced to depersonalize her expectations and instead impose them on a fantasy child equally unprepared to meet them is likely to make more reasonable demands upon herself.

One week after the bulimia workshop weekend, the group has a 3-hour follow-up session. Members also have the option of holding 2½-hour post-workshop sessions with the group leaders, who monitor and reinforce behavior change, further explore feelings, and ease patients into more extensive longer-term treatment or self-help groups. They also provide information on nutrition and health care. Patients are encouraged to continue with these sessions for a year. They meet once a month with the therapists, who also contact them at three-, six- and twelve-month intervals to offer support and follow their progress for research purposes.

Brisman and Schor strongly stress long-term treatment in addition to their workshop and give patients referrals ranging from self-help groups to private psychotherapy, depending on individual needs. They hope to establish an extensive referral system and an ongoing set of self-help groups. They make clear their feelings that the weekend workshop will not help a bulimic who refuses to commit herself to supportive treatment for several months. The weekend provides a magical high followed by depression, an absolute loss at giving up binge-purging that must be filled with more constructive activities. The therapists become targets of anger and must take their patients therapeutically through several phases. As with alcoholism, the follow-up handling of the loss, depression and anger promotes recovery.

Schor reports that many of their patients do experience something of the personal transformation characteristic of successful OA members:

> We're trying to teach these people that they can enjoy things other than food and that feelings need not be so terrifying. You can die from vomiting. You don't usually die from anxiety attacks. Our patients learn to differentiate between self-indulgent misery about binging and real sadnesses they've been hiding from themselves. We see an incredible richness of life experiences that have been stuffed down for years, along with increased hope and self-confidence. The paradox of bulimics is that they seem so together while they feel like derelicts. Once they begin to emerge from the illness, their self-esteem increases dramatically.

The therapists can't estimate their recovery rate because their program is comparatively new. They plan to do follow-up studies on their patients and to have another study done by ANAD.

Someone with severe, chronic bulimia *may* find that a workshop, even with follow-up support, is not enough treatment for her illness. A different kind of program that treats bulimia directly over a longer period of time may be more suitable. Treatment outcome is difficult to predict in advance, so a bulimic who feels attracted to a workshop format should by all means try one; her motivation may be such that a workshop will do the trick regardless of how ill she has been. The point is not to be discouraged if one treatment method doesn't work but rather to try a different one, and to remember that stopping the binge-vomiting is only part of full recovery.

Eating Disorders Clinics

Although they may be found in some large hospitals, eating disorders clinics seem to be springing up primarily at universities all over the country. They tend to have long waiting lists, but a bulimic who can get into a good one has available to her the resources and therapists of a university medical school. Whatever their affiliation, eating disorders clinics produce most of the latest studies and treatment methods for bulimia. Their patients find themselves in programs that are evolving constantly to adjust to new information about the illness. What follows is a look at how two of these clinics are run.

THE UNIVERSITY OF CALIFORNIA AT LOS ANGELES

The Eating Disorders Clinic at UCLA started in November 1980 as a response by Drs. Yager and Rudnick to requests for help from their anorectic patients. It became clear very quickly that the clinic had to expand its program to accommodate bulimics as well. Having treated anorectics at the university for the previous four years, the psychiatrists had ample experience with bulimic behavior in their patients, but they needed to establish what is not an obvious or natural transition to treating pure bulimics. Attempting to handle their patients systematically, they screened them and either placed them in groups or referred them to private therapists, with Dr. Rudnick receiving some of the referrals. Drs. Yager and Rudnick feel that there are three or four times as many pure bulimics as there are either anorectics or bulimic anorectics, and they are working out the most effective ways to treat them.

Bulimics who enroll in the clinic are given a two-pronged evaluation. One is a clinical evaluation by Karen Lee-Benner, the clinic coordinator, and her associates. This involves an intensive personal inventory including psychiatric, eating and family histories. The patients provide this information in part by filling out several questionnaires, the Eating Attitudes Test and similar materials.

Every patient also gets a battery of psychological tests. These measure self-esteem, personality characteristics, feelings of control, gross neurological problems in thinking, depression, perceptions of family background, and borderline personality features. "We are being unusually thorough with these tests because so little is known about bulimia," says Dr. Yager. "We are planning to develop a severity-of-symptom rating scale to judge how people are doing over time."

The therapists also make sure that each patient has an internist. They refer patients to private internists and instruct the physicians which lab tests to do. They likewise refer individual patients to mental-health workers in the community to supplement the clinic programs for bulimia.

After the work-up, each patient's file is presented at a case conference of the clinic staff, held once a week to determine which patients belong in which group. Currently the clinic is running two bulimia groups and one anorexia group, with more coming as staff training and research continue. The groups are run by residents, coordinators and faculty members; they are homogenous because experience has shown the therapists that mixed groups don't work as well. Group size ranges from six to ten people, and the groups have a large turnover. Severely disturbed patients are required to be in individual as well as group therapy, or they are referred to inpatient treatment at the university hospital. Some patients go from inpatient to group therapy, or vice versa.

One of the bulimia groups is dynamically oriented. It has slowly evolved to the point where its members want to stop binge-purging, but some of those who have improved drastically have informed the others that their problems have only just begun. The second group is much more behaviorally oriented; its members may have been a bit healthier to start with, and they have been somewhat (although not dramatically) more successful. This group closely follows certain parameters of group behavioral assessment that they start out with: therapists ask members how often they binge, what the antecedents and consequences of the binge are, and what they can give them to help them stop binging. Group members have been encountering the usual problems of mourning the binging and not knowing what to do with the time that they used to spend on food. But in each group more than half the patients have shown significant improvement in their bulimic symptoms.

The clinicians are also experimenting with medication. They have tried various types of antidepressants and speculate that MAO (monoamine oxidase) inhibitors like Parnate and Nardil (which affect the body's serotonin concentrations) work better than tricyclic antidepressants like Elavil (amitriptyline) and Tofranil. The researchers are also trying Dilantin and Pondimin (fenfluramine) in the hope that if these drugs help to stop binging, the bulimics will feel more control over their behavior. "We have found that between working with their group, in individual therapy and with medication as needed, the majority of our patients seem to improve a great deal," says Dr. Yager.

THE UNIVERSITY OF MINNESOTA

One of the most extensive and structured bulimia programs in the country is offered through the University of Minnesota. Having recognized that individual psychotherapy and inpatient care did not help patients stop binge-vomiting, the university staff began using experimental groups to treat bulimics in March 1979. The groups, which met once a week, included behavior-modification, insight-oriented and unstructured groups. Some were successful; others did not work or fell apart because the women were frustrated that they could not kick their habit. The therapists initially concluded that groups dealing directly with binge-vomiting, followed by support groups dealing with assertiveness, intimacy and independence, seemed to work best. A follow-up study showed that about 40 percent of the bulimics in these groups were abstinent one year after starting treatment. This number is increasing, for some women from the earlier groups have returned to the university for the intensive program on bulimia, which incorporated the most effective techniques.

The intensive program, which began in March 1981, has two purposes: to provide an alternative to hospitalization for people severely ill with bulimia and to approach the problem of binge-purging quickly. Besides educating participants, it provides them with the opportunity to be in a situation that is structured emotionally as well as intellectually and to start to become abstinent.

Each applicant to the program is evaluated by a psychiatrist or psychologist and referred to the group. Gretchen Goff, the clinic coordinator, meets with participants individually and gives them assignments to start recording their binge-vomiting and the circumstances that trigger it. She then has them wait three or four weeks before entering the program to accustom them to the idea of treatment. Some people stop gorge-purging during this preparation time.

The intensive program was originally intended to help participants become abstinent from gorge-purging within two weeks. The group met four hours a night, five nights a week for the first two weeks, for a combination of lectures and group therapy. This was followed by a two-week semi-intensive program involving ninety minutes of group therapy, including talks by abstinent volunteers, three nights a week. Upon completing the intensive program, participants attended a ninety-minute follow-up group meeting each week for a minimum of six months; they were encouraged to stay with their groups for at least a year. They were likewise encouraged to attend OA meetings for additional support and requested to serve as volunteers to new groups of people who were not abstinent, partly because of the beneficent effects this had on their own abstinence. Besides the follow-up groups, the university also ran support groups for women who for some reason had not taken the intensive program and/or were not abstinent. The premise behind this system was that the intensive program just stopped the binge-vomiting and that recovery took place primarily in the follow-up groups. For this reason, six months' attendance was required, and a year was considered more realistic.

In January 1982 the university revised this program. Wanting the change afforded by therapy to occur more gradually and smoothly, the therapists extended the one-month program to two months. Participants now meet five nights the first week, four nights the second, and three nights the third (which involves the issues surrounding relapse). The fourth week they meet three nights, two of them ninety-minute group-therapy meetings, and one a Friday night meeting modeled on OA and run by abstinent volunteers. The fifth through eighth weeks involve two meetings a week, one group therapy and one on Friday night. After completing the intensive program, participants can continue coming to the Friday night meetings in addition to their follow-up groups for free. Besides their initial interview with Gretchen Goff, members also have interviews after the fourth and eighth weeks to help them deal with their individual differences and programs.

The clinic refers them for therapy and has them continue any therapy they might be in.

The program content is comprehensive. Each evening begins with a half hour of exercise or relaxation therapy followed by a one-hour lecture. Lecture topics include:

A factual medical presentation of bulimia to supplement the personal perspectives of its victims

Behavioral cues and chains, teaching the cues for binging and ways to avoid forging a chain of behavior that will cause a binge

Good nutrition, especially the need for three balanced meals a day according to a constructive plan to interrupt the binge patterns

Rational emotive thinking, an identification of the rationalizations for bulimia and techniques for challenging the beliefs that accompany the behavior

Stress and its management

Assertiveness and its relation to bulimia

Family influences and personal relationships

Depression and related behaviors like alcoholism and impulsivity

The course of the illness; bulimia and other eating disorders

Lectures by abstinent volunteers

The participants then spend an hour eating dinner together in the cafeteria, selecting any foods they want that don't contain sugar, and talking informally.

The rest of each evening is spent in group therapy, eight to ten people per group. Each night participants are assigned to call two other group members, to keep a food-intake and a binge-vomit record, and to complete another assignment related to the evening's activities. The groups are attended by abstinent volunteers, who help inspire the others while reinforcing their own abstinence.

The weekly follow-up groups changed with the intensive program. Experience taught the therapists that requiring a six-month commitment, and recommending a full year, worried people who did not want to stay in treatment that long. The therapists also felt that remaining in treatment for a year could foster dependence on the group and result in pressure from people who were still binge-vomiting. The new program, then, has eight different groups, each one meeting weekly for three months, that the participants can join after graduating from intensive treatment. Participants can sign up for more than one group and can either stay with their group for successive three-month periods or move from group to group, since all groups start simultaneously. This system allows members more flexibility in planning their individual programs. It's so much easier for them to contract for three months that many are expected to stay for a year anyway. People who need support between the completion of their intensive program and the start of the groups may continue with the twice-weekly meetings that are part of the intensive program itself.

Groups include a range of topics. A behavioral group and a bulimia support group are designed specifically for people who have been unsuccessful in previous treatments or unable to participate in the intensive program. The goal of these groups is abstinence. An experiential gestalt group is for bulimics who are not abstinent but instead wish to control rather than end their binge-vomiting. This group focuses on resistance to change. Two insight groups, a women's support group, and a structured support group are for abstinent bulimics who wish to avoid relapses while working toward specific personal goals. Finally, a relaxation, stress-management and assertion group is open to both abstinent and nonabstinent bulimics. All of these groups allow members to set and maintain long-range weight goals and teach them to manage stress, to be assertive, to take responsibility for their feelings and actions, to accept themselves, to increase their self-esteem, to be more satisfied with their sexual roles and to start facing intimate relationships. They help victims maintain their abstinence while learning new coping techniques and making new adjustments.

The therapists feel that successful outcome can be predicted by the victim's abstinence from sugar or alcohol, use of the groups and OA for support, willingness to seek help on her own without pressure from relatives or friends, and independence upon entering treatment. So far they have worked with over three hundred and fifty bulimics. Ninety percent of the participants abstained during the intensive program; many of them have never relapsed, although about 10 percent have never been able to maintain abstinence at all. Over 50 percent have been abstinent for at least a month at their six-month follow-up, but this achievement seems related to their determination to eat normally and avoid relapse rather than their being in a support group. Most of them had been in individual or group therapy before the program.

Like other alternatives, the University of Minnesota program may not be right for everyone; it may sound too heavy and time-consuming to some bulimics. The program is open to further change. "It's still experimental," says Gretchen Goff. "We'll stick to it for the time being, since it's effective treatment for a large number of our patients, and modify it as we learn more. We certainly don't have all the answers." Nobody has all the answers to bulimia, but the fact is that bulimics are recovering, and those anticipating treatment should feel optimistic that they can recover too.

Bulimia therapists agree that most bulimics need continued support during their first year of recovery. The University of Minnesota program offers one alternative for getting support without becoming dependent; other programs doubtless have other methods. But this is an important consideration for the prospective patient. Bulimia therapy is a serious and drawn-out process, and before signing up for a program the patient should feel sure that she has explored several options and has picked the one most beneficial to her.

Chapter 13

GETTING (AND GIVING) HELP

"What do you feel is the most important point to be made about bulimia?" Each person quoted in this book answered this question at the end of his or her interview. As might be expected, psychiatrists and psychologists addressed their peers, and bulimics spoke to other bulimics and to the public.

The professionals first want to remind us that the incidence of bulimia among normal-weight women who show no history of psychiatric disturbance is far higher than has been believed. Bulimia is a serious problem, not a discrete condition but one evolving out of personality and family problems. Without treatment it can become progressive and chronic, but it's very difficult to treat. While many quacks are seeking their fortunes from bulimia victims, there are not enough competent therapists to treat all those who need help.

This is partly the fault of mental-health professionals themselves. Psychiatrists, psychologists and social workers should look to universities and large hospitals working with bulimics for training and help. Rather than ignoring patients who mention bulimia or allowing themselves to be shocked by it, they should be confrontive and interested in the disorder. They need not be experts in bulimia to be able to respond well to its victims. They should *not* view it as trivial or talk about underlying problems to "avoid reinforcing it."

Psychiatrists and psychologists must look to all ways possible to deal with bulimia, including easing victims into treatment without pushing them. Nutritionists, for example, are well trained about food and eating and don't carry the stigma attached to seeing a psychiatrist. As such they can serve as bridges between the bulimic and specific treatment. So can the anorexia associations and anyone else in a position to administer preventive medicine. "The media and the diet book writers—whose books can be lethal, some of them are so inaccurate—have a responsibility to be accurate about informing people," says Anita B. Siegman. "We should have seminars for parents on nutrition before their children can become bulimic. They should learn not to destroy the self-esteem of the overweight child."

No matter how ill a bulimic may be, she can hope to recover. Bulimia isn't an easy affliction and may have lifelong repercussions. Recovery will take work, time, continued support, treatment and trust in oneself and others. But bulimics can make life much better for themselves.

Asked to summarize their experiences, bulimic women emphasized that their fellow victims should seek help immediately. Some speak here for the rest. Loretta is twenty-three:

> I'd like to just tell bulimia victims to cut it out right now! Immediately! But to be more practical, the thing to do is to find support. Tell people that you're bulimic so that you can burn your bridges—like if your roommates know, they won't buy your lies about where all the food went. The biggest thing is to be abstinent. Without abstinence your brain will get cloudy—your reasoning will be strange, and you won't be able to be treated effectively.
>
> And I'd like to tell doctors not to be afraid to confront a patient with your suspicions that she might be bulimic. She might be hostile and not admit it—I know that for a time I thought that the behavior was okay—or she might admit it, in which case you can direct her toward help.

Although it's crucial that the bulimic *voluntarily* seek help on her own, Chris agrees with the idea that she should be confronted and encouraged to start treatment:

> It's really sick behavior, and the victim won't be proud of it. Her whole eating behavior becomes secret, and by

the time it's discovered it's far gone. It's so important that someone with this problem be supported, not just with understanding but with encouragement to seek help. I think that even if the person resists, you should make an effort to find out where she can get help, and maybe even take her there. And make her understand that her behavior does not make her a disgusting person—that it's a sickness just like any other, and it's distinct from what she is.

Valerie, age thirty-four, is more imperative:

Get out of your corner and get help. Talk about the bulimia honestly. Maybe you can't be helped by doctors, who are ten times worse than ordinary men and won't be receptive. Stop binge-vomiting first, then worry about the whys of doing it. Get out of the craziness of bulimia so you won't be mad at yourself anymore. I don't know how physically related bulimia is, but I do know that I would go through twenty-five dollars' worth of food in a single binge. You'll need something to fill in the addiction—use the time and the money to do good things for yourself, like making new friends.

Twenty-seven-year-old Maureen picks up on the question of where help can be found:

It's important to recognize that it's not your secret solution to life's problems. You're not alone, and you can't do it on your own. It's really important to get help, but not just anyone can help you.

If you talk to your doctor and he doesn't know about bulimia, don't just stop with him. Ask for a referral. It's such a secret problem that professionals, even really competent younger professionals with broad knowledge, just don't know about it. Many women have a gynecologist as their primary physician, and a gynecologist won't know how to handle it. And many doctors won't deal with chemical-dependency problems, and bulimia is ten times worse than chemical dependency. Keep looking until you find someone who can help you.

Be honest about your bulimia. Get help and support. Become abstinent. And remember, you're not alone. Bulimics repeat these messages over and over again. But how do other bulimics find the road to recovery?

Giving Help

With luck, a bulimic can take her first step to a new life thanks to the intervention of a compassionate physician. Bulimics often say, "I didn't tell my doctor about the bulimia, but he should have known to ask." There's some truth to this statement. Bulimia is becoming so common that physicians should seriously consider incorporating questions about eating behavior into their physical examinations. Any mention of eating habits may make the chronic bulimic so uncomfortable that the physician can then confront her.

If you are a physician (or dentist) who wants to screen for bulimia or suspects it in a patient, what can you do? You can approach the patient indirectly by asking if she has any problems with eating and maintaining her weight. Having broached the subject, you can then ask more direct questions, especially if you have found suspicious signs of binge-purging. If the patient has a distinct symptom like electrolyte imbalance or extensive tooth decay, mention it carefully: "You have this symptom; it's one we usually see in people who induce vomiting or use too many laxatives. Have you ever tried purging like this?" By saying something like this, by being nonjudgmental and locating the symptom in other patients with the same behavior, you can perhaps elicit your patient's honesty without frightening or embarrassing her. Remember that you're revealing your patient's darkest secret, one that makes her feel disgusting. But she may be waiting for someone like you to "rescue" her by a direct confrontation.

If your patient has no definite ill effects but you learn of her bulimia anyway, you should warn her of possible long-term dangers of purging. Together you should discuss matters such as her appropriate weight range and better methods of maintaining it. If your patient is motivated, cooperative and not severely ill, you can perhaps end her binge-purging by working together, or with a nutritionist, on a supervised diet.

If, on the other hand, your patient seems very depressed, anxious and troubled by other problems, you should recommend psychotherapy. If she is not motivated to find a therapist, at least direct her toward the anorexia associations and encourage her to find a self-help group. Remember that hundreds of thousands of women (and men) are experimenting with binge-purging. If you nip such an experiment in the bud, you may save a potential bulimic years of agony.

If you are a bulimic in or through with treatment, how can you help other bulimics? If you know someone who binge-vomits occasionally, point out that you too started binging for fun or vomiting for weight loss, only to regret it later. Explain that little is known at this point about how bulimia develops and that binge-vomiting is an unhealthy and risky practice.

If you know another bulimic who needs treatment, use an indirect approach. Describe your own experience with bulimia, and mention that the disorder is widespread. Treat it as a serious problem, but reassure your listener that it's nothing to be ashamed of and that help is available. If the person seems unwilling to admit to binge-vomiting, say that you'd like to help others recover, and ask her if she knows of anyone with bulimia. It may take some time and eventually some direct questions to get her to confide in you. If she then hesitates to get help, encourage her to join an anorexia nervosa association or a self-help group. Offer to help her work out a food plan. Be supportive, understanding and *patient*—remember how *you* felt in her position!

Getting Help

If you're a bulimic, you will feel less isolated, helpless and out of control as soon as you start seeking treatment. The first step is to educate yourself. Read the materials listed at the end of this book. Join the anorexia associations, and use their newsletters, bibliographies and hotlines as sources of information. Join OA. Write or call the eating disorders clinics for information. An understanding of eating-disorders theories and treatment methods will help prepare you to find a therapist. Your job is to try everything, and keep at it.

ANOREXIA NERVOSA ASSOCIATIONS

The anorexia nervosa associations are good sources of referrals and services. The oldest organization is Anorexia Nervosa and Associated Disorders, Inc. (ANAD), which counsels and informs thousands of victims, families and health professionals about eating disorders. Besides helping form self-help groups all over the country, ANAD has a hotline and a newsletter and serves as an information resource center. They educate by distributing information, by implementing an early detection program and by holding conferences. Their referral list currently has the names of thirteen hundred therapists, hospitals and clinics throughout the United States that treat eating disorders. ANAD makes every effort to evaluate their referrals, but they caution questioners who are given the names, as vice-president Christopher Athas explains:

> There is no registry of therapists treating eating disorders in this country. Our policy is not to endorse anyone or any form of therapy. The world's greatest therapist might not be right for a particular individual. We feel that personal research is very important to delineate someone with whom the person feels that he or she can make progress. Our approach is to encourage people to learn about eating disorders in order to make these evaluations.

ANAD members have participated in two research projects, and the organization encourages further research. Services are free and should not be considered substitutes for medical or psychiatric treatment.

The other associations offer similar services and hope someday to join forces into one national organization. The American Anorexia Nervosa Association, Inc. features general public meetings five times a year to which they have attracted distinguished professionals to speak about eating disorders. They also offer support groups for parents of eating-disorders victims as well as the victims themselves.

The anorexia associations are:

National Association of Anorexia Nervosa and Associated
  Disorders, Inc.
Box 271
Highland Park, IL 60035
(312) 831-3438
(Individuals requesting information should send a self-addressed envelope with $.37 postage; organizations should send $1.00 to cover postage and handling.)

American Anorexia Nervosa Association, Inc.
133 Cedar Lane
Teaneck, NJ 07666
(201) 836-1800 (10 A.M. to 2 P.M. EST)

American Anorexia Nervosa Association of Philadelphia, Inc.
Philadelphia Child Guidance Clinic
Philadelphia, PA 19104
(215) 387-1919

National Anorexic Aid Society
Box 29461
Columbus, OH 43229

Anorexia Nervosa and Related Eating Disorders, Inc.
P.O. Box 5102
Eugene, OR 97405

Anorexia Nervosa Aid Society of Massachusetts, Inc.
Box 213
Lincoln Center, MA 01773

American Anorexia Nervosa Association of Atlanta
3533 Kingsboro Road, NE
Atlanta, GA 30319
(404) 233-7058

OVEREATERS ANONYMOUS

You can find OA in the telephone directory. If it's not listed, write or call:

Overeaters Anonymous Headquarters
World Services Office
2190 West 190th Street
Torrance, CA 90504
(213) 320-7941

Newcomers to OA should arrange to visit their doctors to work out suitable food plans.

EATING DISORDERS CLINICS AND OTHER PROGRAMS

If you live near any of the following major centers, ask about their treatment programs. If they don't suit you, or if their waiting lists are long, ask for referrals.

East Coast

David B. Herzog, M.D., Director
Eating Disorders Unit
Massachusetts General Hospital
Fruit Street
Boston, MA 02114

Katherine A. Halmi, M.D., Director
Eating Disorders Program
New York Hospital–Cornell Medical Center
Westchester Division
21 Bloomingdale Road
White Plains, NY 10605

B. Timothy Walsh, M.D., Director
Eating Disorders Research and Treatment Program
New York State Psychiatric Institute
Columbia Presbyterian Medical Center
722 West 168th Street
New York, NY 10032

Judith Brisman, Ph.D. (or Ellen Schor, Ph.D.)
Center for Bulimia and Related Disorders
31 West 10th Street
New York, NY 10011

William Davis, Ph.D.
Center for the Study of Anorexia and Bulimia
1 West 91st Street
New York, NY 10024

Arnold E. Andersen, M.D., Director
Eating and Weight Disorders Clinic
Henry Phipps Psychiatric Clinic
Johns Hopkins Hospital
600 North Wolfe Street
Baltimore, MD 21205

Midwest

Craig Johnson, Ph.D., Director
Anorexia Nervosa Project
Michael Reese Medical Center
Psychosomatic and Psychiatric Institute
2959 South Cottage Grove
Chicago, IL 60616

Richard L. Pyle, M.D., Director
Behavioral Health Clinic
University of Minnesota
Box 301, Mayo Memorial Building
420 Delaware Street, SE
Minneapolis, MN 55455

West Coast

Joel Yager, M.D., Medical Director
Eating Disorders Clinic
Neuropsychiatric Institute
Center for the Health Sciences
University of California at Los Angeles
760 Westwood Plaza
Los Angeles, CA 90024

Barton J. Blinder, M.D., Director
Eating Disorders Program
Department of Psychiatry and Human Behavior
College of Medicine
University of California at Irvine
Irvine, CA 92717

You may instead be able to locate a therapist on your own. If you live near a medical school or a large hospital, call the psychiatry department, and ask about eating-disorders specialists. Or call your county mental-health or health and social services department, especially if you can't afford private therapy. If you have found a group program that interests you, its graduates will probably be glad to describe it and answer your questions.

If you get nowhere, do as Maureen says—*keep asking*.

SELECTING A THERAPIST

It's not easy to choose a therapist. Most people still find it difficult to evaluate medical care as critically as they would the stereo, car or television that they're about to purchase; long-term therapy can be more expensive than all three. People seeking psychiatric help are probably more vulnerable to outside influences than those just looking for a physician to monitor blood pressure. To make matters worse, you're trying to find someone knowledgeable in a specialized area that little is known about. And if you're bulimic, chances are that you're not assertive to begin with, especially with respect to sizing up the person to whom to entrust your shameful secret. But remember that when you do find a competent therapist, he or she will be fascinated by your problem and anxious to help you work out the therapy contract most appropriate for you.

If you're fortunate enough to find more than one eating-disorders specialist for individual therapy, check them all out— and when you choose one, commit yourself for only half a dozen or so visits until you're sure that the therapy shows promise. You must rely on your own feelings and judgment about the person with whom you're to work. One rule is that he or she should be someone you would enjoy talking to under any circumstances, someone you like and feel you can trust. Examine his or her credentials—just as you would with any other product you buy.

In general, stay away from any therapist

. . . who does not take your eating problem seriously. Any psychiatrist or psychologist should at least know the term *bulimia*. A professional who says, "I'm not qualified to treat you," not only is taking you seriously but is competent enough to know and admit his or her limitations. Ask for a referral.

. . . who tries to engage you in therapy without promising to discuss your bulimia immediately and directly. Avoid a therapist who wants to start with underlying problems. You need help *now*.

. . . who takes advantage of your loneliness and desperation by trying to take you under his or her wing in a fatherly or motherly fashion. This therapist is trying to hook a patient, and the last thing you need is another smothering parent. Look for sincere interest combined with professional detachment.

. . . who tries to convince you that he or she is *the* expert on bulimia. Those therapists most serious about bulimia are the first to admit that nobody knows all about it.

If you can't find an eating-disorders specialist, find a competent therapist you can work with who is willing to research bulimia. (If you are in therapy and doing well, *stick with your therapist,* and try to find another method of treating the bulimia.)

You should schedule a thorough dental examination, and you will also need an internist to work with you and your therapist. As your therapy progresses, you may want to supplement it with hypnotherapy or nutritional counseling. (First discuss these possibilities with your therapist.)

HYPNOTHERAPY

You'll need to find a psychiatrist, psychologist or psychiatric social worker with a background in hypnotherapy. You're looking not for a hypnotist but for someone who can incorporate hypnosis into regular psychotherapy to help you work out the feelings and circumstances that cause you to binge.

To find a qualified local hypnotherapist, contact:

American Society of Clinical Hypnosis
Suite 336
2250 East Devon Avenue
Des Plaines, IL 60018
(312) 297-3317

NUTRITIONAL COUNSELING

Like hypnotherapy, nutritional counseling is best used in combination with psychotherapy. Find a registered dietician or a counselor with a nutrition degree from an accredited college. Your therapist may be able to recommend someone; otherwise check with the outpatient services of your local hospital or call your county or state health department, and ask for their nutrition specialist.

A FINAL NOTE . . .

Bulimia treatment may be the hardest process you'll ever endure, but it's worth it. Don't become discouraged—remember, everyone involved with this book is confident that you can recover. Good luck.

SUGGESTED READING

Articles on bulimia have begun to appear frequently in both popular magazines and medical journals. A few of the more helpful ones are listed here, along with books on related subjects.

Newspaper and Magazine Articles

Boskind-Lodahl, Marlene; and Sirlin, Joyce. "The Gorge-Purging Syndrome." *Psychology Today*. March 1977, pp. 50–52; 82–85.

Brenner, Marie. "Bulimarexia." *Savvy*. June 1980, pp. 54–59.

Brody, Jane E. "An Eating Disorder of Binges and Purges Reported Widespread." The New York *Times*. October 20, 1981. C1; C5.

Gardner, Sandra. "A Subtler Relative of Anorexia Is Gathering Victims." The New York *Times*. January 25, 1981, XI, 2:1.

Squire, Susan. "Why Thousands of Women Don't Know How to Eat Normally Anymore." *Glamour*. October 1981, pp. 244–45; 309–15.

Medical Articles

Halmi, Katherine A., M.D. "Eating Disorders." Kaplan, Harold I., M.D., et al. *Comprehensive Textbook of Psychiatry III*, Vol 3. Baltimore: Williams & Wilkins, 1981, pp. 2598–605.

Johnson, Craig, ed. *International Journal of Eating Disorders*. Florence, Kentucky: Van Nostrand Reinhold, 1981 (quarterly).

Mitchell, James E., M.D., et al. "The Bulimic Syndrome in Normal Weight Individuals: A Review." *International Journal of Eating Disorders.* Winter 1981, pp. 61–73.

Pyle, Richard L., M.D., et al. "Bulimia: A Report of 34 Cases." *Journal of Clinical Psychiatry.* 42:2. February 1981, pp. 60–64.

Russell, Gerald, M.D. "Bulimia Nervosa: An Ominous Variant of Anorexia Nervosa." *Psychological Medicine.* 9 (1979), pp. 429–48.

Books

Bruch, Hilde, M.D. *Eating Disorders: Obesity, Anorexia Nervosa and the Person Within.* New York: Basic Books, Inc., 1973.

———. *The Golden Cage: The Enigma of Anorexia Nervosa.* Cambridge: Harvard University Press, 1978.

Chernin, Kim. *The Obsession: Reflections on the Tyranny of Slenderness.* New York: Harper & Row, 1981.

Levenkron, Steven. *The Best Little Girl in the World.* New York: Warner Books, 1978.

Lindner, Robert. "Solitaire: The Case of Laura." *The Fifty-Minute Hour.* New York: Holt, Rinehart & Winston, Inc., 1954.

Liu, Aimee. *Solitaire: A Young Woman's Triumph over Anorexia Nervosa.* New York: Harper & Row, 1979.

Millman, Marcia. *Such a Pretty Face: Being Fat in America.* New York: Berkeley, 1980.

Orbach, Susie. *Fat Is a Feminist Issue.* New York: Berkeley, 1978.

Vincent, L. M., M.D. *Competing with the Sylph: Dancers and the Pursuit of the Ideal Body Form.* Kansas City: Andrews & McMeel, Inc., 1979.

INDEX

A

B

F

G

H

M

Male bulimics, 147–56
  comparison with female bulimics, 149–51
  incidence impossible to calculate accurately, 147–49
  need for treatment as separate sex group, 149
    feminist perspective discriminatory to men, 156
MAO (monoamine oxidase) inhibitors, 214–15
Massachusetts General Hospital, Eating Disorders Unit,
  24
Meehan, Vivian, 18, 51–52, 60–61, 70, 109, 198
Michael Reese Medical Center, 61
Miller, Estelle, 51, 59, 70, 90–91, 124, 147, 204
Minnesota, University of, 59, 61, 148, 150, 164, 197
  Bulimia Treatment Program, 52, 215–19
  Hospital, 91
Mitchell, Dr. James E., 61, 91–92

N

Nardil, 214–15
National Institute of Health, 91
Neurogenic binge-eating, 79–82
  medication the appropriate cure, 80–82
New York Hospital–Cornell Medical Center, 21, 74
Nutritional counseling, 221–22, 232

O

Obesity, 37, 74, 76
Obsession, The, 135

T

V